Translator's Introduction to Luke

You are about to read the biography of the wonderful Man Jesus Christ. This glorious ospel was penned by one of his early followers, a physician named Luke. All four Gospels in our New Testament are inspired by God, but Luke's is unique. I believe that this could be described as the loveliest book ever written.

We know little about the human author. He was a companion of the apostle Paul for some of his missionary journeys and was possibly one of Paul's early converts. Luke was a literary genius and writes with powerful prose. Some believe Luke was possibly the only non-Jewish writer of the New Testament. Others believe that he was a Syrian Jew who took upon himself a Gentile name. It is obvious that he knew firsthand many of the early followers of Jesus, even the apostles who were chosen to preach his name throughout the nations. Near the end of the apostle Paul's life, when he was facing martyrdom, Paul wrote of his trusted friend, "Only Luke is with me" (2 Timothy 4:11).

This world is a far better place because of the revelation Luke shares with us in his gospel. He gives us a full picture of Jesus' life and ministry and applied scrupulous accuracy to all he wrote, to ensure that what we read is factual. In fact, Luke uses the Greek word for "autopsy" (1:2) for investigating with firsthand knowledge those who had seen what Jesus did and heard what Jesus taught. Dr. Luke performed an "autopsy" on the facts, tracing them all back to their source to make sure what he compiled was of the highest degree of accuracy.

Luke, being a physician, learned the need to exhibit compassion and mercy toward others. It comes through in every chapter. Luke's gospel is perhaps the most compassionate and love-filled account of Jesus' life ever written.

Luke provides us with rich details of Jesus' love of children and the forsaken. Luke writes more about Jesus' ministry to women than the other gospel authors.

This was somewhat controversial in the culture of his day. In fact, Luke uses an alternating narrative of one story about a man and the next story about a woman. Luke begins with the story of Zechariah, then moves to Mary. A focus on Simeon, then on Anna. The Roman centurion, then the widow of Nain. The good Samaritan, then Mary and Martha. This pattern continues throughout his gospel.

Luke shares Jesus' teachings on prayer, forgiveness, and our obligation to demonstrate mercy and grace in dealings with others. Luke's pen was anointed by the Holy Spirit and his book is still read today by the lovers of God, because it is the mercy gospel. It is a book for everybody, for we all need mercy.

Luke writes clearly of the humanity of Jesus—as the servant of all and the sacrifice for all. Every barrier is broken down in Luke's gospel: between Jew and Gentile, men and women, rich and poor. In Luke we see Jesus as the Savior of all who come to him.

A large amount of Luke's gospel is not found in any other gospel narrative. If we did not have the book of Luke, we wouldn't know about the stories of the prodigal son, the good Samaritan, the wedding banquet, and many other amazing teachings. Only in the book of Luke do we find the stories of the shepherds at Bethlehem, the ten lepers who were healed, the young man from Nain who was raised from the dead, and the dying thief on the cross next to Jesus. How thankful I am for the gospel of Luke!

My heart overflows with the joy of seeing this dream realized, of the Word of God being translated with all its passion and fire into contemporary English. I set before you this imperfect but heartfelt attempt to give you the same thrill that must have overwhelmed the first-century readers when they heard the story of Jesus Christ for the first time and without a "religious filter." Unveiled before your eyes will be the glorious Man Jesus Christ and the revelation of his undying love for you. Take all of him into all that you need today and you will not be disappointed.

I present to you, and to every lover of God, the gospel of Luke.

—Dr. Brian Simmons

THE
PASSION
TRANSLATION

Luke AND Acts

TO THE
LOVERS
OF GOD

Translated from Greek and Aramaic Texts

DR. BRIAN SIMMONS

tPt
BIBLE

BroadStreet
P U B L I S H I N G

Luke and Acts: To the Lovers of God, The Passion Translation®
Translated directly from the original Greek and Aramaic texts by Dr. Brian Simmons

Published by BroadStreet Publishing Group, LLC
Racine, Wisconsin, USA
www.broadstreetpublishing.com

© 2014 The Passion Translation®

ISBN-13: 9781424549597 (paperback)
ISBN-13: 9781424549665 (e-book)

Cover and interior design by Garborg Design Works, Inc. | www.garborgdesign.com
Interior typesetting by Katherine Lloyd | www.theDESKonline.com

Printed in the United States of America

Luke

One

——

[1-4]Dear friend,

I am writing for you, mighty lover of God,[a] an orderly account of what Jesus Christ accomplished and fulfilled among us. Several eyewitness biographies have already been written,[b] using as their source material the good news preached among us by Christ's early disciples, who became loving servants of the Living Expression.[c] But now I am passing on to you this accurate compilation of my own meticulous investigation[d] based on numerous eyewitness interviews and thorough research of the story of his life. It is appropriate for me to write this, for he also appeared to me[e] so that I would reassure you beyond any shadow of a doubt the reliability of all you have been taught of him.

The Birth of the Prophet John

[5]During the reign of King Herod the Great over Judea, there was a Jewish priest named Zechariah[f] who served in the temple as part of the priestly order of Abijah.[g] His wife, Elizabeth, was also from a family of priests, being a direct descendant of Aaron. [6]They were both lovers of God, living virtuously and following the commandments of the Lord fully. [7]But they were childless since Elizabeth was barren, and now they both were quite old.

[8-9]One day, while Zechariah's priestly order was on duty and he was serving as priest, it happened by the casting of lots (according to the custom of the

---

a 1:1–4 The Greek text can be translated "most excellent Theophilus." The name Theophilus means "friend of God" or "lover of God." The Greek word means "most honorable" or "mightiest." Many scholars believe there was no individual named Theophilus mentioned in Luke's writings. This becomes instead a greeting to all the lovers of God.

b 1:1–4 It is likely that Matthew and Mark are two of the gospel accounts Luke refers to here.

c 1:1–4 Translated literally from the Aramaic text. The Greek word is *logos*.

d 1:1–4 The Greek word used here is actually "to see with the eye" or "autopsy."

e 1:1–4 Translated literally from the Aramaic text. The Greek text uses the same term for "coming from above" found in John 3:31 and 19:11. Luke is revealing that the Lord Jesus appeared to him and authorized him to compile his inspired gospel.

f 1:5 Zechariah means "God has remembered." Elizabeth means "oath" or "covenant of God."

g 1:5 King David organized the priests into twenty-four divisions, and Abijah was the head of one of the priestly families. See Nehemiah 12:12,17 and 1 Chronicles 24:10.

priesthood) that the honor fell upon Zechariah to enter into the Holy Place[a]and burn incense before the Lord. [10]A large crowd of worshippers had gathered to pray outside the temple at the hour when incense was being offered. [11]All at once an angel of the Lord appeared to him, standing just to the right of the altar of incense.[b]

[12]Zechariah was startled and overwhelmed with fear. [13]But the angel reassured him, saying, "Don't be afraid, Zechariah! God is showing grace to you.[c] For I have come to tell you that your prayer[d] for a child has been answered. Your wife, Elizabeth, will bear you a son and you are to name him John. [14]His birth will bring you much joy and gladness. Many will rejoice because of him. [15]He will be one of the great ones in the sight of God. He will drink no wine or strong drink,[e] but he will be filled with the Holy Spirit even while still in his mother's womb. [16]And he will persuade many in Israel to convert and turn back to the Lord their God. [17]He will go before the Lord as a forerunner, with the same power and anointing[f] as Elijah the prophet. He will be instrumental in turning the hearts of the fathers in tenderness back to their children and the hearts of the disobedient back to the wisdom of their righteous fathers. And he will prepare a united people[g] who are ready for the Lord's appearing."

[18]Zechariah asked the angel, "How do you expect me to believe this? I'm an old man and my wife is too old to give me a child. What sign can you give me to prove this will happen?"[h]

[19]Then the angel said, "I am Gabriel.[i] I stand beside God himself. He has sent me to you to announce this good news. [20]But now, since you did not believe my words, you will be stricken silent and unable to speak[j] until the day

<hr>

a 1:8–9 Some have said there were twenty thousand priests in Christ's time, so that no priest would ever offer incense more than once. This was a once-in-a-lifetime moment for him. The burning of incense before the Lord was done twice daily, once in the morning and once in the afternoon (Exodus 30:7–8).

b 1:10 This would be the south side of the temple, between the altar of incense and the golden lampstand.

c 1:13 Implied in the context and in the name John, which means "God is gracious" or "God shows mercy."

d 1:13 Or "the prayer you don't even pray anymore."

e 1:15 Most likely, John was to be a Nazarite from birth, one totally set apart for God and who would fulfill the Nazarite vow found in Numbers 6:1–12.

f 1:17 Or "spirit."

g 1:17 Implied in the text. The words "united people" are found in the Aramaic text.

h 1:18 Implied in the text.

i 1:19 The name Gabriel means "God's hero" or "God's mighty one."

j 1:20 Since Zechariah asked for a sign rather than believe the word of the Lord, he was given the sign of silence. Unbelief keeps a priest from speaking until faith arises.

my words have been fulfilled at their appointed time and a child is born to you. That will be your sign!"[a]

²¹Meanwhile, the crowds outside kept expecting him to come out. They were amazed over Zechariah's delay,[b] wondering what could have happened inside the sanctuary. ²²When he finally did come out, he tried to talk, but he couldn't speak a word, and they realized from his gestures that he had seen a vision while in the Holy Place. ²³He remained mute as he finished his days of priestly ministry in the temple and then went back to his own home. ²⁴Soon afterward his wife, Elizabeth, became pregnant and went into seclusion for the next five months. ²⁵She said with joy, "See how kind it is of God to gaze upon me[c] and take away the disgrace of my barrenness!"

Angelic Prophecy of Jesus' Birth

²⁶⁻²⁷During the sixth month of Elizabeth's pregnancy, the angel Gabriel was sent from God's presence to an unmarried girl[d] named Mary, living in Nazareth, a village in Galilee.[e] She was engaged[f] to a man named Joseph, a true descendant of King David. ²⁸Gabriel appeared to her and said, "Grace to you, young woman, for our master is with you[g] and so you are anointed with great favor."

²⁹Mary was shocked over the words of the angel and bewildered over what this may mean for her. ³⁰But the angel reassured her, saying, "Do not yield to your fear, Mary, for the Lord has found delight in you and has chosen to surprise you with a wonderful gift. ³¹You will become pregnant with a baby boy, and you are to name him Jesus. ³²He will be supreme[h] and will be known as the Son

---

a 1:20 This is the first spoken message from heaven in more than four hundred years. The last person before Zacharias to receive a message given by angels was also named Zechariah. See Zechariah 1:6.

b 1:21 They were waiting outside for the priest to come out and speak over them the customary Aaronic blessing found in Numbers 6:24–26.

c 1:25 This phrase is translated from the Aramaic text.

d 1:26–27 Many translations have the word "virgin." It is a possible translation of the Greek word *parthenos*, but its most common usage implies "a girl of marriageable age." It is made explicit in Matthew 1:25 and Luke 1:34 that Mary was indeed a virgin.

e 1:25–27 The Aramaic word translated "Galilee" here means "revealed." It is only fitting that God would first be "revealed" in a village in Galilee. Nazareth means "branch." Jesus grew up as the "Branch" of the Lord in the city of the "branch."

f 1:26–27 This betrothal period usually lasted one year, and unfaithfulness on the part of the bride during the engagement was punishable by death.

g 1:28 For Gabriel to say, "Our Master is with you," signifies that Jesus, our Master, had been conceived in her womb. This was what bewildered Mary.

h 1:32 As translated from the Aramaic text.

of the Highest. And the Lord God will enthrone him as King on his ancestor David's throne. ³³He will reign as King of Israel[a] forever, and his reign will have no limit."

³⁴Mary said, "But how could this happen? I am still a virgin!"

³⁵Gabriel answered, "The Spirit of Holiness will fall upon you and the almighty God will spread his shadow of power over you in a cloud of glory![b] This is why the child born to you will be holy,[c] and he will be called the Son of God. ³⁶What's more, your aged aunt,[d] Elizabeth, has also became pregnant with a son. The 'barren one' is now in her sixth month. ³⁷Not one promise from God is empty of power, for with God there is no such thing as impossibility!"[e]

³⁸Then Mary responded, saying, "This is amazing! I will be a mother for the Lord![f] As his servant, I accept whatever he has for me. May everything you have told me come to pass." And the angel left her.

Elizabeth's Prophecy to Mary

³⁹Afterward, Mary arose and hurried off to the hill country of Judea, to the village where Zechariah and Elizabeth lived. ⁴⁰Arriving at their home, Mary entered the house and greeted Elizabeth. ⁴¹At the moment she heard Mary's voice, the baby[g] within Elizabeth's womb jumped and kicked. And suddenly, Elizabeth was filled to overflowing with the Holy Spirit! ⁴²With a loud voice she prophesied with power:[h]

Mary! You are a woman given the highest favor

And privilege above all others.

For your child[i] is destined to bring God great delight.

---

a 1:33 Or "house of Jacob."

b 1:35 The Greek word used as a metaphor, "spread his shadow over you," is also the word used at Jesus' transfiguration when the cloud of glory "overshadowed" Jesus on the mountain (Mark 9:7).

c 1:35 Jesus Christ is holy, born without sin in his bloodline, for his Father was God Almighty. He would become the only perfect sacrifice to take away our sin and remove its power and penalty from us.

d 1:36 The Greek word is "relative." Many scholars believe Elizabeth was Mary's maternal aunt.

e 1:37 This verse can be translated in two different ways: "There is nothing impossible with God" or "The word of God will never fail." The translator has chosen to include both for this verse.

f 1:38 As translated from the Aramaic text.

g 1:39 The Bible calls Elizabeth's yet-to-be-born son, John, a "baby."

h 1:42 Implied in the context.

i 1:42 Or "the fruit of your womb." This is the same word used for the "fruit" of the tree of life in Revelation 22:2. Jesus is "fruit" for us to take in as our life supply.

⁴³How did I deserve such a remarkable honor
To have the mother of my Lordᵃ come and visit me?
⁴⁴The moment you came in the door and greeted me,
My baby danced inside me with ecstatic joy!
⁴⁵Great favor is upon you, for you have believed
Every word spoken to you from the Lord.

Mary's Prophetic Song

⁴⁶And Mary sang this song:

My soul is ecstatic, overflowing with praises to God!
⁴⁷My spirit bursts with joy over my life-giving God!ᵇ
⁴⁸For he set his tender gaze upon me, his lowly servant girl.ᶜ
And from here on, everyone will know
That I have been favored and blessed.
⁴⁹The Mighty One has worked a mighty miracle for me;
Holy is his name!
⁵⁰Mercy kisses all his godly lovers,
From one generation to the next.ᵈ
⁵¹Mighty power flows from him
To scatter all those who walk in pride.
⁵²Powerful princes he tears from their thrones
And he lifts up the lowly to take their place.ᵉ
⁵³Those who hunger for him will always be filled,ᶠ
But the smug and self-satisfied he will send away empty.
⁵⁴Because he can never forget to show mercy,
He has helped his chosen servant, Israel,

---

a 1:43 An obvious prophetic revelation was given to Elizabeth from the Holy Spirit about what had happened with Mary.
b 1:47 Or "Savior." The first recorded person to call Jesus Savior was his mother, Mary. She rejoices in God not simply as her Creator, but as Life Giver and Savior.
c 1:48 The Aramaic text is "He set his gaze upon the willingness of his mother."
d 1:50 Mary is quoting Psalms 103:17 and 111:9.
e 1:52 Implied in the text.
f 1:53 Mary is quoting Psalm 107:9.

⁵⁵Keeping his promises to Abraham^a
And to his descendants forever.

⁵⁶Before going home, Mary stayed with Elizabeth for about three months.^b

The Birth of the Prophet John

⁵⁷When Elizabeth's pregnancy was full term, she gave birth to a son. ⁵⁸All her family, friends, and neighbors heard about it, and they too were overjoyed, for they realized that the Lord had showered such wonderful mercy upon her.

⁵⁹When the baby was eight days old, according to their custom, all the family and friends came together for the circumcision ceremony.^c Everyone was convinced that the parents would name the baby Zechariah, after his father. ⁶⁰But Elizabeth spoke up and said, "No, he has to be named John!"

⁶¹"What?" they exclaimed. "No one in your family line has that name!"

⁶²So they gestured to the baby's father to ask what to name the child. ⁶³After motioning for a writing tablet, in amazement of all, he wrote, "His name is John."^d

⁶⁴Instantly Zechariah could speak again. And his first words were praises to the Lord.

⁶⁵The fear of God then fell on the people of their village, and the news of this astounding event traveled throughout the hill country of Judea. Everyone was in awe over it! ⁶⁶All who heard this news were astonished and wondered, "If a miracle brought his birth,^e what on earth will this child become? Clearly, God's presence is upon this child in a powerful way!"

Zechariah's Prophecy

⁶⁷Then Zechariah was filled to overflowing with the Holy Spirit and he prophesied, saying:

---

a 1:55 Mary understood by revelation that the Christ child would fulfill the promises of mercy that God gave to Abraham. See Genesis 22:16–18.
b 1:56 The cultural practice of the Hebrews was for the mother to do nothing but rest during the first three months of pregnancy.
c 1:59 This ceremony was an important time of celebration in Jewish culture, for another child was born under the covenant of God with Israel. See Genesis 17:4–14 and Leviticus 12:1–3.
d 1:63 The name John means "God's gift" or "God is gracious."
e 1:66 Implied in the text.

⁶⁸Praise be to the exalted Lord God of Israel,
For he has seen us through eyes of grace,
And he comes as our Hero-God to set us free!
⁶⁹He appears to us as a mighty Savior,
A trumpet of redemption[a]
From the house of David, his servant,
⁷⁰Just as he promised long ago
By the words of his holy prophets.
⁷¹They prophesied he would come one day and save us
From every one of our enemies and from
The power of those who hate us.[b]
⁷²Now he has shown us
The mercy promised to our ancestors,
For he has remembered his holy covenant.[c]
⁷³⁻⁷⁵He has rescued us from the power of our enemies!
This fulfills the sacred oath he made with our father Abraham.
Now we can boldly worship[d] God with holy lives,
Living in purity as priests[e] in his presence every day!
⁷⁶And to you I prophesy, my little son,
You will be known as the prophet of the glorious God.
For you will be a forerunner, going before
The face of the Master, Yahweh,[f]
To prepare hearts to embrace his ways.[g]
⁷⁷You will preach to his people the revelation of salvation life,
The cancellation of all our sins, to bring us back to God.[h]
⁷⁸The splendor light of heaven's glorious sunrise[i]

a 1:69 Literal translation of the Aramaic. The Hebrew is "a horn of salvation," which signifies strength and fighting power.
b 1:71 Zechariah is quoting from Psalm 106:10.
c 1:72 There is amazing Hebrew poetry contained in this passage. The names of John, Zechariah, and Elizabeth are all found in this verse. "He has shown us mercy" or "God's gracious gift" is found in the name John. "He has remembered" is the name Zechariah. "His holy covenant" is the name Elizabeth.
d 1:73–75 Or "serve."
e 1:73–75 The word translated as "purity" here is a Hebraic homonym for "priesthood."
f 1:76 Literal translation of the Aramaic.
g 1:76 Zechariah quotes from Malachi 3:1. This "sunrise" is the appearing of Christ, the Messiah.
h 1:77 Implied in the text.
i 1:78 Some believe this is a quote from Malachi 4:2. Jesus the Savior is the dawning light of a new day to this dark world.

Is about to break upon us in holy visitation,
All because the mercy of our God is so very tender.
[79]The manifestation from heaven will come to us[a]
With dazzling light to shine upon those
Who live in darkness, near death's dark shadow.[b]
And he will illuminate the path that leads to the way of peace.

[80]Afterward, their son grew up and was strengthened by the Holy Spirit[c] and he grew in his love for God. John chose to live in the lonely wilderness until the day came when he was to be displayed publicly to Israel.

---

a 1:79 As translated from the Aramaic.
b 1:79 Zechariah is quoting from Isaiah 9:2 and 59:8.
c 1:80 Both of John's parents were full of the Holy Spirit (verses.41, 67). John was raised in a Spirit-filled home.

$$Two$$

The Birth of Jesus

[1-2]During those days, the Roman emperor, Caesar Augustus,[a] ordered that the first census be taken throughout his empire. (Quirinius was the governor of Syria at that time.) [3]Everyone had to travel to his or her hometown to complete the mandatory census. [4-5]So Joseph and his fiancé, Mary, left Nazareth,[b] a village in Galilee, and journeyed to their hometown in Judea, to the village of Bethlehem,[c] King David's ancient home. They were required to register there, since they were both direct descendants of David. Mary was pregnant and nearly ready to give birth.

[6-7]When they arrived in Bethlehem, Mary went into labor, and there she gave birth to her firstborn son. After wrapping the newborn baby in strips of cloth, they laid him in a feeding trough since there was no room in the inn.

An Angelic Encounter

[8]That night, in a field[d] near Bethlehem, there were shepherds watching over their flocks. [9]Suddenly, an angel of the Lord appeared in radiant splendor before them, lighting up the field with the blazing glory of God, and the shepherds were terrified! [10]But the angel reassured them, saying, "Don't be afraid.

---

a 2:1–2 It is ironic that the Roman emperors viewed themselves as "gods" while the little baby born in a feeding trough was the true God incarnate.

b 2:4–5 "Nazareth" is taken from a Hebrew word for "branch" (Isaiah 11:1).

c 2:4–5 The distance from Nazareth to Bethlehem is about sixty-five miles and would have taken a number of days for them to arrive. Bethlehem, or Byt-lehem, means "house of bread," the prophesied birthplace of Messiah. However, the Hebrew word *lechem* is a homonym for "fighter" or "warrior." Jesus was born in "the House of Fighters." This is the city of David, one of the greatest fighters in the entire Bible. Perhaps this is why the people of Jesus' day expected him to fight the Romans and free their land from foreign occupation. Jesus fulfilled both aspects of the meaning of Bethlehem in Gethsemane and on the cross, where he fought the "Goliath" of our souls and won, becoming bread for the world. God controls all events, proven by the prophecy that Jesus would be born in Bethlehem, even though his parents were living in Nazareth. See Micah 5:2.

d 2:8 Many scholars believe that these could be the same fields where sacrificial flocks were kept for temple worship. How fitting that these shepherds would hear the announcement of the birth of the Lamb of God. Others believe these fields could have been near the field of Boaz, or the fields where David once watched over the flocks of his father, Jesse.

For I have come to bring you good news, the most joyous news the world has ever heard! And it is for everyone everywhere! [11]For today in Bethlehem[a] a rescuer was born for you. He is the Lord Yahweh, the Messiah.[b] [12]You will recognize him by this miracle sign: you will find a baby wrapped in strips of cloth and lying in a feeding trough!"[c]

[13]Then all at once, a vast number of glorious angels appeared, the very armies of heaven! And they all praised God, singing:

> [14]**Glory to God in the highest realms of heaven!**
> **For there is peace[d] and a good hope[e] given to the sons of men.**

[15]When the choir of angels disappeared back to heaven, the shepherds said to one another, "Let's go! Let's hurry and find this Manifestation[f] that is born in Bethlehem and see for ourselves what the Lord has revealed to us." [16]So they ran into the village and found their way to Mary and Joseph. And there was the baby, lying in a feeding trough.

[17]Upon seeing this miraculous sign, the shepherds recounted what had just happened. [18]Everyone who heard the shepherds' story was astonished by what they were told.

[19]But Mary treasured all these things in her heart and often pondered what they meant.

[20]The shepherds returned to their flock, ecstatic over what had happened. They praised God and glorified him for all they had heard and seen for themselves, just like the angel had said.

---

a 2:11 The Greek text says, "the city of David."

b 2:11 Translated literally from the Aramaic text. This is one of the most amazing statements found in the Gospels declaring the deity of Jesus Christ.

c 2:12 A baby lying in a feeding trough where animals were kept nearby, wrapped in strips of burial cloths, became a sign of the Man-Savior's life on earth. He entered the world as a lowly baby, and though he is the mighty God, he lived his life on earth in gentleness before all.

d 2:14 Luke's gospel is the gospel of peace. The four prominent sacrifices of the Old Testament are emphasized in the four Gospels. In Matthew we see the death of Christ in the figure of the trespass offering, in Mark the sin offering, in Luke the peace offering, and in John the burnt offering. The peace God gives us is emphasized in Luke's gospel, which is why the angels announced peace and hope. On the day of his resurrection Jesus said, "Peace be unto you."

e 2:14 As translated from the Aramaic. The Greek is "good will."

f 2:15 As translated from the Aramaic text. The Greek is the word *rhema*.

Baby Jesus Dedicated in the Temple

²¹On the day of the baby's circumcision ceremony, eight days after his birth, his parents gave him the name Jesus, the name prophesied by the angel before he was born. ²²After Mary's days of purification had ended, it was time for her to come to the temple with a sacrifice, according to the laws of Moses after the birth of a son.ᵃ So Mary and Joseph took the baby Jesus to Jerusalem to be dedicated before the Lord.ᵇ ²³For it is required in the law of the Lord, **"Every firstborn male shall be a set-apart one for God."**ᶜ ²⁴And, to offer a prescribed sacrifice, **"either a pair of turtledoves or two young pigeons."**ᵈ

²⁵As they came to the temple to fulfill this requirement, an elderlyᵉ man was there waiting—a resident of Jerusalem whose name was Simeon. He was a very good man, a lover of God who kept himself pure, and the Spirit of holiness rested upon him. Simeon believed in the imminent appearing of the one called The Refreshing of Israel.ᶠ ²⁶For the Holy Spirit had revealed to himᵍ that he would not see death before he saw the Messiah, the Anointed One of God. ²⁷For this reason the Holy Spirit had moved him to be in the temple court at the very moment Jesus' parents entered to fulfill the requirement of the sacrifice.

²⁸Simeon cradled the baby in his arms and praised God and prophesied, saying:

> ²⁹⁻³¹**Lord and Master, I am your loving servant,**
> **And now I can die content,**
> **For your promise to me has been fulfilled.**
> **With my own eyes I have seen your Manifestation,**ʰ

---

a 2:22 This comes from Leviticus 12:1–7. When a son was born, the mother went through a forty-day period of purification, and then she was to offer a sacrifice to complete the process.

b 2:22 The ark of the covenant, signifying the presence of God, had been absent from the temple since 587 BC, when the Babylonians destroyed the temple. Herod's temple had no ark of covenant until Jesus came into the temple that day. God returned to the temple when Mary carried her baby into its courts. What a dramatic moment! See Malachi 3:1–2.

c 2:23 Exodus 13:2, 12.

d 2:24 Because Joseph and Mary were rather poor, not yet having received the gifts brought by the wise men, they offered a pair of doves or pigeons instead of a lamb (Leviticus 12:8). Mary offered a sin offering, showing her need of a Savior. Jesus would one day be offered as her true Lamb.

e 2:25 Implied in the context.

f 2:25 The Refreshing of Israel is a name for Jesus that can also be translated "The Encourager of Israel."

g 2:26 Simeon's name means "He who hears."

h 2:31 As translated from the Aramaic text.

> The Savior you sent into the world.
> [32] He will be glory for your people Israel,
> And the Revelation Light
> For all people everywhere![a]

[33]Mary and Joseph stood there, awestruck over what was being said about their baby.

Simeon then blessed them and prophesied over Mary, saying:

> [34-35]A painful sword[b] will one day pierce your inner being,
> For your child will be rejected by many in Israel.
> And the destiny of your child is this:
> He will be laid down[c] as a miracle sign
> For the downfall[d] and resurrection of many in Israel.
> Many will oppose this sign, but it will expose to all
> The innermost thoughts of their hearts before God.

[36-37]A prophetess named Anna was also in the temple court that day. She was from the Jewish tribe of Asher and the daughter of Phanuel.[e] Anna was an aged widow who had been married only seven years before her husband passed away. After he died she chose to worship God in the temple continually. For the past eighty-four years[f] she had been serving God with night-and-day prayer and fasting.

[38]While Simeon was prophesying over Mary and Joseph and the baby, Anna walked up to them and burst forth with a great chorus of praise to God for the child. And from that day forward she told everyone in Jerusalem who was waiting for their redemption that the anticipated Messiah had come![g]

a 2:32 This is a fulfillment of many Old Testament prophesies, such as those found in Isaiah 9:2, 40:5, 42:6, 49:6, 51:4, and 60:1–3.

b 2:34–35 This is a unique Greek word used for "sword." Literally, it means "a large broadsword."

c 2:34–35 The Greek word translated "appointed" actually means "to lie down." Jesus was laid in a tomb for us and rose again for us.

d 2:34–35 The Greek word translated "falling" can also be translated "downfall" or "destruction." Perhaps this was a prophecy of the cross of Jesus Christ, where many will rise or fall depending on what they do with Jesus' death and resurrection. We are all destined to be joined to him in his death and resurrection (Galatians 2:20). Every believer experiences both a "downfall" and a "resurrection."

e 2:36–37 The name Asher means "blessed." Phanuel means "the face of God."

f 2:36–37 Some Greek manuscripts make her age to be eighty-four. But the most reliable Greek and Aramaic texts state that she had been in the temple for eighty-four years. If so, this would make her at that time to be about one hundred six. God is faithful to those who wait in faith. Both Simeon and Anna were privileged to touch the Christ before they died in faith.

g 2:38 The Greek text literally says that Anna told everyone "who was looking for the redemption of Jerusalem." This is a figure of speech for the one who would come and set them free; i.e., the Messiah. What amazing prophetic words came through Simeon and Anna!

³⁹When Mary and Joseph had completed everything required of them by the law of Moses, they took Jesus and returned to their home^a in Nazareth in Galilee. ⁴⁰The child grew more powerful in grace, for he was being filled with wisdom, and the favor of God was upon him.

At Age Twelve Jesus Visits the Temple

⁴¹Every year Jesus' parents went to worship at Jerusalem during the Passover festival. ⁴²When Jesus turned twelve,^b his parents took him to Jerusalem to observe the Passover, as was their custom. ⁴³A full day after they began their journey home, Joseph and Mary realized that Jesus was missing. ⁴⁴They had assumed he was somewhere in their entourage, but he was nowhere to be found. After a frantic search among relatives and friends, ⁴⁵Mary and Joseph returned to Jerusalem to search for him.

⁴⁶After being separated from him for three days, they finally found him in the temple, sitting among the Jewish teachers,^c listening to them and asking questions. ⁴⁷All who heard Jesus speak were astounded at his intelligent understanding of all that was being discussed and at his wise answers to their questions.

⁴⁸His parents were shocked to find him there, and Mary scolded him, saying, "Son, your father and I have searched for you everywhere! We have been worried sick over not finding you. Why would you do this to us?"

⁴⁹Jesus said to them, **"Why would you need to search for me? Didn't you know that it was necessary for me to be here in my Father's house, consumed with him?"**^d

⁵⁰Mary and Joseph didn't fully understand what Jesus meant.

---

a 2:39 Luke omits their journey to Egypt to spare Jesus from the death decree of Herod. That information is given to us by Matthew. But none of the Gospels gives all the details of this period. Luke also has nothing about the visit of the wise men (Matthew 2:1–12), and Matthew tells nothing of the shepherds or of Simeon and Anna (Luke 2:8–28). All four Gospels supplement one another. A long period of time likely transpired between verse 38 and verse 39.

b 2:42 At the age of twelve, a boy was called by the Jews a "son of the law." The number twelve is found often in the Bible and is linked to God's perfect administration and our human alignment to it. God's family of Israel was made up of twelve tribes, twelve sons of Jacob. Jesus chose twelve apostles, there are twelve months in the yearly cycle, and there are twenty-four elders around God's throne (twelve times two). Jesus coming into the house of God at age twelve points to the perfect alignment he had with his Father as the Apostle of our faith. See Hebrews 3:1.

c 2:46 Or "rabbis."

d 2:49 The first recorded words of Jesus, when he was only twelve, are given to us here.

⁵¹Jesus went with them back home to Nazareth and was obedient to them. His mother[a] treasured Jesus' words deeply in her heart. ⁵²As Jesus grew, so did his wisdom and maturity. The favor of men increased upon his life, for he was loved greatly by God.[b]

---

a 2:51 Mary was an amazing woman and should be honored as the mother of our Lord Jesus Christ. She was the only human being who was with Jesus all the way from his birth to his death. She is also mentioned in Acts 1:14.

b 2:52 We know virtually nothing about the eighteen years between Luke 2 and Luke 3, when Jesus went to the Jordan to be baptized by the prophet John. We knew he grew in favor with God and men. He served his earthly father in a carpenter's shop. It is likely that Joseph, Jesus' earthly father, died during this season of his life. This left Jesus with the responsibility as firstborn to provide for his family. Amazing mysteries surround this one who is too marvelous for words!

Three

John the Baptizer

¹⁻²A powerful message from God came to John, Zechariah's son, when he was living out in the lonely wilderness.^a This prophetic commission came to John during the fifteenth year of the reign of Emperor Tiberius, son of Caesar. Pontius Pilate was governor over Judea at that time. Antipas, son of Herod, was governor over Galilee, Herod's brother Philip was over the region of Ituraea and Trachonitis, and Lysanias was over Abilene.^b This happened during the days of two high priests, Annas and Caiaphas.^c

³John went preaching and baptizing throughout the Jordan Valley. He persuaded people to turn away from their sins and turn to God^d for the freedom of forgiveness.^e

⁴This was to fulfill what was written in the book of the prophet Isaiah:

> **"Listen! You will hear a thunderous voice in the lonely wilderness telling you to wake up and get your heart ready for the coming of the Lord Jehovah.^f Every twisted thing in your lives**

---

a 3:1–2 Some believe that John may have been a member of the Qumran community of Jewish Essenes, who lived in the wilderness because they viewed the Jewish religious system as corrupt.

b 3:1–2 A region west of Ituraea.

c 3:1–2 As the forerunner of Jesus Christ, the prophet John was a hinge of human history who forever changed the world. Luke carefully dates this event by giving us six markers. Historians have dated the reign of Tiberius Caesar as beginning in AD 14. The fifteenth year of his reign would be AD 28–29. Regarding Annas and Caiaphas, never in Jewish history had there been two high priests. The priesthood was corrupt. Even though Caiaphas, Annas's son-in-law, was the high priest, Annas remained the real authoritative leader behind the scenes (John 18:13; Acts 4:6).

d 3:3 This is the definition of repentance, and it has two concepts. One is turning away from sin; the other is turning to God for freedom. They are linked together as one word, translated "repentance." The Aramaic word has the concept of returning to God, to unite with Unity.

e 3:3 John's message was revolutionary, for the religion of the day taught that forgiveness could only be found temporarily by offering sacrifices in the temple. John, an Essene, told the people that forgiveness of sin was a heart issue, not gained by an animal sacrifice offered in the corrupt religious system of the day. Repentance, breaking open the heart, is more important than gaining forgiveness by religious acts.

f 3:4 Translated from the Aramaic.

must be made straight. ⁵⁻⁶Every dark way must be brought to the light. Wrongs righted. Injustices removed. Every heart of pride will be humbled low before him. Every deception will be exposed and replaced by the truth[a] so that everyone everywhere will be ready to see the Life of God!"[b]

⁷John kept preaching to the many crowds who came out to be baptized, "You are nothing but the offspring of poisonous snakes, full of deception! Have you been warned to repent before the coming wrath of God? ⁸Then turn away from your sins, turn to God, and prove it by a changed life. Don't think for a moment that it's enough to simply be the favored descendants of Abraham. That's not enough to save you.[c] I'm telling you, God could make more sons of Abraham out of stones if he chose to!

⁹"Even now God's axe of judgment is poised to chop down your barren tree right down to its roots! And every tree that does not produce good fruit will be leveled and thrown into the fire."

¹⁰The crowd kept asking him, "What then are we supposed to do?"

¹¹John told them, "Give food to the hungry, clothe the poor, and bless the needy."[d]

¹²Even the despised tax collectors came to John to be baptized, and they asked him, "What are we to do to prove our hearts have changed?"

¹³"Be honest," he replied. "Don't demand more taxes than what you are required to collect."[e]

¹⁴"And us?" asked some soldiers.[f] "What about us?"

John answered them, "Be content with what you earn. Never extort money or terrify others by threats of violence or be guilty of accusing the innocent."

---

a 3:5–6 The Greek text, quoting from Isaiah 40:3–5, is literally translated "Wake up and make lines for the Lord, make his side alleys straight. Every ravine will be filled, every mountain and hill shall be leveled, the crooked straightened, rough ways smoothed, and all flesh shall see the salvation of God." Every honest scholar recognizes this as more than a road construction project, implying a spiritual renewal in hearts.

b 3:5–6 Translated from the Aramaic. The Aramaic word translated "life" often refers to salvation.

c 3:8 Implied in the context. God values reformation over ritual. John's ministry was to prepare people for the appearing of Jesus Christ through repentance and baptism. Repentance breaks open the heart and changes our attitudes toward God. Baptism was a burial of those who repented, preparing them for the germination of Christ coming to live within by the new birth.

d 3:11 The Greek text is literally "The one with two tunics is to share with him who has none, and he who has food is to do likewise."

e 3:13 True repentance is tied to actions, a change of heart and deeds, not just words.

f 3:14 They were likely temple police.

¹⁵During those days, everyone was gripped with messianic expectations, believing the Messiah could come at any moment, and many began to wonder if John might be the Christ.

¹⁶But John made it clear by telling them, "There is one coming who is mightier than I. He is supreme.^a In fact, I'm not worthy of even being his slave.^b I can only baptize you in this river, but he will baptize you into the Spirit of holiness and into his raging fire.^c ¹⁷He has in his hands the authority to judge your hearts and the power to sift and cleanse you. He will separate the valuable within you from that which is worthless.^d The valuable he will store up for use in his kingdom, but he will burn the worthless in a fire that no one can ever put out!"

¹⁸John used many similar warnings as he preached the good news and prepared^e the people. ¹⁹He even publicly rebuked Antipas, son of Herod, the governor of Galilee, for the many wicked things he had done. He fearlessly reprimanded him for seducing and marrying his sister-in-law, Herodias.

²⁰Adding to his many other sins, Herod had John seized and locked up in prison.

The Baptism of Jesus

²¹⁻²²One day Jesus came to be baptized^f along with all the others. As he was consumed with the spirit of prayer,^g the heavenly realm ripped open above him and the Holy Spirit descended from heaven in the visible, tangible form of

---

a 3:16 The word translated "supreme" is found only in the Aramaic text. John was a true prophet who pointed others to the Supreme One. Before John came on the scene, there had not been a prophet in Israel for four hundred years.

b 3:16 Or "loose his sandal strap," which only a slave would do.

c 3:16 The Aramaic text reads, "He will baptize you into the Spirit of the Holy One and in light." A baptism of light or fire would cleanse and change a life, giving new power to live for God and deal with every issue that hinders love and passion from burning in our hearts. It is the baptism of the Holy Spirit that is needed today.

d 3:17 The text is literally, "a winnowing fork is in his hand." This was a small pitchfork used to separate the chaff from the grain.

e 3:18 Translated from the Aramaic text.

f 3:21–22 Jesus identified with sinners, even at his baptism. Although he had no sin, he chose to become one with sinners and was washed by John as a preview of what would come when he became sin and was judged for our sins at the cross.

g 3:21–22 We read about Jesus praying eight times in Luke's gospel. 1) At his baptism Jesus prayed and the heavens were opened, revealing his sonship. Jesus asked the Father to send the Holy Spirit to strengthen him for his wilderness temptations [3:21–23]. 2) Jesus prayed in solitude, and miracles broke loose in his ministry [5:16–17]. 3) Jesus prayed all night before he chose his twelve companions [6:12–16]. 4) Jesus prayed for his apostles to receive the full revelation of who he is [9:18–22]. 5) When Jesus was about to be glorified in splendor on the mountain, he prayed, and his face glowed with a flashing light [9:28–29]. 6) Jesus prayed that he would be an example to every one of his disciples [11:1]. 7) Jesus prayed for Peter's restoration and future ministry [22:31–32]. 8) Jesus prayed in Gethsemane for strength and glory as the terrors of Calvary lay before him [22:41–46].

a dove[a] and landed on him. Then God's audible voice was heard, saying, **"My Son, you are my beloved one.[b] Through you I am fulfilled."[c]**

The Ancestry of Jesus Christ

[23-38]Jesus, assumed to be Joseph's son, was about thirty years old when he began his ministry.[d] Here are the names of Mary's[e] ancestors, from her father traced all the way back to Adam:

Eli,[f] Matthat, Levi, Melki, Jannai, Joseph, Mattathias, Amos, Nahum, Esli, Naggai, Maath, Mattathias, Semein, Josech, Joda,

Joanan, Rhesa, Zerubbabel, Shealtiel, Neri, Melchi, Addi, Cosam, Elmadam, Er, Joshua, Eliezer, Jorim, Matthat, Levi, Simeon, Judah, Joseph, Jonam, Eliakim, Melea, Menna, Mattatha, Nathan, David, Jesse, Obed, Boaz, Salmon, Nahshon, Amminadab, Admin, Arni, Hezron, Perez, Judah, Jacob, Isaac, Abraham, Terah, Nahor, Serug, Reu, Peleg, Eber, Shelah, Kenan, Arphaxad, Shem, Noah, Lamech, Methuselah, Enoch, Jared, Mahalaleel, Cainan, Enos, Seth, and Adam, who was created by God.[g]

a 3:21–22 After the flood, Noah released doves from the ark. The final one he released never returned. Similarly, the Holy Spirit flew over the patriarchs and prophets for generations, yet there was no one upon whom he could land and rest—not until Jesus, the Lamb of God. What a beautiful picture: a dove resting on a lamb. To have the power of the Spirit (dove), we need to have the nature of the Lamb (Jesus). Although Jesus had the Holy Spirit from his immaculate conception, at his baptism he received the abiding presence of the Holy Spirit to fulfill his ministry. God gives more and more of his Spirit to those who love him and obey him.

b 3:21–22 The heavenly voice confirms the identity of Jesus as Messiah. God quoted Psalm 2:7 and Isaiah 42:1, both of which are considered as speaking of the Christ. God publicly stated that Jesus was the long-awaited and much-loved Son, the Christ. The Trinity is clearly seen in this passage: Jesus, the Holy Spirit, and the Father.

c 3:21–22 As translated from the Aramaic text. The Greek text states, "in whom I am greatly pleased." When the presence of the Holy Spirit came upon the Son of God, those around him heard the voice of the Father. We see from this a picture of the triune God, three in one.

d 3:23–38 Old Testament priests could not begin their ministry until they were thirty years old. The number thirty is the biblical number of maturity. Both Joseph and David were promoted to the place of honor when they were thirty.

e 3:23–38 Matthew gives us the genealogy of Jesus from Joseph's family, while Luke's genealogy is from Mary's side. Luke is the only gospel writer who gives much attention to women. Neither Matthew nor Luke gives a complete genealogy.

f 3:23–38 Matthew identifies Joseph's father as Jacob (Matthew 1:16), while Luke says he was Eli's (Heli's) son (Luke 3:23). The ancient world often referred to a man's sons-in-law as his own sons. Thus it is possible that Eli was Mary's father and Joseph's father-in-law.

g 3:38 As translated from the Aramaic. The Greek text states, "the son of God."

Four

Jesus Tested in the Wilderness

[1-2]From the moment of his baptism, Jesus was overflowing with the Holy Spirit. He was taken by the Spirit from the Jordan into the lonely wilderness of Judea[a] to experience the ordeal of testing[b] by the accuser[c] for forty days.[d] He ate no food during this time and ended his forty-day fast very hungry. [3]It was then the Devil said to him, "If you are really the Son of God, command this stone to turn into a loaf of bread for you."

[4]Jesus replied, **"I will not!**[e] **For it is written in the Scriptures,**[f] **'Life does not come only from eating bread but from God. Life flows from every revelation from his mouth.'"**[g]

[5]The Devil lifted Jesus high into the sky[h] and in a flash showed him all the kingdoms and regions of the world. [6-7]The Devil then said to Jesus, "All of this, with all its power, authority, and splendor, is mine to give to whomever I wish. Just do one thing and you will have it all. Simply bow down to worship me and it will be yours! You will possess everything!"

---

a   4:1–2 The Holy Spirit's leading is not always into comfort and ease. The Spirit may lead us, as he did Jesus, into places where we will be proven, tested, and strengthened for our future ministry. After Jesus' greatest affirmation from heaven came a great time of testing.

b   4:1–2 The Greek word here means "to test with a sinister motive." This test was more than proving that Jesus could overcome this ordeal. It proved that Satan was defeated by Christ's appearing.

c   4:1–2 The words "accuser" and "devil" are used interchangeably in this translation.

d   4:1–2 Jesus' baptism and the forty days of wilderness temptations that followed evoke parallels with the historical narrative of the Hebrew exodus through the Red Sea and the forty years of wilderness testing.

e   4:4 Jesus refused to turn stones to bread, yet today he transforms the stony hearts of human beings and converts us into living bread to give to the nations.

f   4:4 Jesus, the living Word, is quoting from the written Word (Deuteronomy 8:3). If the living Word used the written Word against the Enemy's temptations, how much more do we need the revelation of what has been written so we can stand against all his snares?

g   4:4 This is implied by both the Greek and Aramaic texts. Although this last clause is missing in some Greek manuscripts, it is included in the Aramaic.

h   4:5 Implied, for the Greek text simply says, "took him up," without telling us where.

⁸Jesus rebuked him and said, **"Satan, get behind me!ᵃ For it is written in the Scriptures, 'Only one is worthy of your adoration. You will worship before the Lord your God and love him supremely.'"ᵇ**

⁹Next, the Devil took Jesus to Jerusalem and set him on the highest point of the temple and tempted him there, saying, "If you really are the Son of God, jump down in front of all the people. ¹⁰⁻¹¹For isn't it written in the Scriptures, **'God has given his angels instructions to protect you from harm. For the hands of angels will hold you up and keep you from hurting even one foot on a stone'?"ᶜ**

¹²Jesus replied, **"It is also written in the Scriptures, 'How dare you provoke the Lord your God!'"ᵈ**

¹³That finished the Devil's harassment for the time being. So he stood off at a distance, retreating until the time came to return and tempt Jesus again.

¹⁴Then Jesus, armed with the Holy Spirit's power, returned to Galilee, and his fame spread throughout the region. ¹⁵He taught in the meeting placesᵉ and offered everyone glory.ᶠ

¹⁶⁻¹⁷When he came to Nazareth,ᵍ where he had been raised, he went into the meeting house, as he always did on the Sabbath day. When Jesus came to the front to read the Scriptures,ʰ they handed him the scroll of the prophet Isaiah. He unrolled the scroll and read where it is written, ¹⁸⁻¹⁹**"The Spirit of the Lord is upon me, and he has anointed me to be hopeⁱ for the poor, freedom for the brokenhearted, and new eyesʲ for the blind, and to preach to prisoners,ᵏ**

---

a 4:8 This is found in the majority of later manuscripts. See also Matthew 4:10.
b 4:8 This is taken from Deuteronomy 6:13 and 10:20.
c 4:8 The Devil is quoting from Psalm 91:11–12, but he misapplies it.
d 4:10–11 Jesus was not deceived. He quotes here from Deuteronomy 6:16.
e 4:14 This was the Jewish synagogue, the meeting place for the Jewish people. Every village that had at least ten families would erect a meeting house where they would come and hear visiting teachers expound the Scriptures.
f 4:14 As literally translated from the Aramaic text.
g 4:15–17 This is Netzaret, which is taken from the Hebrew word for "branch" or "sprout."
h 4:15–17 It was the custom of the day to read the Scriptures in Hebrew and then paraphrase it into Aramaic, the common language of that day.
i 4:18–19 Or "good news."
j 4:18–19 The Greek word is translated "looking up to heaven" in Mark 6:41.
k 4:18–19 Literally, "prisoners of war."

'You are set free!' I have come to share the message of Jubilee,[a] for the time of God's great acceptance[b] has begun."[c]

²⁰After he read this he rolled up the scroll, handed it back to the minister, and sat down. Everyone stared at Jesus, wondering what he was about to say. ²¹Then he added, **"These Scriptures came true today in front of you."**

²²Everyone was impressed by how well Jesus spoke, in awe of the beautiful words of grace that came from his lips. But they were surprised at his presumption to speak as a prophet,[d] so they said among themselves, "Who does he think he is?[e] This is Joseph's son, who grew up here in Nazareth."[f]

²³Jesus said to them, "I suppose you'll quote me the proverb, 'Doctor, go and heal yourself before you try to heal others.' And you'll say, 'Work the miracles here in your hometown that we heard you did in Capernaum.' ²⁴But let me tell you, no prophet is welcomed or honored in his own hometown.

²⁵"Isn't it true that there were many widows in the land of Israel during the days of the prophet Elijah when he locked up the heavens for three and a half years and brought a devastating famine over all the land? ²⁶But he wasn't sent to any of the widows living in that region. Instead, he was sent to a foreign place, to a widow in Zarephath of Sidon.[g] ²⁷Or have you not considered that the prophet Elisha healed only Naaman,[h] the Syrian, rather than one of the many Jewish lepers living in the land?"

²⁸When everyone present heard those words, they erupted with furious rage.[i] ²⁹They mobbed Jesus and threw him out of the city, dragging him to the edge of the cliff on the hill on which the city had been built, ready to hurl him off. ³⁰But he walked right through the crowd, leaving them all stunned.[j]

---

a 4:18–19 Implied in the text. See Leviticus 25:8–17, Isaiah 58:6, and 61:1–2. The Isaiah passage is associated with the proclamation of the Year of Jubilee. The Greek word used here implies a cycle of time. Jesus clearly defined his mission by reading these words of the prophet Isaiah.

b 4:18–19 Or "favor." This phrase can be translated "the years when God will accept man."

c 4:18–19 This is quoted from Isaiah 61:1.

d 4:22 Implied in the context.

e 4:22 This is the inferred meaning of their criticism of Jesus. His true Father was not Joseph, but Yahweh.

f 4:22 Implied in the text.

g 4:26 Zarephath means "the place of refining." Sidon means "fishery" and was a Phoenician seaport city.

h 4:27 Both the Aramaic and Greek texts have "Naaman the Aramean" or "descendant of Aram." The Arameans inhabited what is now Syria. Naaman means "pleasantness."

i 4:28 Jesus' listeners got the point of his sermon. His statements implied that he would take his miracle ministry to non-Jewish people. Jubilee had come, not only for them, but for those they hated. This infuriated them enough to want to kill Jesus.

j 4:30 The Greek text clearly implies it was a supernatural event. After hearing Jesus' first sermon, they wanted to throw him off a cliff!

Jesus Confronts a Demonized Man

³¹Jesus went to Capernaum in Galilee and taught the people on the Sabbath day. ³²His teachings stunned and dazed[a] them, for he spoke with penetrating words that manifested great authority.

³³In the congregation there was a demonized man, who screamed out with a loud voice, ³⁴"Hey, you! Go away and leave us alone. I know who you are. You're Jesus of Nazareth, God's holy one. Why are you coming to meddle with us? Have you come to destroy us already?"[b]

³⁵Just then the demon hurled the man down on the floor in front of them all. But Jesus rebuked the demon, **"Be quiet and come out of him!"** And the demon came out of him without causing him any harm.

³⁶Great astonishment swept over the people, and they said among themselves, "What kind of man is this who has such power and authority? With a mere word he commands demons to come out and they obey him!" ³⁷

The reports about Jesus spread like wildfire throughout every community in the surrounding region.

Jesus Heals Many

³⁸After leaving the meeting that day, Jesus went into Simon's house, where Simon's mother-in-law was sick with a high fever. The disciples begged Jesus to help her. ³⁹Jesus stood over her and rebuked the fever,[c] and she was healed instantly. Then she got up and began to serve them.

⁴⁰At sunset,[d] the people brought all those who were sick to Jesus to be healed. Jesus laid his hands on them one by one, and they were all healed of different ailments and sicknesses.

⁴¹Demons also came out of many of them. The demons knew that Jesus was the Anointed One, so they shouted while coming out, "You are the

a 4:32 The Greek word used here, *ekplesso*, is a strong verb that means "struck with amazement, astonished, panic stricken, shocked" or "something that takes your breath away (like being hit with a blow)" or "to expel, to drive out." Jesus spoke with such glory and power emanating from him that his words were like thunderbolts into their hearts. May we hear his words in the same way today.

b 4:34 This is not a question but an assertive statement.

c 4:39 Five times in this chapter Jesus corrects and rebukes various things and persons. He rebuked Satan (verse 8) and the unbelieving people in his hometown (verses 23–27). Twice he rebuked demons (verses 35 and 41). And in this verse he rebukes fever.

d 4:40 People came before dark. The Sabbath, which was to be a day of rest for every Jew, began at sunset on Friday and ended at sunset on Saturday.

Messiah, the Son of El Shaddai!"[a] But Jesus rebuked them and commanded them to be silent.

[42] At daybreak the next morning, the crowds came and searched everywhere for him, but Jesus had already left to go to a secluded place. When they finally found him, they held him tightly, begging him to stay with them in Capernaum. [43] But Jesus said, **"Don't you know there are other places I must go to and offer them the hope found in the kingdom of God?[b] This is what I have been sent to do."**

[44] Jesus continued to travel and preach in the Jewish meeting places throughout the land.

a 4:41 Or "Son of God." El Shaddai is used to emphasize the Hebraic word for God Almighty. See footnote on Psalm 91:1.
b 4:43 The gospel includes the hope of an eternal kingdom. Conversion is not found in believing an historical event but in the change of heart that is found in the revelation of God's kingdom that changes our hearts.

Five
———

The Miracle Catch of Fish

[1]On one occasion, Jesus was preaching to the crowds on the shore of the Sea of Galilee.[a] There was a vast multitude of people pushing to get close to Jesus to hear the word of God. [2]He noticed two fishing boats at the water's edge, with the fishermen nearby, rinsing their nets. [3]Jesus climbed into the boat belonging to Simon Peter and asked him, **"Let me use your boat. Push it off a short distance away from the shore so I can speak to the crowds."**

[4]Jesus sat down and taught the people from the boat. When he had finished, he said to Peter, **"Now row out to deep water to cast your nets and you will have a great catch."**

[5]"Master," Peter replied, "we've just come back from fishing all night and didn't catch a thing. But if you insist, we'll go out again and let down our nets because of your word."

[6]When they pulled up their nets, they were shocked to see a huge catch of fish, so much that their nets were ready to burst! [7]They waved to their business partners in the other boat for help. They ended up completely filling both boats with fish until their boats began to sink![b]

[8]When Simon Peter saw this astonishing miracle,[c] he knelt at Jesus' feet and begged him, "Go away from me, Master, for I am a sinful man!"

[9-10]Simon Peter and the other fishermen—including his fishing partners, James and John, the sons of Zebedee—were awestruck over the miracle catch of fish.

---

a 5:1 Or "Gennesaret," which is known as the Sea of Galilee.
b 5:7 It has been estimated that this was a catch of nearly one ton of fish, what was normally caught in two weeks. The miracle is even greater when we consider that fishing was normally only done at night.
c 5:8 Implied in the text.

Jesus answered, **"Do not yield to your fear, Simon Peter. From now on you will catch men for salvation!"**[a]

[11]After pulling their boats to the shore, they left everything behind and followed Jesus.

Jesus, the Healer

[12]One day, while Jesus was ministering in a certain city, he came upon a man covered with leprous sores. When the man recognized Jesus, he fell on his face at Jesus' feet and begged to be healed, saying, "If you are only willing, you could completely heal me."

[13-14]Jesus reached out and touched him[b] and said, **"Of course I am willing to heal you, and now you will be healed."** Instantly the leprous sores were healed and his skin became smooth.

Jesus said, **"Tell no one what has happened, but go to the priest and show him you've been healed. And to show that you are purified, make an offering for your cleansing, just as Moses commanded. You will become a living testimony to them!"**

[15]After this miracle the news about Jesus spread even farther. Massive crowds continually gathered to hear him speak and to be healed from their illnesses. [16]But Jesus often slipped away from them and went into the wilderness to pray.

[17]One day many Jewish religious leaders, known as "separated ones,"[c] along with many religious scholars came from every village of Galilee, throughout Judea, and even from Jerusalem to hear Jesus teach. And the power of the Lord God surged through him to instantly heal.

[18]Some men came to Jesus, carrying a paraplegic man on a stretcher. They attempted to bring him in past the crowd to set him down in front of Jesus. [19]But because there were so many people crowding the door, they had no way to bring him inside. So they crawled onto the roof, dug their way through the roof

---

a 5:10 Translated literally from the Aramaic text. The Greek word *zoogreo* is a compound word of *zoos* (meaning "life") and *agreuo* (meaning "to catch"). Fishermen catch fish for death and to be consumed, but Peter was to catch men for life and to be set free.

b 5:13-14 For the religious Jew, touching a leper was forbidden because of the contamination. Jesus was not defiled in touching the leper; rather, the leper was healed.

c 5:17 Literally, "Pharisees," which means "separated ones."

tiles, and lowered the man, stretcher and all, into the middle of the crowd, right in front of Jesus.

[20]Seeing the demonstration of their faith, Jesus said to the paraplegic man, **"My friend, your sins are forgiven!"**

[21]The Jewish religious leaders and the religious scholars[a] whispered objections among themselves. "Who does this man think he is to speak such blasphemy? Only God can forgive sins. Does he think he is God?"

[22-23]Jesus, knowing their thoughts, said to them, **"Why do you argue in your hearts over what I do and think that it is blasphemy for me to say his sins are forgiven? Let me ask you, which is easier to prove: when I say, 'Your sins are forgiven,' or when I say, 'Stand up, carry your stretcher, and walk'?"**

Jesus turned to the paraplegic man and said, [24]**"To prove to you all that I, the Son of Man,[b] have the lawful authority on earth to forgive sins, I say to you now, stand up! Carry your stretcher and go on home, for you are healed."**

[25]In an instant, the man rose right before their eyes. He stood, picked up his stretcher, and went home, giving God all the glory with every step he took.

[26]The people were seized with astonishment and dumbfounded over what they had just witnessed. And they all praised God, remarking over and over, "Incredible! What an unbelievable miracle[c] we've seen today!"

Jesus Calls Matthew to Follow Him

[27]Afterward, Jesus went out and looked for a man named Matthew.[d] He found him sitting at his tax booth, for he was a tax collector. Jesus said to him, **"Be my disciple and follow me."** [28]That very moment, Matthew got up, left everything behind, and followed him.

[29-30]Matthew wanted to throw a banquet to honor Jesus. So he invited Jesus to his home for dinner, along with many tax collectors and other notable sinners. While they were all sitting together at the table, the Jewish religious

---

a 5:21 Or "scribes." They were the experts in the law of Moses.

b 5:24 This is the title Jesus uses for himself more than any other, especially in Luke. This refers to the vision of Daniel when he saw the Ancient of Days, and walking before the Ancient of Days was one like the Son of Man who would be given the right to judge the world. Calling himself the Son of Man was Jesus' claim to heavenly authority. It was more of an exalted and heavenly concept than being a human, the "son of a man." See Daniel 7:13 and Matthew 16:13-20.

c 5:26 Or "things we never expected," or "paradox."

d 5:27 The Greek text is "Levi," another name for Matthew.

leaders and experts of the law complained to Jesus' disciples, "Why would you defile yourselves by eating and drinking with tax collectors and sinners? Doesn't Jesus know it's wrong to do that?"[a]

[31] Jesus overheard their complaining and said, **"Who goes to the doctor for a cure? Those who are well or those who are sick?**[b] **[32] I have not come to call the 'righteous,' but to call those who fail to measure up and bring them to repentance."**

A Question about Fasting

[33] Jesus' critics questioned him. "John the prophet is known for leading his disciples to frequently fast and pray. As the religious leaders of the land, we do the same. Why do you and your disciples spend most of your time feasting at banquets?"[c]

[34] Jesus replied, **"Should you make the sons of the bridal chamber fast while celebrating with the Bridegroom? [35] But when the Bridegroom is taken away from them, then you will see them fasting."**

[36] And he gave them this illustration: **"No one rips up a new garment to make patches for an old, worn-out one. If you tear up the new to make a patch for the old, it will not match the old garment. [37] And who pours new wine into an old wineskin? If someone did, the old wineskin would burst and the new wine would be lost. [38] New wine must always be poured into new wineskins.**[d] **[39] Yet you say, 'The old ways are better,' and you refuse to even taste the new that I bring."**

---

a 5:29–30 Implied in the text.

b 5:31 The word used here is the Greek word for "evil." Sickness is a form of evil in God's eyes. Jesus came to heal the "evil" or sicknesses of earth.

c 5:33 It is likely that Matthew held his banquet on one of the Jewish fast days.

d 5:38 Christ is our new garment (righteousness) and our new wine that is poured into a new wineskin (our new life and divine nature). Many today are trying to patch up their old garments (self-righteousness), hoping their old lives can hold the new wine of the Spirit.

Six

Jesus and Religious Traditions

¹One Sabbath day, Jesus and his disciples were walking through a field of ripe wheat. His disciples plucked some heads of grain and rubbed the husks off with their hands and ate it. ²This infuriated some of the Jewish religious leaders. They said to Jesus, "Why are you allowing your disciples to harvest grain on the Sabbath day? Don't you know it's not permissible according to the law?"

³Jesus replied, **"Haven't you read the Scriptures? Haven't you read what King David did when he was hungry? ⁴He entered the sanctuary of God, took the bread of God's presence right off the sacred table, and shared it with his men.ᵃ It was only lawful for the priests to eat the bread of God's presence. ⁵You need to know that the Son of Man is no slave to the Sabbath day, for I am master over the Sabbath."**

⁶⁻⁷On another Sabbath day, Jesus was teaching in the Jewish meeting house. In the room with him was a man with a deformed right hand. Everyone watched Jesus closely, especially the Jewish religious leaders and the religious scholars, to see if Jesus would heal on a Sabbath day, for they were eager to find a reason to accuse him of breaking the Jewish laws.

⁸Jesus, knowing their every thought, said to the man with the deformed hand, "Come and stand here in the middle of the room." So he got up and came forward.

⁹Jesus said to all who were there, **"Let me ask you a question. Which is better: to heal or to do harm on the Sabbath day? I have come to save a life, but you have come to find a life to destroy."ᵇ**

---

a 6:4 This incident is found in 1 Samuel 21:1–6. Jesus referred to this story to prove to the Pharisees that they were hypocrites who were willing to overlook David's "violation" of the Sabbath but not Jesus' supposed "violation."

b 6:9 Jesus knew there were some present who wanted to "destroy" his life and would soon crucify him. He came to heal; they came to kill. They were the real Sabbath breakers.

[10]One by one Jesus looked into the eyes of each person in the room. Then he said to the man, **"Stretch out your arm and open your hand!"**

With everyone watching intently, he stretched out his arm, and his hand was completely healed!

[11]The room erupted with bitter rage because of this Sabbath-day healing. And from that moment on, the religious leaders plotted among themselves about how they might harm Jesus.

Jesus Chooses Twelve Apostles

[12]After this, Jesus went up into the high hills to spend the whole night in prayer to God.[a] [13]At daybreak he called together all of his followers and selected twelve from among them, and he appointed them to be his apostles.[b]

[14-16]Here are their names: Simon, whom he named Peter; Andrew, Peter's brother; James; John; Philip; Bartholomew;[c] Matthew; Thomas; James the son of Alpheus; Simon, known as a fiery political zealot; Judah the son of James;[d] and Judas the locksmith,[e] who later betrayed Jesus.

[17]Jesus and his apostles came down from the hillside to a level field, where a large number of his disciples waited, along with a massive crowd of people who had gathered from all over Judea, Jerusalem, and the coastal district of Tyre and Sidon.[f] [18]They had all come to listen to the Manifestation so that they could be healed of their diseases[g] and be set free from the demonic powers that tormented them. [19]The entire crowd eagerly tried to come near Jesus so they could touch him and be healed, because a tangible supernatural power emanated from him, healing all who came close to him.

---

a 6:12 This was the pattern of Jesus in the gospel accounts. Before he made important decisions and before great events in his life, he sought the Father. Once he saw what the Father wanted, Jesus obeyed as the perfect Son.

b 6:13 Apostle means "ambassador," "missionary," or "sent one." The apostles were all different in their personalities and came from different backgrounds. The people Jesus chooses today don't all look, act, or sound alike. The first ministry Jesus established was the apostolic. See 1 Corinthians 12:28 and Ephesians 4:11.

c 6:14–16 Many scholars believe that Bartholomew was the Nathanial mentioned in John 1:45–46.

d 6:14–16 He is also called Thaddeus, as mentioned in Matthew 10:3 and Mark 3:18.

e 6:14–16 The name Judas is actually Judah. Iscariot is not his last name, but could be taken from the name of the town, Kerioth, twelve miles south of Hebron. More plausibly, it is from a Hebrew word meaning "lock": Judah the locksmith. Most likely he was chosen to lock the collection bag, which means he had the key and could pilfer the funds at will. Sadly, he wanted to lock up Jesus and control him for his own ends.

f 6:17 The non-Jewish people flocked to hear Jesus, and he healed them all.

g 6:18 This is the literal translation of the Aramaic text.

Jesus Taught Them What Matters Most

[20]Looking intently at his followers, Jesus began his sermon. "**How enriched**[a] **you become when you are poor,**[b] **for you will experience the reality of the kingdom realm of God.**

[21]"How filled you become when you are consumed with hunger and desire, for you will be completely satisfied.

"How content you become when you weep with complete brokenness,[c] for you will laugh with unrestrained joy.

[22]"How favored you become when you are hated, excommunicated, or slandered, or when your name is spoken of as evil because of your love for me, the Son of Man.

[23]"I promise you that as you experience these things, you will celebrate and dance with overflowing joy. And the heavenly reward of your faith will be abundant, because you are being treated the same way as your forefathers the prophets.

[24]"But what sorrows await those of you who are rich in this life only. For you have already received all the comfort you'll ever get.

[25]"What sorrows await those of you who are complete and content with yourselves. For hunger and emptiness will come to you.

"What sorrows await those of you who laugh now, having received all your joy in this life only. For grief and wailing will come to you.

[26]"What sorrows await those of you who are always honored and lauded by others. For that's how your forefathers treated every other false prophet."

Love Your Enemies

[27]"But if you will listen, I say to you, love your enemies and do something wonderful[d] for them in return for their hatred. [28]When someone curses you, bless that person in return. When you are mistreated and harassed by others, accept it as your mission to pray for them. [29]To those who despise you,

---

a 6:18 Or "blessed." The Aramaic word for "blessed" can also be translated "ripe."
b 6:20 The Aramaic word for "poor" is *miskeneh*, which means "more poverty stricken." It can also mean "meek, humble" or "those who are poor in pride."
c 6:21 Implied in the text.
d 6:27 As translated from the Aramaic text.

continue to serve them and minister to them.[a] If someone takes away your coat, give him as a gift your shirt as well. ³⁰When someone comes to beg from you, give to that person what you have. When things are wrongly taken from you, do not demand they be given back. ³¹However you wish to be treated by others is how you should treat everyone else.

³²"Are you really showing true love by only loving those who love you back? Even those who don't know God will do that. ³³Are you really showing compassion when you do good deeds only to those who do good deeds to you? Even those who don't know God will do that.

³⁴"If you lend money only to those you know will repay you, what credit is that to your character? Even those who don't know God do that. ³⁵But love your enemies and continue to treat them well. When you lend money, don't despair[b] if you are never paid back, for it is not lost. You will receive a rich reward and you will be known as true children of the Most High God, having his same nature. For your Father is famous for his kindness to heal[c] even the thankless and cruel. ³⁶Show mercy and compassion for others, just as your heavenly Father overflows with mercy and compassion for all."

Judging Others

³⁷Jesus said, "Forsake the habit of criticizing and judging others, and then you will not be criticized and judged in return. Don't look at others and pronounce them guilty, and you will not experience guilty accusations yourself. Forgive over and over and you will be forgiven over and over. ³⁸Give generously and generous gifts will be given back to you, shaken down to make room for more. Abundant gifts will pour out upon you with such an overflowing measure that it will run over the top! Your measurement of generosity becomes the measurement of your return."

³⁹Jesus also quoted these proverbs: "What happens when a blind man pretends to guide another blind man? They both stumble into a ditch! ⁴⁰And how could the apprentice know more than his master, for only after he is fully

---

a 6:29 As literally translated from the Aramaic text. The Greek text states, "If someone strikes you on one side of your jaw, offer the other side too."

b 6:35 The Aramaic is literally "Do not cut off the hope of man."

c 6:35 Literal translation of the Aramaic text.

qualified will he be at that level. [41]Why do you focus on the flaw in someone else's life and fail to notice the glaring flaws of your own life?[a] [42]How could you say to your friend, 'Here, let me show you where you're wrong,' when you are guilty of even more than he is? You are overly critical, splitting hairs and being a hypocrite! You must acknowledge your own blind spots and deal with them before you will be able to deal with the blind spot of your friend."[b]

The Fruit of Your Life

[43]"You'll never find choice fruit hanging on a bad, unhealthy tree. And rotten fruit doesn't hang on a good, healthy tree. [44]Every tree will be revealed by the quality of fruit that it produces. Figs or grapes will never be picked off of thorn trees. [45]People are known in this same way. Out of the virtue stored in their hearts, good and upright people will produce good fruit. But out of the evil hidden in their hearts, evil ones will produce what is evil. For the overflow of what has been stored in your heart will be seen by your fruit and will be heard in your words.

[46]"What good does it do for you to say I am your Lord and Master if what I teach you is not put into practice? [47]Let me describe the one who truly follows me and does what I say. [48]He is like a man who chooses the right place to build a house and then lays a deep and secure foundation. When the storms and floods rage against that house, it continues to stand strong and unshaken through the tempest, for it has been wisely built on the right foundation. [49]But the one who has heard my teaching and does not obey it is like a man who builds a house without laying any foundation whatsoever. When the storms and floods rage against that house, it will immediately collapse and become a total loss. Which of these two builders will you be?"[c]

---

a 6:41 Or "Why do you see a speck in your brother's eye but fail to see the beam of wood sticking out of your own eye?"

b 6:42 Or "You hypocrite, why don't you first remove the beam sticking out of your own eye? Then you can see clearly to remove the small speck out of your brother's eye." Jesus is teaching that our blind spots prevent us from accurately evaluating the needs of others.

c 6:49 This last question is an important summary implied in the context.

$$Seven$$

Jesus Heals

[1]After Jesus finished giving revelation[a] to the people on the hillside, he went on to Capernaum.[b] [2-3]There he found a Roman military captain who had a beloved servant he valued highly, and the servant was sick to the point of death. When the captain heard that Jesus was in the city, he sent some respected Jewish elders to plead with him to come and heal his dying servant. [4]So they came to Jesus and told him, "The Roman captain is a wonderful man. If anyone deserves to have a visit from you, it is him. Won't you please come to his home and heal his servant? [5]For he loves the Jewish people, and he even built our meeting hall for us."

[6-7]Jesus started off with them, but on his way there, he was stopped by friends of the captain, who gave this message: "Master, don't bother to come to me in person, for I am not good enough for you to enter my home. I'm not worthy enough to even come out to meet one like you. But if you would just release the manifestation of healing right where you are, I know that my young servant will be healed.

[8]"Unlike you,[c] I am just an ordinary man. Yet I understand the power of authority, and I see that authority operating through you.[d] I have soldiers under me who obey my every command. I also have authorities over me whom I likewise obey. So Master, just speak the word and healing will flow."

[9]Jesus marveled at this. He turned around and said to the crowd who had followed him, **"Listen, everyone! Never have I found even one among the people of God a man like this who believes so strongly in me."** [10]Jesus then spoke

---

a 7:1 Or "teaching." The Greek word used here is *rhema*.
b 7:1 This is literally "the hamlet of Nahum," the village where Nahum the prophet lived.
c 7:8 The text implies that the Roman captain acknowledged that Jesus was more than a man.
d 7:8 Implied in the text.

the healing word from a distance.[a] When the man's friends returned to the home, they found the servant completely healed and doing fine.

Jesus Raises the Dead

[11]Shortly afterward, Jesus left on a journey for the village of Nain,[b] with a massive crowd of people following him, along with his disciples. [12]As he approached the village, he met a multitude of people in a funeral procession, who were mourning as they carried the body of a young man to the cemetery. The boy was his mother's only son and she was a widow. [13]When the Lord saw the grieving mother, his heart broke for her. With great tenderness he said to her, **"Please don't cry."** [14]Then he stepped up to the coffin and touched it. When the pallbearers came to a halt, Jesus said to the corpse, **"Young man, I say to you, arise and live!"**

[15]Immediately, the young man moved, sat up, and spoke to those nearby. Jesus presented the son to his mother, alive! [16]A tremendous sense of holy mystery swept over the crowd as they witnessed this miracle of resurrection.[c] They shouted praises to God, saying, "God himself has visited us to bless his people! A great prophet has appeared among us!"

[17]The news of Jesus and this miracle raced throughout Judea and the entire surrounding region.

The Prophet John's Question

[18]John's disciples reported to him in prison[d] about all the wonderful miracles and the works Jesus was doing. [19]So John dispatched two of his disciples to go and inquire of Jesus. [20]When they came before the Master, they asked him, "Are you the coming Messiah we've been expecting, or are we to continue to look for someone else? John the prophet has sent us to you to seek your answer."

[21]Without answering,[e] Jesus turned to the crowd and healed many of their incurable diseases. His miracle power freed many from their suffering. He

---

a 7:10 Implicit in the miracle was that Jesus released the word of healing for the servant.
b 7:11 *Nain* means "pleasant." The Prince of Life was about to enter the gate of the city when death came out. There at the gates where life and death meet, life wins and death is defeated. Just outside of Jerusalem one day, death and life met again, and life won forevermore.
c 7:16 Implied in the text.
d 7:18 Implied in the context. See also Luke 3:20 and Matthew 11:2–19.
e 7:21 Or "at that time."

restored the gift of sight to the blind, and he drove out demonic spirits from those who were tormented.

²²Only then did Jesus answer the question posed by John's disciples. **"Now go back and tell John what you have just seen and heard here today. The blind are now seeing. The crippled are now walking. Those who were lepers are now cured. Those who were deaf are now hearing. Those who were dead are now raised back to life. The poor and broken**[a] **are given the hope of salvation.**[b] ²³**And tell John these words: 'The blessing of heaven comes upon those who never lose their faith**[c] **in me no matter what happens.'"**

²⁴After John's messengers departed, Jesus spoke about John to the audience crowded around him, saying, **"What kind of man did you expect to see out in the wilderness? Did you expect to see a man who would be easily influenced and shaken by the shifting opinions of others?** ²⁵**Who did you really go there to see? Did you expect to see a man decked out in the splendid fashion of the day?**[d] **They are the ones who live in the lap of luxury, embracing the values of this world.** ²⁶**Or did you discover a true prophet out in the lonely wilderness? Yes, John was a legitimate prophet. Even more than that,** ²⁷**he was the fulfillment of this Scripture:**

> **See, I am sending my prophetic messenger**[e]
> **Who will go ahead of me**
> **And prepare hearts to receive me.**[f]

²⁸**"Throughout history there was never found a man as great as John the Baptizer. Yet those who now walk in God's kingdom realm, though they appear to be insignificant, will become even greater than he."**

²⁹When the common and disreputable people among the audience heard Jesus say this, they acknowledged that it was the truth, for they had already experienced John's baptism. ³⁰But the hearts of the Jewish religious leaders and experts of the Law had rejected the clear purpose of God by refusing to be baptized by John.

---

a 7:22 This fulfills many Old Testament references to the coming of the Messiah, including Isaiah 29:18–19, 35:5–6, and 61:1.
b 7:22 Jesus is assuring John that the message he brings is life and salvation, not judgment and wrath.
c 7:23 The Greek text is literally "Blessed are those who are not offended over me."
d 7:25 See Matthew 3:4.
e 7:27 Or "angel."
f 7:27 This is quoted from Malachi 3:1.

[31] Jesus continued, saying, "How could I describe the people of this generation? Can't you see? [32] You're like children playing games on the playground, complaining to friends, 'You don't like it when we want to play Wedding. And you don't like it when we want to play Funeral. Why will you neither dance nor mourn?'[a]

[33] "When the prophet John came fasting and refused to drink wine, you said, 'He's crazy! There's a demon in him.' [34] Yet when the Son of Man came and went to feasts and drank wine, you said, 'Look as this man! He is nothing but a glutton and a drunkard. He spends all his time with tax collectors and other notorious sinners.'

[35] "Nevertheless, I say to you, the wisdom of God[b] will be proven true by the expressions of godliness in everyone who follows me."

Extravagant Worship

[36] Afterward, a Jewish religious leader named Simon[c] asked Jesus to his home for dinner. Jesus accepted the invitation. When he went to Simon's home, he took his place at the table.

[37] In the neighborhood there was an immoral woman of the streets, known to all to be a prostitute. When she heard about Jesus being in Simon's house, she took an exquisite flask made from alabaster,[d] filled it with the most expensive perfume, went right into the home of the Jewish religious leader, and knelt at the feet of Jesus in front of all the guests. [38] Broken and weeping, she covered his feet with the tears that fell from her face. She kept crying and drying his feet with her long hair. Over and over she kissed Jesus' feet. Then she opened her flask and anointed his feet[e] with her costly perfume as an act of worship.

[39] When Simon saw what was happening, he thought, *This man can't be*

---

a 7:32 Christ and John the Baptist both offered people the "wedding," yet the Pharisees didn't want to dance. They both offered a funeral to the old, dead ways of religion, yet the Pharisees refused to attend. Grace offered them salvation, but they rejected it.

b 7:35 Or more literally, 'Wisdom is vindicated by all her children.'

c 7:36 The name Simon is supplied from verse 40.

d 7:37 This is a soft, cream-colored stone often used for jars and vases.

e 7:38 Six times in Luke we find someone at Jesus' feet (described as "beautiful" in Isaiah 52:7). 1) The sinful woman mentioned in this verse who poured out her worship and tears at Jesus' feet. 2) The demonized man who worshiped at Jesus' feet [8:35]. 3) Jairus, who fell at his feet pleading for a miracle for his daughter [8:41]. 4) Mary, who sat at his feet and received his word [10:39]. 5) The healed leper who fell at his feet in deep gratitude [17:15–16]. 6) Those who worshipped Jesus at his resurrection when he showed them his hands and his feet [24:39–40].

a true prophet. If he were really a prophet, he would know what kind of sinful woman is touching him.[a]

⁴⁰Jesus said, **"Simon, I have a word for you."**

"Go ahead, Teacher. I want to hear it," he answered.

⁴¹**"It's a story about two men who were deeply in debt. One owed the bank one hundred thousand dollars,**[b] **and the other only owed ten thousand dollars. ⁴²When it was obvious that neither of them would be able to repay their debts, the kind banker graciously wrote off the debts and forgave them all that they owed. Tell me, Simon, which of the two debtors would be the most thankful? Which one would love the banker most?"**

⁴³Simon answered, "I suppose it would be the one with the greatest debt forgiven."

"You're right," Jesus agreed. ⁴⁴Then he spoke to Simon about the woman still weeping at his feet.

"Don't you see this woman kneeling here? She is doing for me what you didn't bother to do. When I entered your home as your guest, you didn't think about offering me water to wash the dust off my feet. Yet she came into your home and washed my feet with her many tears and then dried my feet with her hair. ⁴⁵You didn't even welcome me into your home with the customary kiss of greeting, but from the moment I came in she has not stopped kissing my feet. ⁴⁶You didn't take the time to anoint my head with fragrant oil, but she anointed my head and feet with the finest perfume. ⁴⁷She has been forgiven of all her many sins. This is why she has shown me such extravagant love. But those who assume they have very little to be forgiven will love me very little."

⁴⁸Then Jesus said to the woman at his feet, **"All your sins are forgiven."**[c]

⁴⁹All the dinner guests said among themselves, "Who is the one who can even forgive sins?"

⁵⁰Then Jesus said to the woman, **"Your faith in me has given you life. Now you may leave and walk in the ways of peace."**

a 7:39 Simon thought Jesus should have known the sinfulness of the woman, but Simon should have known the love of the one next to him, who was ready to forgive and restore. Religion focuses on the sinfulness of a person, but faith sees the glory of the one who forgives and heals.

b 7:41 The Greek text uses the monetary term "denarius." The point is that one person owed more than a year's wages, the other much less.

c 7:48 Twice in Luke's gospel we hear Jesus say, "All your sins are forgiven." Once he says it to a man (Luke 5:20) and once here to a woman. The proof of her sins being forgiven is her love; with the healed man it was his life, for he took up his bed and walked.

Eight

Jesus Ministers throughout the Land

[1]Soon afterward, Jesus began a ministry tour throughout the country, visiting cities and villages to announce the fantastic news of God's kingdom realm. His twelve disciples traveled with him [2]and also a number of women who had been healed of many illnesses under his ministry and set free from demonic power. Jesus had cast out seven demons from one woman.[a] Her name was Mary Magdalene, for she was from the village of Magdala.[b] Among the women were Susanna and [3]Joanna, the wife of Chusa, who managed King Herod's household.[c] Many other women who supported Jesus' ministry from their own personal finances also traveled with him.[d]

Mysteries of God's Kingdom Realm

[4]Massive crowds gathered from many towns to hear Jesus, and he taught them using metaphors and parables,[e] such as this:

[5]**"A farmer went out to sow seeds for a harvest. As he scattered his seed, some of it fell on the hard pathway and was quickly trampled down and unable to grow and became nothing but bird seed. [6]Some fell on the gravel, and though it sprouted it couldn't take root; it withered for lack of moisture. [7]Other seed fell where there was nothing but weeds. It too was unable to grow**

---

a 8:2 The number seven means completeness. Mary was completely possessed by demons, but Jesus restored her true self and cast out her demons.

b 8:2 Implied by the word Magdalene. The ancient village of Magdala has recently been discovered near the current town of Migdol.

c 8:3 Some scholars believe that Chusa was the government official mentioned in John 4:46–53.

d 8:3 To travel with a rabbi was considered a high honor. Yet it was not permitted in the culture and time of Jesus' ministry for a woman to be mentored by a rabbi. Jesus elevated women into a place of honor and respect, in spite of the cultural limitations. It was these wealthy women who provided for Jesus' care. Luke is the one gospel writer who brings out the many times Jesus honored women. These women would later be present at the crucifixion (Matthew 27:56; Mark 15:40–41; Luke 23:49, 55) and at the resurrection (Luke 24:1–11). Mary Magdalene was the first human being to see the risen Christ (John 20:11–18).

e 8:4 Jesus' preferred teaching method was through story (Matthew 13:34). A parable required the listener to be humble, teachable, and open to truth. Revelation from God can be found through the doorway of an allegory. This parable is described in the Aramaic as "the parable of the seed."

to full maturity, for it was choked out by the weeds. ⁸Yet some of the seed fell into good, fertile soil, and it grew and flourished until it produced more than a hundredfold harvest, a bumper crop." Then Jesus added, shouting out to all who would hear, **"Listen with your heart and you will understand!"**

⁹Later his disciples came to Jesus and asked him privately what deeper meaning was found in this parable. ¹⁰He said, **"You have been given a teachable heart to perceive the secret, hidden mysteries of God's kingdom realm. But to those who don't have a listening heart, my words are merely stories. Even though they have eyes, they are blind to the true meaning of what I say,ᵃ and even though they listen, they won't receive full revelation.**

¹¹**"Here, then, is the deeper meaning to my parable: The word of Godᵇ is the seed that is sown into hearts. ¹²The hard pathway represents the hard hearts of men who hear the word of God but the slandererᶜ quickly snatches away what was sown in their hearts to keep them from believing and experiencing salvation. ¹³The seed falling on the gravel represents those who initially respond to the Manifestation with joy, but soon afterward, when a season of harassment of the Enemy and difficulty come to them, they whither and fall away, for they have no root in the truth and their faith is temporary.ᵈ ¹⁴The seed that falls into the weeds represents the hearts of those who hear the Manifestation of God but their growth is quickly choked off by their own anxious cares, the riches of this world, and the fleeting pleasures of this life. This is why they never become mature and fruitful. ¹⁵The seed that fell into good, fertile soil represents those lovers of truth who hear it deep within their hearts. They respond by clinging to the word, keeping it dear as they endure all things in faith. This is the seed that will one day bear much fruit in their lives."**

The Revelation Light

¹⁶**"No one lights a lamp and then hides it, covering it over or putting it where its light won't be seen. No, the lamp is placed on a lampstand so others are able to benefit from its brightness. ¹⁷Because this revelation lamp now shines**

---

a   8:10 This is taken from Isaiah 6:9–10. See also Jeremiah 5:21 and Ezekiel 12:2.
b   8:11 Or "Manifestation of God."
c   8:12 Or 'the Devil.' The Greek word *diabolos* (also translated "devil") means 'the slanderer.'
d   8:13 From the Aramaic text.

within you, nothing will be hidden from you—it will all be revealed. Every secret of the kingdom[a] will be unveiled and out in the open, made known by the revelation light. [18]So pay careful attention to your hearts as you hear my teaching, for to those who have open hearts, even more revelation will be given to them until it overflows. And for those who do not listen with open hearts, what little light they imagine to have will be taken away."[b]

Jesus' True Family

[19]Mary, Jesus' mother, and her other sons[c] came to where Jesus was teaching, but they couldn't get through the crowd that had gathered around him. [20]So he was told, "Your mother and brothers[d] are standing outside, wanting to speak with you."

[21]Jesus told them, **"These who come to listen to me are like my mothers and my brothers. They're the ones who long to hear and to put God's word into practice."**

Peace in the Storm

[22-23]One day Jesus said to his disciples, **"Let's get in a boat and go across to the other side of the lake."** So they set sail. Soon Jesus fell asleep. The wind rose, and the fierce wind became a violent squall that threatened to swamp their boat. [24]So the disciples woke Jesus up and said, "Master, Master, we're sinking! Don't you care that we're going to drown?"

With great authority Jesus rebuked the howling wind and surging waves, and instantly they stopped and became as smooth as glass. [25]Then Jesus said to them, **"Why are you fearful? Have you lost your faith in me?"[e]**

Shocked and shaken, they said with amazement to one another, "Who is this man[f] who has authority over winds and waves that they obey him?"

---

a 8:17 Implied in the context of Jesus' teaching on the mysteries of God's kingdom (verse 10).

b 8:18 This verse contains a complicated ellipsis, which is a literary function of omitting certain information to invite discovery. The ellipsis of the text has been supplied by making explicit what is implicit in the context. The parables of the sower and of the lamp are similar, in that they speak of the heart that receives truth. The Manifestation of the kingdom is a "seed" that grows within us and a "lamp" that glows within us.

c 8:19 Mary had other sons and daughters. These were the half-brothers/sisters of Jesus. Jesus' father was not Joseph, but the Father of Eternity. See also Mark 6:3.

d 8:20 See John 7:5.

e 8:25 Implied in the text.

f 8:25 The answer to that question is found in Jeremiah 31:35, "He is the Lord of hosts!"

A Demonized Man Set Free

²⁶⁻²⁹As soon as they stepped ashore on the eastern side of the lake in the land of the Gerasenes, the disciples were confronted by a demon-possessed madman from a nearby town. Many times he had been put under guard and bound with chains, but repeatedly the many demons inside him had thrown him into convulsions, breaking his shackles and driving him out of the town into the countryside. He had been demonized for a long time and was living naked in a cemetery among the tombs. When he saw Jesus, he fell at his feet and screamed out, "What are you doing here? You are Jesus, the Son of the Most High God!"

Jesus commanded the demons to come out of him, and they shouted, "We beg you, don't torture us!"

³⁰Jesus asked the man, **"What is your name?"**

"Mob," the demons answered. "We are a mob,ᵃ for there are many of us here in this man. ³¹We beg you, don't banish us to the bottomless pit of the Abyss!"ᵇ

³²On the hillside nearby, there was a large herd of pigs, and the demons pled with Jesus, "Let us enter into the pigs." ³³So Jesus ordered all the "mob" of demons to come out of the man and enter the pigs. The crazed herd of swine stampeded over the cliff into the lake and all of them drowned.

³⁴When the herders tending the pigs saw what had happened, they ran off in fear and reported it to the nearby town and throughout the countryside. ³⁵Then the people of the region came out to see for themselves what had happened. When they came to where Jesus was, they discovered the notoriousᶜ madman totally set free. He was clothed, speaking intelligently, and sitting at the feet of Jesus. They were shocked!³⁶ Then eyewitnesses to the miracle reported all that they had seen and how the demonized man was completely delivered from his torment.

After hearing about such amazing power, the townspeople became frightened. ³⁷Soon all the people of the region of the Gerasenes and the surrounding

---

a 8:30 The Greek word used for "mob" is literally "legion," which was the largest unit of the Roman military and represented up to 6,800 soldiers.
b 8:31 See Revelation 9:1 and 20:1–3. The Abyss is the place of imprisonment for Satan and his demons.
c 8:35 Implied in the context.

country begged Jesus to leave them, for they were gripped with fear. So Jesus got into the boat, intending to return to Galilee. ³⁸But the man who had been set free begged Jesus over and over not to leave, saying, "Let me be with you!"

Jesus sent him away with these instructions: ³⁹**"Return to your home and your family, and tell them all the wonderful things God has done for you."** So the man went away and preached to everyone who would listen about the amazing miracle Jesus had worked in his life.

More Miracles of Healing

⁴⁰When Jesus returned to Galilee, the crowds were overjoyed, for they had been waiting for him to arrive. ⁴¹⁻⁴²Just then, a man named Jairus, the leader of the local Jewish congregation, fell before Jesus' feet. He desperately begged him to come and heal his twelve-year-old daughter, his only child, because she was at the point of death.

Jesus started to go with him to his home to see her, but a large crowd surrounded him. ⁴³In the crowd that day was a woman who had suffered greatly for twelve years[a] from slow bleeding. Even though she had spent all that she had on "healers,"[b] she was still suffering. ⁴⁴Pressing in through the crowd, she came up behind Jesus and touched the tassel[c] of his prayer shawl. Instantly her bleeding stopped and she was healed.

⁴⁵Jesus suddenly stopped and said to his disciples, **"Someone touched me. Who is it?"**[d]

While they all denied it, Peter pointed out, "Master, everyone is touching you, trying to get close to you. The crowds are so thick[e] we can't walk through all these people without being jostled."

⁴⁶Jesus replied, **"Yes, but I felt power surge through me. Someone touched me to be healed, and they received their healing."**

---

a   8:43 The daughter of Jairus was twelve years old; this woman had suffered for twelve years. Jesus touched the girl; the woman touched Jesus.

b   8:43 Translated from the Aramaic text, which states literally, "the house of healers." This phrase is not found in many Greek texts.

c   8:44 This was on the corner of the prayer shawl, and the tassel was meant to symbolize all of the commandments and promises of God. The woman was laying hold of a promise for healing.

d   8:45 Jesus already knew the answer to his question. He wanted the woman to come forward and acknowledge her healing.

e   8:45 There were many crowds around Jesus, the living Word. Many today crowd around the Bible, the written Word. But only those who "touch" the Scriptures in faith receive its promises, just like the sick woman received her healing.

⁴⁷When the woman realized she couldn't hide any longer, she came and fell trembling at Jesus' feet. Before the entire crowd she declared, "I was desperate to touch you, Jesus, for I knew if I could just touch even the fringe of your robe[a] I would be healed."

⁴⁸Jesus responded, **"Beloved daughter, your faith in me has released your healing. You may go with my peace."**

⁴⁹While Jesus was still speaking to the woman, someone came from Jairus's house and told him, "There's no need to bother the Master any further. Your daughter has passed away. She's gone."

⁵⁰When Jesus heard this, he said, **"Jairus, don't yield to your fear. Have faith in me and she will live again."**

⁵¹When they arrived at the house, Jesus allowed only Peter, John, and James—along with the child's parents—to go inside. ⁵²Jesus told those left outside, who were sobbing and wailing with grief, **"Stop crying. She is not dead; she's just asleep and must be awakened."**

⁵³They laughed at him,[b] knowing for certain that she had died.

⁵⁴Jesus approached the body, took the girl by her hand, and called out with a loud voice, **"My sleeping child, awake! Rise up!"**

⁵⁵⁻⁵⁶Instantly her spirit returned to her body and she stood up.[c]

Jesus directed her stunned parents to give her something to eat and ordered them not to tell anyone what just happened.

---

a 8:47 She was touching the hem of the robe of our anointed High Priest, Jesus. See Psalm 133:2.
b 8:53 They did not realize that Jesus was using "sleep" as a metaphor for death.
c 8:55–56 This chapter contains four great miracles of Jesus Christ: (1) over nature, for he stilled the wind and waves, (2) over demons, for he cast out a mob of evil spirits, (3) over disease, for he healed the hemorrhaging woman, and (4) over death, for he restored the life of this twelve-year-old girl.

Nine

Jesus Sends Out His Apostles

[1]Jesus summoned together his twelve apostles[a] and imparted to them authority over every demon and the power to heal every disease. [2]Then he commissioned them to preach the kingdom realm of God and to heal the sick to demonstrate that the kingdom had arrived. As he sent them out, he gave them these instructions: [3]**"Take nothing extra on your journey.**[b] **Just go as you are. Don't carry a staff, a backpack, food, money, not even a change of clothes.** [4]**Whatever home welcomes you as a guest, remain there and make it your base of ministry.** [5]**And wherever your ministry is rejected and not welcomed, you are to leave that town and shake the dust off your shoes as a testimony before them."**[c]

[6]The apostles departed and went into the villages with the wonderful news of God's kingdom realm, and they instantly healed diseases wherever they went.

Herod Perplexed

[7]Now, Herod, the governor, was confused and perplexed when he heard the reports of all the miracles of Jesus and his apostles. Many were saying, "John the Baptizer has come back to life!" [8]Others said, "This has to be Elijah who has reappeared or one of the prophets of old who has risen from the dead." These were the rumors circulating throughout the land.

Herod exclaimed, [9]"Who is this Man? I keep hearing about him over and

---

a 9:1 As translated from certain Greek manuscripts and implied in the context.

b 9:3 Why did Jesus tell them to go empty-handed? To trust and walk in faith. But also because they already had the five items they were told not to bring, as their spiritual counterparts are found in him (i.e., he is our treasure, our strength, our living bread, our provider, and our righteousness).

c 9:5 Shaking the dust off their feet would be a statement against the people who had rejected the gospel, that the messengers would not be responsible for their fate. More than a metaphor, this was an actual custom of the day. However, the words against them can also be translated "before them." Shaking the dust off their feet did not mean they were to stomp off offended and angry, but that they would move on with no defilement or unforgiveness in their hearts toward those who rejected their message. If they did not do that, they would take the "dust" of that offense to the next place they ministered.

over. It can't be the prophet John; I had him beheaded!"[a] Herod was very eager to meet Jesus.

Jesus Feeds Thousands

[10]Months later,[b] the apostles returned from their ministry tour and told Jesus all the wonders and miracles they had witnessed. Jesus, wanting to be alone with the Twelve, quietly slipped away with them toward Bethsaida.[c] [11]But the crowds soon found out about it and took off after him. When they caught up with Jesus, he graciously welcomed them all, taught them more about the kingdom of God, and healed all who were sick.

[12]As the day wore on, the Twelve came to Jesus and told him, "It's getting late. You should send the crowds away to the surrounding villages and farms to get something to eat and find shelter for the night. There's nothing to eat here in the middle of nowhere."

[13]Jesus responded, **"You have the food to feed them."**[d]

They replied, "All we have are these five small loaves of bread and two dried fish. Do you really expect us to go buy food for all these people? [14]There are nearly five thousand men here, with women and children besides!"[e]

He told his disciples, **"Have them all sit down in groups of fifty each."**[f]

[15-16]After everyone was seated, Jesus took the five loaves and two fish, and gazing into the heavenly realm he gave thanks for the food. Then, in the presence of his disciples, he broke off pieces of bread and fish, and kept giving more to each disciple to give to the crowd. It was multiplying[g] before their eyes! [17]So everyone ate until they were filled, and afterward the disciples gathered up the leftovers—it came to exactly twelve baskets full!

---

a 9:9 See Mark 6:14–29.

b 9:10 Implied in the context. Matthew infers that they had been sent north and east, possibly as far as Persia to preach to the Jewish residents there, which would take them months to return.

c 9:10 Bethsaida means "House of Fishing."

d 9:13 In the Greek text, the word "you" here is emphatic. Jesus told his disciples they had food to give to others. Because Jesus lives within us, we can give others the living bread and, if need be, multiply food for others to eat. We are to focus on what we have, not what we don't have.

e 9:14 Implied in the text. There were likely ten thousand people whom Jesus miraculously fed that day.

f 9:14 There is an interesting correlation between seating the people in groups of fifty and the feast of Pentecost. Fifty was the number of days between Passover and Pentecost.

g 9:16 This is supplied information, a summary statement, implied in the text.

Jesus Prophesies His Death and Resurrection

¹⁸One time, when Jesus was praying in a quiet place with his disciples nearby, he came over to them and asked, **"Who do people think I am?"**

¹⁹They answered, "Some are convinced you're the prophet John who has returned. Others say you are Elijah, or perhaps one of the Jewish prophets brought back from the dead."

²⁰Jesus asked them, **"But who do you believe that I am?"**

Peter said, "You are the Anointed One, God's Messiah!"

²¹Jesus gave them strict orders not to tell this to anyone yet, saying, ²²**"The Son of Man**ᵃ **is destined to experience great suffering and face complete rejection by the Jewish leaders and religious hierarchy.**ᵇ **He will be killed and raised back to life on the third day."**

What it Means to Follow Jesus

²³Jesus said to all of his followers, **"If you truly desire to be my disciple, you must disown your life completely, embrace my 'cross'**ᶜ **as your own, and surrender to my ways.**ᵈ ²⁴**For if you choose self-sacrifice, giving up your lives for my glory, you will embark on a discovery of more and more of true life. But if you choose to keep your lives for yourselves, you will lose what you try to keep.** ²⁵**Even if you gained all the wealth and power of this world, everything it could offer you, yet lost your soul in the process, what good is that?** ²⁶**So why then are you ashamed of being my disciple? Are you ashamed of the revelation truth**ᵉ **I give to you?**

"I, the Son of Man, will one day return in my radiant brightness, with the holy angels and in the splendor and majesty of my Father, and I will be ashamed of all who are ashamed of me. ²⁷**But I promise you this: there are some of you standing here right now who will not die until you have witnessed the presence and the power of the kingdom realm of God."**ᶠ

---

a 9:22 Or "the true Man."

b 9:22 The Greek text is literally "the elders, chief priests, and scribes." These three groups were represented in the religious hierarchy of the Sanhedrin, a council of seventy-one leaders.

c 9:23 This could also mean being willing to suffer and die for Christ.

d 9:23 Implied in the text.

e 9:26 The Greek word is *logos*.

f 9:27 This was a prophecy of what was about to take place with Peter, James, and John on the Mountain of Transforming Glory. This promise was fulfilled when they experienced the power of the kingdom of God and the cloud of glory.

The True Glory of Jesus

28Eight days later, Jesus took Peter, James, and John and climbed a high mountain to pray. 29As he prayed, his face began to glow until it was a blinding glory streaming from him. His entire body was illuminated with a radiant glory. His brightness[a] became so intense that it made his clothing blinding white, like multiple flashes of lightning.

30-31All at once, two men appeared in glorious splendor: Moses and Elijah. They spoke with Jesus about his soon departure[b] from this world and the things he was destined to accomplish in Jerusalem.

32Peter and his companions had become very drowsy, but they became fully awake when they saw the glory and splendor of Jesus standing there and the two men with him.

33As Moses and Elijah were about to return to heaven, Peter impetuously blurted out, "Master, this is amazing to see the three of you together! Why don't we stay here in the glory and set up three shelters: one for you, one for Moses, and one for Elijah?"

34While Peter was still speaking, a radiant cloud of glory formed above them and overshadowed them. As the glory cloud enveloped them, they were struck with fear. 35Then the voice of God thundered from within the cloud, **"This is my Son, my Beloved One.[c] Listen carefully to all he has to say."**

36When the thunderous voice faded away and the cloud disappeared, Jesus was standing there alone. Peter, James, and John were speechless and awestruck. But they never said a word to anyone about what they had seen.

The Power of Faith

37The next day, when they came down from the mountain, a massive crowd was waiting there to meet them. 38And a man in the crowd shouted desperately, "Please, Teacher, I beg of you, do something about my boy. He's my only child. 39He's possessed by an evil spirit that makes him scream out in torment. This demon rarely leaves him and only after a long struggle. It throws him into

---

a 9:29 Implied in the context of what was taking place. The Greek text says, "The appearance of his face was altered." The light shined through his clothing as his glorified body became brilliant with light. This is called Jesus' transfiguration.

b 9:30-31 The actual word in Greek is translated "exodus."

c 9:35 Several Greek manuscripts have "My Chosen One."

convulsions and he foams at the mouth. And when it finally does leave him, he's left with horrible bruises. ⁴⁰I begged your disciples to drive it out of him, but they didn't have enough power to do it."

⁴¹Jesus responded, **"You are an unbelieving people with no faith! Your lives are twisted with lies that have turned you away from doing what is right. How much longer should I remain here, offering you hope?"**ᵃ Then he said to the man, **"Bring your son to me."**

⁴²As the boy approached, the demon slammed him to the ground, throwing him into violent convulsions. Jesus sternly commanded the demon to come out of the boy, and immediately it left. Jesus healed the boy of his injuries and returned him to his father, saying,ᵇ **"Here is your son."**

⁴³Everyone was awestruck. They were stunned seeing the power and majesty of God flow through Jesus.

⁴⁴While everyone marveled, trying to process what they had just witnessed, Jesus turned to his disciples and said, **"This is very important, so listen carefully and remember my words. The Son of Man is about to be betrayed and given over to the authority of men."**

⁴⁵But the disciples were unable to perceive what he was saying, for it was a veiled mystery to them, and they were too embarrassed to ask him to explain it.

True Greatness

⁴⁶The disciples began to argue and became preoccupied over who would be the greatest one among them. ⁴⁷Fully aware of their innermost thoughts, Jesus called a little child to his side and said to them, ⁴⁸ **"If you tenderly care for this little child**ᶜ **on my behalf, you are tenderly caring for me. And if you care for me, you are honoring my Father who sent me. For the one who is least important in your eyes is actually the most important one of all."**

⁴⁹The disciple John said, "Master, we found someone who was casting out demons using your name and we tried to stop him, because he doesn't follow you like we do."

---

a 9:41 As translated from Aramaic text. Some translate this phrase "How long must I endure you?" However, the Aramaic root word for "endure" is *sebar*, which means "hope or good news."
b 9:42 Implied in the text.
c 9:48 The little child is representative of unimportant people in general. Treating the least with care and respect makes us truly great.

[50]Jesus responded, **"You shouldn't have hindered him, for anyone who is not against you is your friend."**[a]

Jesus' Journey to Jerusalem

[51]Jesus passionately determined to leave for Jerusalem and let nothing distract Him from fulfilling[b] his mission there, for the time for him to be lifted up was drawing near.[c] [52]So he sent messengers[d] ahead of him as envoys to a village of the Samaritans. [53]But as they approached the village, they were turned away. They would not allow Jesus to enter, for he was on his way[e] to worship in Jerusalem.

[54]When the disciples James and John realized what was happening, they came to Jesus and said, "Lord, if you wanted to, you could command fire to fall down from heaven just like Elijah did[f] and destroy all these wicked people."

[55]Jesus rebuked them sharply, saying, **"Don't you realize what comes from your hearts when you say that? For the Son of Man did not come to destroy life, but to bring life to the earth."**[g]

[56]So they went to another village instead.

The Cost to Follow Jesus

[57]On their way, someone came up to Jesus and said, "I want to follow you wherever you go."

[58]Jesus replied, **"Yes, but remember this: even animals in the field have holes in the ground to sleep in and birds have their nests, but the Son of Man has no place here to lay down his head."**

---

a 9:50 Jealousy blinds our hearts. Nine disciples combined could not cast out a demon spirit (verse 40), but they were jealous of this one who did.

b 9:51 Implied in the context.

c 9:51 This refers to the cross, where Jesus was lifted up on a tree to bear the sins of all humankind. His exaltation into glory was through the sacrifice of his life on Calvary's cross. Nothing would turn him aside from being our sin-bearer and Redeemer.

d 9:52 The most literal translation is "He sent angels before his face."

e 9:53 The Samaritans had their own place of worship on Mount Gerizim, and they were hostile toward Jews, who wanted to worship in Jerusalem. There were many cultural, religious, and ethnic hostilities between Jews and Samaritans.

f 9:54 This sentence is translated from the Aramaic. The earliest Greek manuscripts do not include "just like Elijah did." Some Greek texts state that the disciples asked, "Do you want us to call down fire and destroy them?"

g 9:55 Translated from Aramaic and a few Greek manuscripts. This pericope reveals the mercy of Jesus. Although the Samaritans refused entry to Jesus and his disciples, in the next chapter Jesus uses an example of a good Samaritan who cared for a stranger. Jesus saw in the Samaritan outcasts a redemptive future (Luke 10:25–37). He knew the Father had the grace to change even the most stubborn individuals. An entire Samaritan village received Jesus through the witness of a woman (John 4:39–42), and later, as recorded in the book of Acts, the entire region of the Samaritans received the gospel (Acts 8:9–25). We can never give up on those who seem to be wayward.

⁵⁹Jesus then turned to another and said, **"Come be my disciple."**

He replied, "Someday I will, Lord, but first let me fulfill my duty as a good son[a] and wait until my father passes away."

⁶⁰Jesus told him, **"Don't wait for your father's burial. Let those who are already dead wait for death. But as for you, go and proclaim everywhere that God's kingdom has arrived."**

⁶¹Still another said to him, "Lord, I want to follow you too. But first let me go home and say good-bye to my entire family."

⁶²Jesus responded, **"Why do you keep looking backward to your past and have second thoughts about following me? When you turn back you are useless to the kingdom realm of God."**

---

a 9:59 The text is literally "Allow me first to go and bury my father." This is an idiom for waiting until his father passed away. He wanted an inheritance in this life as his security.

Ten

Labor Shortage

[1]After this, the Lord Jesus formed thirty-five teams among the other disciples. Each team was two disciples, seventy in all,[a] and he commissioned them to go ahead of him into every town he was about to visit. [2]He released them with these instructions:

"The harvest is huge and ripe. But there are not enough harvesters to bring it all in. As you go, plead with the Owner of the Harvest to drive out[b] into his harvest fields many more workers. [3]Now, off you go! I am sending you out even though you feel as vulnerable as lambs going into a pack of wolves. [4]You won't need to take anything[c] with you—trust in God alone. And don't get distracted from my purpose by anyone you might meet along the way.

[5]"Once you enter a house, speak to the people there and say, 'God's blessing of peace be upon this house!' [6]If a lover of peace[d] resides there, your peace will rest upon that household.[e] But if you are rejected, your blessing of peace will come back upon you. [7]Don't feel the need to shift from one house to another, but stay put in one home during your time in that city. Eat and drink whatever they serve you. Receive their hospitality, for you are my harvester, and you deserve to be cared for.

---

a 10:1 The text states they were "other" (i.e., other than the Twelve). A few Greek manuscripts have "seventy-two." The number seventy is a key numerical symbol in the Bible. Seventy nations are listed in Genesis 10, seventy of Jacob's clan went into Egypt (Exodus 1:5), seventy palm trees refreshed God's people at Elim (Exodus 15:27), seventy elders served with Moses (Exodus 24:1), seventy princes are mentioned in Judges 9:56, seventy men sat on the council of the Sanhedrin, and Jesus sent out seventy apostles to preach the message of the kingdom.

b 10:2 This is the term used many times in the Gospels for driving out or casting out demons. The Lord of the Harvest must cast them forth. The Holy Spirit is the Director of the Harvest.

c 10:3 The text states literally, "Take no money, no knapsack, no sandals." The implication is that they were to trust in God alone for all their needs to be met.

d 10:6 Literally, "son of peace," which is a way of saying, "a godly man."

e 10:6 Or as translated from the Aramaic, "Let him rest upon your peace."

[8]"When you enter into a new town, and you have been welcomed by its people, follow these rules: Eat[a] what is served you. [9]Then heal the sick, and tell them all, 'God's kingdom realm has arrived and is now within your reach!' [10]But when you enter a city and they do not receive you, say to them publicly, [11]'We wipe from our feet the very dust of your streets as a testimony before you![b] Understand this: the kingdom realm of God came within your reach and yet you have rejected God's invitation!'"

[12]Jesus continued, "Let me say it clearly: on the day of judgment the wicked people of Sodom will have a lesser degree of judgment than the city that rejects you, for Sodom did not have the opportunity that was given to them."[c]

Jesus Condemns the Unrepentant Cities

[13]"How disastrous it will be for the city of Korazin! How horrible for the city of Bethsaida! For if the powerful miracles that I performed in Korazin and Bethsaida had been done in Tyre and Sidon, they would have humbled themselves and repented, and turned from their sins. [14]Tyre and Sidon[d] will face a lesser degree of judgment than you will on the day of judgment. [15]And Capernaum! Do you really think you'll be highly exalted because of the great things I have done there? No! You'll be brought down to the depths of hell[e] because of your rejection of me!"

[16]Jesus concluded his instructions to the seventy with these words: "Remember this: Whoever listens to your message is actually listening to me. And anyone who rejects you is rejecting me, and not only me but the one who sent me."

The Seventy Return

[17]When the seventy missionaries returned to Jesus, they were ecstatic with joy, telling him, "Lord, even the demons obeyed us when we commanded them in your name!"

---

a 10:8 This instruction to "eat what was served" was given twice, for the Jewish dietary laws were not meant not to be a hindrance in their ministry, nor were the disciples to demand certain foods.

b 10:11 See footnote on Luke 9:5.

c 10:12 Implied in the context.

d 10:14 Tyre and Sidon (present-day Lebanon) were two Gentile cities on the Mediterranean coast that were known for their wickedness.

e 10:15 See Isaiah 14:13–15.

[18]Jesus replied, "While you were ministering, I watched Satan topple until he fell suddenly from heaven like lightning to the ground. [19]Now you understand that I have imparted to you all my authority to trample over his kingdom. You will trample upon every demon before you and overcome every power[a] Satan possesses. Absolutely nothing will be able to harm you as you walk in this authority. [20]However, your real source of joy isn't merely that these spirits submit to your authority, but that your names are written in the journals of heaven and that you belong to God's kingdom. This is the true source of your authority."

[21]Then Jesus, overflowing with the Holy Spirit's anointing of joy, exclaimed, "Father, thank you, for you are Lord Supreme over heaven and earth! You have hidden the great revelation of this authority from those who are proud, those wise in their own eyes, and you have shared it with these who humbled themselves. Yes, Father. This is what pleases your heart and the very way you've chosen to extend your kingdom: to give to those who become like trusting children.

[22]Father, you have entrusted me with all that you are and all that you have. No one fully knows the Son except the Father. And no one fully knows the Father except the Son. But the Son is able to introduce and reveal the Father to anyone he chooses.

[23]When Jesus was alone with the Twelve, he said to them, **"You are very privileged to see and hear all these things. [24]Many kings and prophets of old longed to see these days of miracles that you've been favored to see. They would have given everything to hear the revelation you've been favored to hear. Yet they didn't get to see as much as a glimpse or get to hear even a whisper."**

Loving God, Loving Others

[25]Just then a religious scholar stood before Jesus in order to test his doctrines. He posed this question: "Teacher, what requirement must I fulfill if I want to live forever in heaven?"

[26]Jesus replied, **"What does Moses teach us? What do you read in the Law?"**

---

a   10:19 The Greek text is literally "snakes and scorpions," which are emblems of demonic powers.

²⁷The religious scholar answered, "It states, 'You must love the Lord God with all your heart, all your passion, all your energy, and your every thought. And you must love your neighbor as well as you love yourself.'"

²⁸Jesus said, **"That is correct. Now go and do exactly that and you will live."**

²⁹Wanting to justify himself, he questioned Jesus further, saying, "What do you mean by 'my neighbor'?"

³⁰Jesus replied, **"Listen and I will tell you. There was once a Jewish**ᵃ **man traveling from Jerusalem to Jericho when bandits robbed him along the way. They beat him severely, stripped him naked, and left him half dead.**

³¹**"Soon, a Jewish priest walking down the same road came upon the wounded man. Seeing him from a distance, the priest crossed to the other side of the road and walked right past him, not turning to help him one bit.**

³²**"Later, a religious man, a Levite,**ᵇ **came walking down the same road and likewise crossed to the other side to pass by the wounded man without stopping to help him.**

³³**"Finally, another man, a Samaritan,**ᶜ **came upon the bleeding man and was moved with tender compassion for him.** ³⁴**He stooped down and gave him first aid, pouring olive oil on his wounds, disinfecting them with wine, and bandaging them to stop the bleeding. Lifting him up, he placed him on his own donkey and brought him to an inn. Then he took him from his donkey and carried him to a room for the night.** ³⁵**The next morning he took his own money from his wallet and gave it to the innkeeper with these words: 'Take care of him until I come back from my journey. If it costs more than this, I will repay you when I return.'**ᵈ ³⁶**So, now, tell me, which one of the three men who saw the wounded man proved to be the true neighbor?"**

³⁷The religious scholar responded, "The one who demonstrated kindness and mercy."

Jesus said, **"You must go and do the same as he."**

a 10:30 Although the text does not describe him as Jewish, it is clearly implied in the context.
b 10:32 The Levites were temple assistants, helping the priests (1 Chronicles 23:28–32).
c 10:33 There was racial tension in those days between Jews and Samaritans. The Samaritans were considered to be a mixed race by the religious Jews. A Samaritan would be the most unlikely person to stop and help a Jewish man. The word *Samaritan* does not refer to people who lived in a geographical place, but is the Hebrew-Aramaic word *Samarim*, which means "keeper of the law."
d 10:35 Jesus is the Good Samaritan. He stoops down to touch us, heal us, lift us up, carry us on our journey, and pay our debts, and he promises to return and reward those who do his will.

Jesus Visits Martha and Mary

38-39As Jesus and the disciples continued on their journey, they came to a village where a woman welcomed Jesus into her home. Her name was Martha and she had a sister named Mary. Mary sat down attentively before the Master, absorbing every revelation he shared. 40But Martha became exasperated by finishing the numerous household chores in preparation for her guests, so she interrupted Jesus and said, "Lord, don't you think it's unfair that my sister left me to do all the work by myself? You should tell her to get up and help me."

41The Lord answered her, **"Martha, my beloved Martha. Why are you upset and troubled, pulled away by all these distractions? Are they really that important? 42Mary has discovered the one thing most important by choosing the most beautiful place of sitting at my feet. She is undistracted, and I won't take this privilege from her."**

Eleven

Jesus Teaches about Prayer

[1]One day, as Jesus was in prayer, one of his disciples came over to him as he finished and said, "Would you teach us a model prayer[a] that we can pray, just like John did for his disciples?"

[2]So Jesus taught them this prayer: **"Our heavenly Father,[b] may the glory of your name be the center on which our life turns.[c] May your Holy Spirit come upon us and cleanse us.[d] Manifest your kingdom on earth.** [3]**And give us each day[e] what is needed for that day.** [4]**Forgive our sins as we ourselves release forgiveness to those who have wronged us. And rescue us every time we face tribulations."[f]**

[5]Then Jesus gave this illustration: **"Imagine what would happen if you were to go to one of your friends in the middle of the night and pound on his door and shout, 'Please! Do you have some food you can spare?** [6]**A friend just arrived at my house unexpectedly and I have nothing to serve him.'[g]** [7]**But your friend says, 'Why are you bothering me? The door's locked and my family and I are all in bed. Do you expect me to get up and give you our food?'** [8]**But listen—because of your shameless impudence, even though it's the middle of the night, your friend will get up out of his bed and give you all that you need.** [9-10]**So it is with your prayers. Ask and you'll receive. Seek and you'll discover. Knock on heaven's door, and it will one day open for you. Every persistent**

---

a 11:1 Implied in the text.
b 11:2 Some Greek manuscripts read simply, "Father." The Aramaic is *Abba*.
c 11:2 An alternate reading of the Aramaic text. The Aramaic word for "name" is *shema* (or the Hebrew word, *shem*), a word with multiple meanings. It can also be translated as "light, sound, or atmosphere." Placing a light in an enclosed space, like a lantern, magnifies that light. This is the meaning here of God's name being made sacred and magnified as we focus our lives on him.
d 11:2 Translated from some of the earliest Greek manuscripts.
e 11:3 The text is literally "Give us our needed bread for the coming day."
f 11:4 Or "Do not let us enter into ordeals."
g 11:6 It was the culture of the day to honor every guest and provide a meal when they arrived.

person will get what he asks for. Every persistent seeker will discover what he needs. And everyone who knocks persistently will one day find an open door.

[11]"Let me ask you this: Do you know of any father who would give his son a snake on a plate when he asked for a serving of fish?[a] Of course not! [12]Do you know of any father who would give his daughter a spider when she had asked for an egg? Of course not! [13]If imperfect parents know how to lovingly take care of their children and give them what they need, how much more will the perfect heavenly Father give the Holy Spirit's fullness when his children ask him."

Jesus Responds to Controversy

[14]One day there was a crowd gathered around Jesus, and among them was a man who was mute. Jesus drove out of the man the spirit that made him unable to speak. Once the demon left him, the mute man's tongue was loosed and he was able to speak again. The stunned crowd saw it all and marveled in amazement over this miracle!

[15]But there were some in the crowd who protested, saying, "He casts out demons by the power of Satan,[b] the demon king." [16]Others were skeptical and tried to persuade Jesus to perform a spectacular display of power to prove that he was the Messiah.[c]

[17]Jesus, well aware of their every thought, said to them, **"Every kingdom that is split against itself is doomed to fail and will eventually collapse. [18]If it is true that Satan casts out his own demons through me, how could his kingdom remain intact? [19]If Satan gives me the power to cast out his demons, who is it that gives your exorcists[d] their power? Let them become your judges! Go and ask them and they will tell you. [20]Yet if I am casting out demons by God's mighty power,[e] the kingdom realm of God is now released upon you—but you still reject it![f]**

a 11:11 Some manuscripts substitute the word "fish" with "loaf" (bread) and the word "snake" with "a stone."
b 11:15 The word used here is "Beelzebul," which was an Aramaic word for "the prince of devils" and was worshipped by the Philistines.
c 11:16 Implied in the context.
d 11:19 Literally, "your sons," which is a figure of speech for their followers.
e 11:20 The text literally states, "in the finger of God," a Hebrew phrase denoting God's power. See Exodus 8:19 and 31:18.
f 11:20 Implied in the context.

²¹"Satan's belongings are undisturbed as he stands guard over his fortress kingdom, strong and fully armed with an arsenal of many weapons. ²²But when one stronger than he comes to attack and overpower him, the stronger one will empty the arsenal in which he trusted. The conqueror will ransack his kingdom and distribute all the spoils of victory. ²³This is a war,ᵃ and whoever is not on my side is against me, and whoever does not gather the spoils with me will be forever scattered.

²⁴"When a demon is cast out of a person, it goes to wander in the waterless realm, searching for rest. But finding no place to rest it says, 'I will go back to the body of the one I left.' ²⁵When it returns, it finds the person like a house that has been swept clean and made tidy but is empty.ᵇ ²⁶Then it goes and enlists seven demons more evil than itself, and they all enter and possess the person, leaving that one with a much worse fate than before."ᶜ

²⁷While he was saying all this, a woman shouted from the crowd, "God bless the one who gave you birth and nursed you as a child!"

²⁸"Yes," said Jesus. "But God will bless all who listen to the Manifestation of Godᵈ and carefully obey everything they hear."

The Miracle Sign of Jonah the Prophet

²⁹As the crowds swelled even more, Jesus went on to say, "How evil is this generation! For when you demand a mighty display of power simply to prove who I am, you demonstrate your unbelief.ᵉ The only sign given you will be a repeat of the miracle of Jonah. ³⁰For in the same way Jonah became a sign to the people of Nineveh, so the Son of Man will be a sign to this generation.ᶠ

³¹"The Queen of Shebaᵍ will rise up on the day of judgment to accuse and condemn this generation for its unbelief. She journeyed from a far and distant land just to listen to the wisdom of King Solomon. There is one greater

---

a 11:23 Implied in the context.
b 11:25 Implied in the text is the truth that if a person is delivered from a demon but does not receive Christ and become filled with him, that individual's condition can become even worse. True conversion fills a life with Christ and his Spirit.
c 11:26 Christ's power is still available for all. Even Mary Magdalene had seven demons cast out of her. See Luke 8:2.
d 11:28 Taken from the literal Aramaic text. The Greek word is *logos*.
e 11:29 Implied in the context.
f 11:30 The Aramaic is "tribe." See verse 31. The Ninevites were a different Semitic tribe from the Jews.
g 11:31 Literally, "the queen of the south." See 1 Kings 10:1–13. Sheba is modern-day Yemen.

than Solomon speaking with you today, but you refuse to listen.[a] [32]Yes, the people of Nineveh will also rise up on the day of judgment to accuse and condemn this generation.[b] For they all repented when they heard the preaching of Jonah, but you refuse to repent. Yet there is one greater than Jonah who is preaching to you today."

Revelation Light

[33]"No one would think of lighting a lamp and then hiding it in the basement where no one would benefit. A lamp belongs on a lampstand, where all who enter may see its light. [34]The eyes of your spirit allow revelation light[c] to enter into your being. When your heart is open the light floods in.[d] When your heart is hard and closed, the light cannot penetrate and darkness takes its place. [35]Open your heart and consider my words. Watch out that you do not mistake your opinions for revelation light! [36]If your spirit burns with light, fully illuminated with no trace of darkness, you will be a shining lamp, reflecting rays of truth by the way you live."

Jesus Warns Hypocrites

[37-38]After Jesus finished saying this, a Jewish religious leader, one of the "separated ones," asked him to come for a meal at his home. When everyone had been seated at the table, the religious leader noticed that Jesus hadn't performed the cleansing ritual[e] before he began eating. He was shocked.

[39]The Lord said, "You Pharisees are religiously strict to your customs and obsessed with the peripheral issues. You are like one who will wipe clean only the outside of a cup or bowl, leaving the inside filthy.[f] [40]You are foolish to ignore the greed and wickedness within you! Shouldn't the one who cleans

---

a 11:31 Implied in the text here and in verse 32.

b 11:32 The Aramaic is "tribe." The Ninevites were of Semitic origin, and although they were pagans, after the preaching of one prophet they converted. The people of Israel had many prophets throughout their history, and the greatest prophet of all was now preaching to them, yet they refused to listen.

c 11:34 The teachings of Jesus are the "revelation light" referred to here.

d 11:34 The literal Greek text reads, "Your eye is the lamp of your body. If your eye is healthy, your whole body is full of light; but if it is sick, your body is full of darkness." The eye becomes a metaphor for spiritual perception. The body is our spirit. The lamp is Jesus' teachings. The darkness is formed by the lies and opinions that blind us. These metaphors have been made explicit.

e 11:37-38 This was not required by the law of Moses, but was a rule imposed by the Pharisees.

f 11:39 Implied in the text.

the outside also be concerned with cleaning the inside?[a] [41]If you free your heart of greed, showing compassion and true generosity to the poor, you have more than clean hands; you will be clean within.

[42]"You Pharisees are hopeless frauds! For you are obsessed with peripheral issues, like paying meticulous tithes on the smallest, most insignificant part of your income.[b] These matters you should do. Yet when you unjustly cheat others, you ignore the most important duty of all: to walk in the love of God. Readjust your values and place first things first.[c]

[43]"You Pharisees are hopeless frauds! For you love to be honored before men with your titles of respect, seeking public recognition[d] as you aspire to become important among others.[e]

[44]"You Pharisees, what hopeless frauds! Your true character is hidden, like an unmarked grave that hides the corruption inside, defiling all who come in contact with you."[f]

[45]Just then a specialist in interpreting religious law blurted out, "But Teacher, don't you realize that your words insult me and those of my profession? You're being rude to us all!"

[46]Jesus responded, "Yes, and you are also hopeless frauds, you experts of the law! For you crush people beneath the burden of obeying impossible religious regulations, yet you would never even think of doing them yourselves.[g] What hypocrites! [47]What hopeless frauds! You build monuments to honor the prophets of old, yet it was your murdering ancestors who killed them. The only prophet you'll honor is a dead one![h] [48]In fact, by erecting monuments to the prophets they killed, you demonstrate your agreement with your murdering ancestors and bear witness to their deeds. You're no better than they! [49]That accounts for the wisdom of God, saying, 'I will send to them apostles

a 11:40 Translated from the Aramaic text.
b 11:42 Literally, "You pay tithes even on mint and dill and every other garden herb."
c 11:42 Implied in the context.
d 11:43 Literally, "greeted with respect in the marketplaces."
e 11:43 The Aramaic text states, "You aspire to leadership of the synagogues."
f 11:44 The strictly religious Jew could not touch a dead body or walk over a grave. It was common to whitewash the grave so no one would walk on it and be ceremonially defiled. Jesus taught that people who followed the example of the Pharisees would become morally unclean.
g 11:46 The Greek text is literally "You compel men to carry burdens that you yourselves do not touch."
h 11:47 Implied by the tone and irony of the context.

and prophets though some they will murder and others they will chase away.'

[50]"This generation will be held accountable for every drop of blood shed by every murdered prophet from the beginning of time until now, [51]from the blood of Abel, who was killed by his brother, to the blood of Zechariah,[a] who was murdered in the middle of the temple court. Yes, the blood-guilt of all your ancestors will be laid before you in this generation.

[52]"You are nothing but hopeless frauds, you experts of religion! You take away from others the key that opens the door to the house of knowledge. Not only do you lock the door and refuse to enter, you do your best to keep others from the truth."

[53-54]The religious leaders and experts of the law became enraged and began to furiously oppose him. They harassed Jesus all the way out the door, spewing out their hostility, arguing over everything he said—wanting nothing more than to find a reason to entrap him with his own words.

---

a 11:51 2 Chronicles 24:21–22. Second Chronicles is the last book in the Hebrew order of the Old Testament.

Twelve

Jesus Warns against Hypocrisy

¹By now a crowd of many thousands had gathered around Jesus. So many people pushed to be near him, they began to trample on one another.

Jesus turned to his disciples and warned them, **"Make sure you are not influenced by the hypocrisy and phoniness of the religious leaders. It permeates everything they do and teach, for they are merely serving their own interests.**ᵃ **²Everything hidden and covered up will soon be exposed. For the facade is falling down, and nothing will be kept secret for long. ³Whatever you have spoken in private will be public knowledge, and what you have whispered secretly behind closed doors will be broadcast far and wide for all to hear.**

⁴**"Listen, my beloved friends, don't fear those who may want to take your life but nothing more. It's true that they may kill your body, but they have no power over your soul. ⁵The one you must fear is God, for he has both the power to take your life and the authority to cast your soul into hell.**ᵇ **Yes, the only one you need to fear is God.**

⁶⁻⁷**"What is the value of your soul to God? Could your worth be defined by an amount of money? God doesn't abandon or forget even the small sparrow he has made. How then could he forget or abandon you? What about the seemingly minor issues of your life? Do they matter to God? Of course they do! So you never need to worry, for you are more valuable to God than anything else in this world.**ᶜ

⁸**"I can assure you of this: If you don't hold back, but freely declare in public that I am the Son of Man, the Messiah, I will freely declare to all the angels**

---

a 12:1 "Serving their own interests" is found in the Aramaic text.

b 12:5 The Greek text is literally "the Valley of Hinnom." This was a valley along the south side of Jerusalem where excrement and rubbish was burned continually. It became a Jewish metaphor for the place of eternal punishment.

c 12:6–7 The translator has chosen to make explicit the figures of speech and metaphors of these verses. The literal Greek text reads, "Do not five sparrows sell for two copper coins? Not one is overlooked before God. Indeed, the very hairs of your head are numbered. Stop fearing—you are more valuable than many sparrows."

of God that you are mine. ⁹But if you publicly pretend that you don't know me, I will deny you before the angels of God. ¹⁰If anyone speaks evil of me, the Son of Man, he can be forgiven. But if anyone scornfully speaks against the Holy Spirit, it will never be forgiven. ¹¹And remember this: When people accuse you before everyone[a] and forcefully drag you before the religious leaders and authorities, do not be troubled. Don't worry about defending yourself or be concerned about how to answer their accusations. ¹²Simply be confident and allow the Spirit of Wisdom access to your heart, and he will reveal in that very moment what you are to say to them."

Jesus Condemns Greed

¹³Just then someone spoke up from the crowd and said, "Master, you should tell my older brother that he has to divide the family inheritance and give me my fair share!"

¹⁴Jesus answered,[b] "My friend, you can't expect me to help you with this. It's not my business to settle arguments between you and your brother—that's yours to settle."

¹⁵Speaking to the people, Jesus continued, "Be alert and guard your heart from greed and always wishing for what you don't have. For your life can never be measured by the amount of things you possess."

¹⁶Jesus then gave them this illustration: "A wealthy land owner had a farm that produced bumper crops. In fact, it filled his barns to overflowing! ¹⁷He thought, *What should I do now that every barn is full and I have nowhere else to store more? ¹⁸I know what I'll do! I'll tear down the barns and build one massive barn that will hold all my grain and goods. ¹⁹Then I can just sit back, surrounded with comfort and ease. I'll enjoy life with no worries at all.*

²⁰"God said to him, 'What a fool you are to trust in your riches and not in me. This very night the messengers of death[c] are demanding to take your life. Then who will get all the wealth you have stored up for yourself?' ²¹This is what will happen to all those who fill up their lives with everything but God."

---

a 12:11 The Greek text adds, "in the synagogues."
b 12:14 In the Jewish culture of that day, rabbis would be asked to mediate disputes such as this. However, the man did not want mediation but representation.
c 12:20 The Greek text is simply "they."

Don't Worry

²²Jesus taught his disciples, saying, "Listen to me. Never let anxiety enter your hearts. Never worry about any of your needs, such as food or clothing. ²³For your life is infinitely more than just food or the clothing you wear. ²⁴Take the carefree birds as your example. Do you ever see them worry? They don't grow their own food or put it in a storehouse for later. Yet God takes care of every one of them, feeding each of them from his love and goodness. Isn't your life more precious to God than a bird? Be carefree in the care of God![a]

²⁵"Does worry add anything to your life? Can it add one more year, or even one day? ²⁶So if worrying adds nothing, but actually subtracts from your life, why would you worry about God's care of you?

²⁷"Think about the lilies. They grow and become beautiful, not because they work hard or strive to clothe themselves. Yet not even Solomon, wearing his kingly garments of splendor, could be compared to a field of lilies. ²⁸If God can clothe the fields and meadows with grass and flowers, can't he clothe you as well, O struggling one with so many doubts?[b] ²⁹I repeat it: Don't let worry enter your life. Live above the anxious cares about your personal needs. ³⁰People everywhere seem to worry about making a living, but your heavenly Father knows your every need and will take care of you. ³¹Each and every day he will supply your needs as you seek his kingdom passionately, above all else. ³²So don't ever be afraid, dearest friends! Your loving Father joyously gives you his kingdom realm with all its promises!

³³"So, now, go and sell what you have and give to those in need, making deposits in your account in heaven, an account that will never be taken from you. Your gifts will become a secure and unfailing treasure, deposited in heaven forever. ³⁴Where you deposit your treasure, that is where your thoughts will turn to—and your heart will long to be there also."

Be Ready

³⁵"Be prepared for action[c] at a moment's notice. ³⁶Be like the servants who anticipate their master's return from a wedding celebration. They are ready

---

a 12:24 Implied in the context.
b 12:28 This Greek word means "little faiths."
c 12:35 The Greek is literally "Let your loins be girded and keep your lamps burning."

to unlock and open the door for him at a moment's notice. ³⁷What great joy is ahead for the awakened ones who are waiting for the Master's return! He himself will become their servant and wait on them at his table as he passes by. ³⁸He may appear at midnight or even later, but what great joy for the awakened ones whenever he comes! ³⁹Of course, if they knew ahead of time the hour of the master's appearing, they would be alert, just as they would be ready if they knew ahead of time that a thief was coming to break into their house. ⁴⁰So keep being alert and ready at all times. For I can promise you that the Son of Man will surprise you and will appear[a] when you don't expect him."

The Faithful Servant

⁴¹"Lord," Peter asked, "does this apply only to the twelve of us, or is it for everyone else as well?"

⁴²The Lord said, **"A trustworthy and thoughtful manager who understands the ways of his master will be given a ministry of responsibility in his master's house, serving others exactly what they need at just the right time. ⁴³⁻⁴⁴And when the master returns, he will find that his servant has served him well. I can promise you, he will be given a great reward and will be placed as an overseer of everything the master owns.**

⁴⁵**"But what if that servant says in his heart,** *My master delays his coming, and who knows when he will return?* **Because of the delay, the servant elevates himself and mistreats those in his master's household. Instead of caring for the ones he was appointed to serve, he abuses the other servants, both men and women. He throws drunken parties for his friends and gives himself over to every pleasure.** ⁴⁶**Let me tell you what will happen to him. His master will suddenly return at a time that shocks him, and he will remove the abusive, selfish servant from his position of trust. He will be severely punished and assigned a portion with the unbelievers.**

⁴⁷**"Every servant who knows full well what pleases his master, yet who does not make himself ready and refuses to put his master's will to action, will be punished with many blows.** ⁴⁸**But the servant who does not know his master's will**[b] **and unwittingly does what is wrong will be punished less**

---

a 12:40 The Greek word can also be translated "become."
b 12:48 Implied in the text.

severely. For those who have received a greater revelation from their master are required a greater obedience. And those who have been entrusted with great responsibility will be held more responsible to their master."

Jesus Brings Fire to the Earth

[49]"I have come to set the earth on fire. And how I long for every heart to be already ablaze with this fiery passion for God! [50]But first I must be immersed into the baptism of God's judgment,[a] and I am consumed with passion as I await its fulfillment. [51]Don't think for a moment that I came to grant peace and harmony to everyone. No, for my coming will change everything and create hostility among you. [52]From now on, even family members will be divided over me and will choose sides[b] against one another. [53]Fathers will be split off against sons and sons against fathers; mothers will be against daughters and daughters against mothers; mothers-in-law will be against brides and brides against mothers-in-law—all because of me."

Discerning the Time

[54]Jesus then said to the crowds gathered around him, "When you see a cloud forming in the west, don't you say, 'A storm is brewing'? And then it arrives. [55]And when you feel the south wind blowing, you say, 'A heat wave is on the way.' And so it happens. [56]What hypocrites![c] You are such experts at forecasting the weather, but you are totally unwilling to understand the spiritual significance[d] of the time you're living in.

[57]"You can't even judge for yourselves what is good and right.

[58]"When you are wrong, it is better that you agree with your adversary and settle your dispute before you have to go before a judge. If not, you may be dragged into court, and the judge may find you guilty and [59]throw you into prison until you have paid off your fine entirely."

---

a 12:50 The implication of the context is that Jesus was drawing closer to his time of experiencing God's judgment for our sins on the cross. It is a "baptism" of judgment that we deserved.

b 12:52 The Greek text is literally "Among five in one house, three will be against two and two will be against three."

c 12:56 There is an amazing play on words found in the Aramaic text. The word translated "hypocrites" is literally "accepter of faces." The Aramaic states that the Pharisees looked at the "face" of the sky and the "faces" of men, living superficially, not seeing what was happening spiritually around them.

d 12:56 Implied in the context.

Thirteen

The Need for True Repentance

¹Some of those present informed Jesus that Pilate had slaughtered some Galilean Jews[a] while they were offering sacrifices at the temple, mixing their blood with the sacrifices they were offering.

²Jesus turned and asked the crowd, **"Do you believe that the slaughtered Galileans were the worst sinners of all the Galileans? ³No, they weren't! So listen to me. Unless you all repent,[b] you will perish as they did. ⁴Or what about the eighteen who perished when the tower of Siloam[c] fell upon them? Do you really think that they were more guilty than all of the others in Jerusalem? ⁵No, they weren't. But unless you repent, you will all eternally perish, just as they did."**

The Parable of the Barren Tree

⁶Then Jesus told them this parable: **"There was a man who planted a fig tree in his orchard. But when he came to gather fruit from his tree he found none, for it was barren and had no fruit. ⁷So he said to his gardener, 'For the last three years I've come to gather figs from my tree but it remains fruitless. What a waste! Go ahead and cut it down!'**

⁸**"But the gardener said, 'Sir, we should leave it one more year. Let me fertilize and cultivate it, then let's see if it will produce fruit. ⁹If it doesn't bear fruit by next year, we'll cut it down.'"[d]**

---

a 13:1 It is likely that Pilate viewed these Jews as rebellious to his rule. This was indeed an atrocious act by Pilate.
b 13:3 The Greek term for repentance means "to change your mind and amend your ways."
c 13:4 Siloam was the name of a pool or reservoir for the city of Jerusalem near the junction of the south and east walls of the city.
d 13:9 This parable was an obvious picture of the nation of Israel. The owner was the Father and the gardener was Jesus, who had come to them and for three years had longed to have true spiritual fruit from his spiritual vine (Isaiah 5:1–7). The warning is that it would be cut down if it did not bear the fruits of repentance. The purpose of the parable was to warn people that they were in their last year of God's grace toward them.

Jesus Heals on the Sabbath Day

[10]One Sabbath day, while Jesus was teaching in the Jewish meeting house, [11]he encountered a seriously handicapped woman. She was crippled and had been doubled over for eighteen years. Her condition was caused by a demonic spirit of bondage[a] that had left her unable to stand up straight.

[12-13]When Jesus saw her condition, he called her over and gently laid his hands on her. Then he said, **"Dear woman, you are free. I release you forever from this crippling spirit."**

Instantly she could stood straight and tall, and she overflowed with glorious praise to God!

[14]The Jewish leader who was in charge of the meeting house was infuriated over Jesus healing on the Sabbath day. "Six days you are to work," he shouted angrily to the crowd. "Those are the days you should come here for healing, but not on the seventh day!"

[15]The Lord said, **"You hopeless frauds! Don't you care for your animals on the Sabbath day, untying your ox or donkey from the stall and leading it away to water? [16]If you do this for your animals, what's wrong with allowing this beloved daughter of Abraham, who has been bound by Satan for eighteen long years, to be untied and set free on a Sabbath day?"**

[17]When they heard this, his critics were completely humiliated. But the crowds shouted with joy over the glorious things Jesus was doing among them.

Parables of Jesus

[18]Jesus taught them this parable: **"How can I describe the kingdom of God? Let me illustrate it this way. [19]It is like the smallest of seeds that you would plant in a garden. And when it grows, it becomes a huge tree, with so many spreading branches that various birds[b] make nests there."**

[20]Jesus taught them another parable: **"How can I describe the kingdom of God? Let me give you this illustration: [21]It is like something as small as yeast**

---

a 13:11 Literally, "spirit of weakness."
b 13:19 See Ezekiel 17:23. The obvious meaning of this parable is that the kingdom of God will begin small but it will expand, grow, and mature. People from every nation will come and make a "nest" in the kingdom of God.

that a woman kneads into a large amount of dough. It works unseen until it permeates[a] the entire batch and rises high."

The Way of the Kingdom

[22]Jesus ministered in one town and village after another,[b] teaching the people as he made his way toward Jerusalem. [23]A bystander asked him, "Lord, will only a few have eternal life?"

Jesus said to the crowd, [24]"There is a great cost[c] for anyone to enter through the narrow doorway to the kingdom of God. I tell you, there will be many who will want to enter but won't be able to. [25]For once the head of the house has shut and locked the door, it will be too late. Even if you stand outside knocking, begging to enter, and saying, 'Lord, Lord, open the door for us,' he will say to you, 'I don't know who you are. You are not a part of my family.'[d]

[26]"Then you will reply, 'But Lord, we dined with you and walked with you as you taught us.' [27]And he will reply, 'Don't you understand? I don't know who you are, for you are not a part of my family. You cannot enter in. Now, go away from me! For you are all disloyal to me and do evil.'[e]

[28]"You will experience great weeping and great anguish when you see Abraham, Isaac, and Jacob, along with all the prophets of Israel, enjoying the kingdom of God while you yourselves are barred from entering. [29]And you will see people streaming from the four corners of the earth, accepting the invitation to feast in God's kingdom, while you are kept outside[f] looking in! [30]And take note of this: There are some who are despised and viewed as the least important now, but will one day be placed at the head of the line. And there are others who are viewed as 'elite' today who will become least important then."

---

a 13:21 The meaning of this parable is that something small can impact and penetrate something great. It is the pervading influence of virtue and truth that is highlighted here. A transformation takes place when the hidden yet pervasive kingdom impacts every part of culture and society around us.

b 13:22 Jesus now visits the places where his disciples had already been sent to. See Luke 10:1–11.

c 13:24 The Greek word used here is actually "agonize."

d 13:25 Implied in the text.

e 13:27 This is quoted from Psalm 6:8. Though they were acquaintances, they had not responded to his message with repentance. The word "disloyal" is taken from the Aramaic. The question to ask is not simply "Will the saved be few?" (verse 23) but rather, "Will it be you?"

f 13:29 Implied in the text.

Jesus' Sorrow for Jerusalem

³¹Just then some Jewish religious leaders came to Jesus to inform him that Herod was out to kill him and urged him to flee from that place. ³²Jesus told them, **"Go and tell that deceiver**ᵃ **that I will continue to cast out demons and heal the sick today and tomorrow, but on the third day I will bring my work to perfection. ³³For everyone knows I am safe until I come to Jerusalem, for that is where all the prophets have been killed. ³⁴O city of Jerusalem, you are the city that murders your prophets! You are the city that pelts to death with stones the very messengers**ᵇ **who were sent to deliver you! So many times I have longed to gather your wayward children together around me, as a hen gathers her chicks under her wings—but you were too stubborn to let me. ³⁵And now it is too late, since your house will be left in ruins.**ᶜ **You will not see me again until you are able to say, 'We welcome the one who comes to us in the name of the Lord.'"**ᵈ

---

a 13:32 Or "fox."
b 13:34 Or "apostles."
c 13:35 See Jeremiah 12:7.
d 13:35 See Psalm 118:26.

Fourteen

Jesus Heals on the Sabbath

¹One day Jesus was on his way to dine with a prominent Jewish religious leader for a Sabbath meal. Everyone was watching him to see if he would heal anyone on the Sabbath. ²Just then, standing right in front of him was a man suffering with his limbs swollen with fluid.

³Jesus asked the experts of the law and the Pharisees who were present, **"Is it permitted within the law to heal a man on the Sabbath day? Is it right or wrong?"** ⁴No one dared to answer. So Jesus turned to the sick man, took hold of him, and released healing to him, then sent him on his way.

⁵Jesus said to them all, **"If one of your children or one of your animals fell into a well, wouldn't you do all you could to rescue them even if it was a Sabbath day?"**

⁶There was nothing they could say—all were silenced.

Humility and Hospitality

⁷When Jesus noticed how the guests for the meal were all vying for the seats of honor, he shared this story with the guests around the table:

⁸**"When you are invited to an important social function, don't be quick to sit near the head of the table, choosing the seat of honor. What will happen when someone more distinguished than you arrives? ⁹The host will then bring him over to where you are sitting and ask for your seat, saying in front of all the guests, 'You're in the wrong place. Please give this person your seat.' Disgraced, you will have to take whatever seat is left. ¹⁰Instead, when you're invited to a banquet, you should choose to sit in the lowest place**ᵃ **so that when your host comes and sees you there, he may say, 'My friend, come with**

a 14:10 See Proverbs 25:6–7.

me and let me seat you in a better place.' Then, in front of all the other guests at the banquet, you will be honored and seated in the place of highest respect.

[11]"Remember this: everyone with a lofty opinion of who he is and who seeks to raise himself up will be humbled before all. And everyone with a modest opinion of who he is and chooses to humble himself will be raised up before all."

[12]Then Jesus turned to his host and said, **"When you throw a banquet, don't just invite your friends, relatives, or rich neighbors—for it is likely they will return the favor. [13-14]It is better to invite those who never get an invitation. Invite the poor to your banquet, along with the outcast, the handicapped, and the blind—those who could never repay you the favor. Then you will experience a great blessing in this life, and at the resurrection of the godly you will receive a full reward."**

[15]When they heard this, one of the dinner guests said to Jesus, "Someday God will have a kingdom feast,[a] and how happy and privileged will be the ones who get to share in that joy!"

[16]Jesus replied with this parable:

"There was a man who invited many to join him in a great feast. [17]When the day for the feast arrived, the host instructed his servant to notify all the invited guests and tell them, 'Come, for everything is now ready for you!' [18]But one by one they all made excuses. One said, 'I can't come. I just bought some property and I'm obligated to go and look it over.' [19]Another said, 'Please accept my regrets, for I just purchased five teams of oxen[b] and I need to make sure they can pull the plow.' [20]Another one said, 'I can't come because I just got married.'

[21]"The servant reported back to the host and told him of all their excuses. So the master became angry and said to his servant, 'Go at once throughout the city and invite anyone you find—the poor, the blind, the disabled, the hurting, and the lonely—and invite them to my banquet.'

[22]"When the servant returned to his master, he said, 'Sir, I have done what you've asked, but there's still room for more.'

[23]"So the master told him, 'All right. Go out again, and this time bring them all back with you. Persuade the beggars on the streets, the outcasts,

---

a 14:15 The guest at the dinner assumed the kingdom of God was coming one day, but Jesus' parable explained that it had already begun with the invitation to come to him, the King.
b 14:19 This implies he was a wealthy man who foolishly chose possessions over Christ.

even the homeless. Urgently insist that they come in and enjoy the feast so that my house will be full.'

[24]"I say to you all, the one who receives an invitation to feast with me and makes excuses will never enjoy my banquet."

The Cost of Following Jesus

[25]As massive crowds followed Jesus, he turned to them and said, [26]"When you follow me as my disciple, you will appear to others as though you hate your father, your mother, your wife, your sisters, your brothers—yes, you will even seem as though you hate your own life. This is the price you'll pay to be considered one of my followers. [27]And anyone who comes to me must be willing to share my cross and experience it as his own, or he cannot be considered to be my disciple. [28]So don't follow me without considering what it will cost you. For who would construct a house[a] before first sitting down to estimate the cost to complete it? [29]Otherwise he may lay the foundation and not be able to finish. The neighbors will ridicule him, saying, [30]'Look at him! He started to build but couldn't complete it!'

[31]"Have you ever heard of a commander[b] who goes out to war without first sitting down with strategic planning to determine the strength of his army to win the war[c] against a stronger opponent? [32]If he knows he doesn't stand a chance of winning the war, the wise commander will send out delegates to ask for the terms of peace. [33]Likewise, unless you surrender all to me, giving up all you possess, you cannot be one of my disciples.

[34]"Salt is good for seasoning. But if salt were to lose its flavor,[d] how could it ever be restored? [35]It will never be useful again, not even fit for the soil or the manure pile![e] If you have ears opened by the Spirit, then hear the meaning of what I have said and apply it to yourselves."[f]

---

a 14:28 Or "tower."
b 14:31 Or "king."
c 14:31 The Greek text states, "With ten thousand he will be able to go up against twenty thousand."
d 14:34 Or "become foolish." Both Greek and Aramaic use a word that can mean "foolish." If salt that has lost its flavor is foolish, then the salt that keeps its flavor is equal to wisdom. Rabbinical literature equates salt with wisdom. (Eduard Schweizer," *The Good News According to Matthew*, Atlanta: John Knox Press, 1975.) After speaking of salt, Jesus speaks of lighting a lamp. It was a common practice in the time of Jesus to put salt on the wick of a lamp to increase its brightness. The "salt" of wisdom will make our light shine even brighter. (W. A. Elwell and P. W. Comfort, *Tyndale Bible Dictionary*, Tyndale reference library, Wheaton, Ill.: Tyndale House, 2001, 797–798.)
e 14:35 Followers of Jesus who are unwilling to pay the price of discipleship are like worthless salt, unable to affect anything or anyone.
f 14:35 Implied in the text.

The Parable of the Lost Lamb

¹Many dishonest tax collectors and other notorious sinners often gathered around to listen as Jesus taught the people. ²This raised concerns with the Jewish religious leaders and experts of the law. Indignant, they grumbled and complained, saying, "Look at how this man associates with all these notorious sinners and welcomes them all to come to him!"

³In response, Jesus gave them this illustration:

⁴⁻⁵"**There once was a shepherd with a hundred lambs, but one of his lambs wandered away and was lost. So the shepherd left the ninety-nine lambs out in the open field and searched in the wilderness for that one lost lamb. He didn't stop until he finally found it. With exuberant joy he raised it up and placed it on his shoulders,**ᵃ **carrying it back with cheerful delight!** ⁶**Returning home, he called all his friends and neighbors together and said, 'Let's have a party! Come and celebrate with me the return of my lost lamb. It wandered away, but I found it and brought it home.'"**

⁷Jesus continued, "**In the same way, there will be a glorious celebration in heaven over the rescue of one lost sinner who repents, comes back home, and returns to the fold—more so than for all the righteous people who never strayed away.**"

The Parable of the Lost Coin

⁸Jesus gave them another parable:

"**There once was a woman who had ten**ᵇ **valuable silver coins. When she**

ᵃ 15:4–5 What a wonderful picture this gives us our "Good Shepherd." He doesn't beat the lost sheep for wandering away. He raises it up and carries it home!

ᵇ 15:8 The silver coin was a *zuza* (Aramaic). Although there are differing opinions as to its value, it could be equal in today's currency to more than twelve hundred US dollars. Notice the change of numbers in the three parables in this chapter: one out of a hundred for the sheep, one out of ten for the coins, and one out of two for the sons. This progressively shows the extraordinary value that Jesus places on every lost soul. Although the coin was lost, it never lost its value.

lost one of them, she swept her entire house, diligently searching every corner of her house for that one lost coin. [9]When she finally found it, she gathered all her friends and neighbors for a celebration, telling them, 'Come and celebrate with me! I had lost my precious silver coin, but now I've found it.' [10]That's the way God responds[a] every time one lost sinner repents and turns to him. He says to all his angels, 'Let's have a joyous celebration, for that one who was lost I have found!'"[b]

The Loving Father

[11]Then Jesus said, "Once there was a father with two sons. [12]The younger son came to his father and said, 'Father, don't you think it's time to give me the share of your estate that belongs to me?'[c] So the father went ahead and distributed among the two sons their inheritance.[d] [13]Shortly afterward, the younger son packed up all his belongings and traveled off to see the world. He journeyed to a far-off land where he soon wasted all he was given in a binge of extravagant and reckless living.

[14]"With everything spent and nothing left, he grew hungry, for there was a severe famine in that land. [15]So he begged a farmer in that country to hire him. The farmer hired him and sent him out to feed the pigs. [16]The son was so famished, he was willing to even eat the slop given to the pigs,[e] because no one would feed him a thing.

[17]"Humiliated, the son finally realized what he was doing and he thought, *There are many workers at my father's house who have all the food they want with plenty to spare. They lack nothing. Why am I here dying of hunger, feeding these pigs and eating their slop? [18]I want to go back home to my father's house, and I'll say to him, 'Father, I was wrong. I have sinned against you. [19]I'll never be worthy to be called your son. Please, Father, just treat me like one of your employees.'*

a 15:10 Jesus used the woman in this parable as a metaphor for God. This alone would incite anger from the Pharisees. In the next parable, God is unveiled as the extravagant Father who forgives his wayward son.
b 15:10 The silver coin had an image of Roman authority on it. We have been stamped with the image of God. Even when we are "lost," that image is still present, needing only to be "found" by grace and redeemed.
c 15:12 In the light of Middle Eastern culture, it was a great offense for a son to ask his father for his inheritance. It would be equivalent to saying, "I wish you were already dead!"
d 15:12 The Greek is literally "He gave them his life" (Greek *bios*).
e 15:16 This would be degrading to anyone, but especially to a Jew, who was forbidden to raise swine.

[20]"So the young son set off for home. From a long distance away, his father saw him coming, dressed as a beggar,[a] and great compassion swelled up in his heart for his son who was returning home. So the father raced out to meet him. He swept him up in his arms, hugged him dearly, and kissed him over and over with tender love.

[21]"Then the son said, 'Father, I was wrong. I have sinned against you. I could never deserve to be called your son. Just let me be—'

The father interrupted and said,[b] 'Son, you're home now!'

[22]"Turning to his servants, the father said, 'Quick, bring me the best robe, my very own robe, and I will place it on his shoulders. Bring the ring, the seal of sonship,[c] and I will put it on his finger. And bring out the best shoes[d] you can find for my son. [23]Let's prepare a great feast[e] and celebrate. [24]For this beloved son of mine was once dead, but now he's alive again. Once he was lost, but now he is found!' And everyone celebrated with overflowing joy.

[25]"Now, the older son was out working in the field when his brother returned, and as he approached the house he heard the music of celebration and dancing. [26]So he called over one of the servants and asked, 'What's going on?'

[27]"The servant replied, 'It's your younger brother. He's returned home and your father is throwing a party to celebrate his homecoming.'

[28]"The older son became angry and refused to go in and celebrate. So his father came out and pleaded with him, 'Come and enjoy the feast with us!'[f]

[29]"The son said, 'Father, listen! How many years have I been working like a slave for you, performing every duty you've asked as a faithful son?[g] And I've never once disobeyed you. But you've never thrown a party for me because of my faithfulness. Never once have you even given me a goat that I could feast on and celebrate with my friends like he's doing now. [30]But look at this son of

a 15:20 Implied in the context of the Greek text and stated more explicitly in the Aramaic.
b 15:21 This poetic description is made explicit from the cultural and spiritual implication of the text.
c 15:22 Culturally, this ring was an emblem of authority, giving the son authority to transact business in the father's name. This was a token of the seal of the Holy Spirit (Ephesians 1:14).
d 15:22 Or "bring sandals for his feet." Slaves were barefoot.
e 15:23 Implied in the text. The Greek text is "kill the grain-fatted calf." This is a picture of feasting upon Christ, who was sacrificed for us.
f 15:28 In the culture of that era, hospitality was of supreme importance. To refuse to go in to the feast, when it was his responsibility culturally to cohost the event with his father, was a humiliating rejection to the father.
g 15:29 While the younger brother pursued self-discovery, the older brother believed in moral conformity, earning favor from his father. Both needed the revelation of grace.

yours! He comes back after wasting your wealth on prostitutes and reckless living, and here you are throwing a great feast to celebrate—for him!'

[31]"The father said, 'My son, you are always with me by my side. Everything I have is yours to enjoy. [32]It's only right to celebrate like this and be overjoyed, because this brother of yours was once dead and gone, but now he is alive and back with us again. He was lost but now he is found!'"[a]

---

a   15:32 Jesus spoke three parables unveiling and revealing how the Trinity desires to bring people back through the Son, by the Spirit, to the Father. The Son came as a shepherd, seeking and sacrificing to find the lost sinner. The Spirit seeks the lost like the woman with the light of illumination for the lost coin until she found it. And the Father welcomes the returning sinner back to his house. It is the work of the Trinity to bring us back to God. In Matthew 28:19, it is the sequence of the Father, the Spirit, and the Son. Here in Luke 15, it is the Son, the Spirit, and the Father.

Sixteen

The Dishonest Manager

[1] Jesus taught his disciples using this story:

"There was once a very rich man who hired a manager to run his business and oversee all his wealth. But soon a rumor spread that the manager was wasting his master's money. [2] So the master called him in and said, 'Is it true that you are mismanaging my estate? You need to provide me with a complete audit of everything you oversee for me. I've decided to dismiss you.'

[3] "The manager thought, *Now what am I going to do? I'm finished here. I can't hide what I've done,*[a] *and I'm too proud to beg to get my job back.* [4] *I have an idea that will secure my future. It will win me favor and secure friends who can take care of me and help me when I get fired!*

[5] "So the dishonest manager hatched his scheme. He went to everyone who owed his master money, one by one, and he asked them, 'How much do you owe my master?' [6-7] One debtor owed twenty thousand dollars, so he said to him, 'Let me see your bill. Pay me now and we'll settle for twenty percent less.' The clever manager scratched out the original amount owed and reduced it by twenty percent. And to another who owed two hundred thousand dollars, he said, 'Pay me now and we'll reduce your bill by fifty percent.' And the clever manager scratched out the original amount owed and reduced it by half.

[8] "Even though his master was defrauded, when he found out about the shrewd way this manager had feathered his own nest, he congratulated the clever scoundrel for what he'd done to lay up for his future needs."

---

a 16:3 The manager's words include an ancient Aramaic figure of speech, "I can't dig," which means it can't be buried or hidden.

Jesus continued, "Remember this: The sons of darkness are more shrewd than the sons of light in their interactions with others. [9]It is important that you use the wealth of this world to demonstrate your friendship with God by winning friends and blessing others. Then, when this world fails and falls apart, your generosity will provide you with an eternal reward.[a]

[10]"The one who manages the little he has been given with faithfulness and integrity will be promoted and trusted with greater responsibilities. But those who cheat with the little they have been given will not be considered trustworthy to receive more. [11]If you have not handled the riches of this world with integrity, why should you be trusted with the eternal treasures of the spiritual world? [12]And if you've not been proven faithful with what belongs to another, why should you be given wealth of your own? [13]It is impossible for a person to serve two masters at the same time. You will be forced to love one and reject the other. One master will be despised and the other will have your loyal devotion. It is no different with God and the wealth of this world.[b] You must enthusiastically love one and definitively reject the other."

[14]Now, the Jewish religious leaders who were listening to Jesus were lovers of money. They laughed at what he said and mocked his teachings.

[15]So Jesus addressed them directly. "You always want to look spiritual in the eyes of others, but you have forgotten the eyes of God, which see what is inside you. The very things that you approve of and applaud are the things God despises. [16]The laws of Moses and the revelation of the prophets have prepared you for the arrival of the kingdom realm announced by John. And now, when this wonderful news of the kingdom realm of God is preached, people's hearts burn with extreme passion to press in and receive it. [17]Heaven and earth will disintegrate before even the smallest detail of the word of God will fail or lose its power.

[18]"It is wrong for you to divorce to cover your lust for another wife—that is adultery. And when you take that one you have lusted after as your wife, and contribute to the breakup of her marriage, you are once again guilty of adultery."

---

a 16:9 Or "You will be welcomed to the tents of eternity."
b 16:13 The word used here is "Mammon," which is money personified as a god and worshipped.

The Rich Man and Lazarus

[19]Jesus continued. "There once was a very rich man who had the finest things imaginable,[a] living every day enjoying his life of opulent luxury. [20-21]Outside the gate of his mansion[b] was a poor beggar named Lazarus.[c] He lay there every day, covered with boils, and all the neighborhood dogs would come and lick his open sores. The only food he had to eat was the garbage that the rich man threw away.

[22]"One day poor Lazarus died, and the angels of God came and escorted his spirit into Paradise.[d]

[23]The day came that the rich man also died. In hell he looked up from his torment and saw Abraham in the distance, and Lazarus the beggar was standing beside him in the glory. [24]So the rich man shouted, 'Father Abraham! Father Abraham! Have mercy on me. Send Lazarus to dip his finger in water and come to cool my tongue, for I am in agony in these flames of fire!'

[25]"But Abraham responded, 'My friend, don't you remember? While you were alive, you had all you desired, surrounded in luxury, while Lazarus had nothing. Now Lazarus is in the comforts of Paradise and you are in agony. [26]Besides, between us is a huge chasm that cannot be bridged, keeping anyone from crossing from one realm to the other, even if he wanted to.'

[27]"So the rich man said, 'Then let me ask you, Father Abraham, to please send Lazarus to my relatives. [28]Tell him to witness to my five brothers and warn them not to end up where I am in this place of torment.'

[29]"Abraham replied, 'They've already had enough warning. They have the teachings of Moses and the prophets, and they must obey them.'

[30]"'But what if they're not listening?' the rich man added. 'If someone from the dead were to go and warn them, they would surely repent.'

[31]"Abraham said to him, 'If they won't listen to Moses and the prophets, neither would they believe even if someone[e] was raised from the dead!'"

---

a 16:19 The Greek text is literally "He was dressed in a purple robe." This is a figure of speech that refers to the luxury that surrounded him. This was the kind of robe worn only by kings.
b 16:20–21 Implied by the context.
c 16:20–21 Lazarus is a form of the name Eleazar and means "God helps."
d 16:22 The Greek text is literally "Abraham's bosom," which is a metaphor for Paradise.
e 16:31 Translated from the Aramaic. Jesus is that "someone" who rose from the grave, yet many still will not listen and believe.

Seventeen

Faith and Forgiveness

[1]One day Jesus taught his disciples this: **"Betrayals[a] are inevitable, but great devastation will come to the one guilty of betraying others. [2]It would be better for him to have a heavy boulder tied around his neck and be hurled into the deepest sea than to face the punishment of betraying one of my dear ones! So be alert to your brother's condition, [3]and if you see him going the wrong direction, cry out and correct him. If there is true repentance on his part, forgive him. [4]No matter how many times in one day your brother sins against you[b] and says, 'I'm sorry; I am changing; forgive me,' you need to forgive him each and every time."**

[5]Upon hearing this, the apostles said to Jesus, "Lord, you must increase[c] our measure of faith!"

[6]Jesus responded, **"If you have even the smallest measure of authentic faith, it would be powerful enough to say to this large[d] tree, 'My faith will pull you up by the roots and throw you into the sea,' and it will respond to your faith and obey you."[e]**

[7-8]Jesus continued, **"After a servant has finished his work in the field or with the livestock, he doesn't immediately sit down to relax and eat. No, a true servant prepares the food for his master and makes sure his master is served his meal before he sits down to eat his own. [9]Does the true servant expect to be thanked for doing what is required of him? [10]So learn this lesson: After doing all that is commanded of you, simply say, 'We are mere servants,**

---

a 17:1 As translated from the Aramaic. Other Greek texts use the word "temptation" or "to stumble."
b 17:4 The Greek text states explicitly, "seven times." But this is used as a metaphor for unlimited forgiveness.
c 17:5 The Greek text is literally "Add faith to us."
d 17:6 The Greek text is "mulberry" or "sycamore tree," which is known to grow to about thirty-five feet high.
e 17:6 Implied conclusion of the text. The apostles had faith; they simply needed to use it.

undeserving of special praise, for we are just doing what is expected of us and fulfilling our duties.'"

Jesus Heals Ten Lepers

¹¹Jesus traveled on toward Jerusalem and passed through the border region between Samaria and Galilee. ¹²As he entered one village, ten men approached him, but they kept their distance, for they were lepers. ¹³They shouted to him, "Mighty Lord, our wonderful Master!ᵃ Won't you have mercy on us and heal us?"ᵇ

¹⁴When Jesus stopped to look at them, he spoke these words: **"Go to be examined by the Jewish priests."**ᶜ

They set off, and they were healed while walking along the way.¹⁵

One of them, a foreigner from Samaria,ᵈ when he discovered that he was completely healed, turned back to find Jesus, shouting out joyous praises and glorifying God. ¹⁶When he found Jesus, he fell down at his feet and thanked him over and over, saying to him, "You are the Messiah."ᵉ

¹⁷**"So where are the other nine?"** Jesus asked. **"Weren't there ten who were healed? ¹⁸They all refused to return to give thanks and give glory to God except you, a foreigner from Samaria?"**

¹⁹Then Jesus said to the healed man lying at his feet, **"Arise and go. It was your faith that brought you salvation and healing."**

God's Kingdom Realm within You

²⁰Jesus was once asked by the Jewish religious leaders, "When will the kingdom of God come?"ᶠ

Jesus responded, **"The kingdom realm of God does not come simply by**

a 17:13 The Greek word used here for "Master" is not the usual word used for "Teacher" or "Master." It denotes one with supernatural authority and power.
b 17:13 It is implied that they were seeking a healing from Jesus.
c 17:14 This was what was required. See Leviticus 13:19 and 14:1–11. What a step of faith for these lepers as they stepped out on only the word Jesus spoke to them. They were to go the priest, who would confirm their healing and declare them ceremonially clean and approved to go into the temple to worship God.
d 17:15 This information is supplied from verse 16. For a Samaritan man to give thanks to a Jewish man was indeed peculiar. Since he likely had no "priest," he turned to the only one he knew to be a priest for him, Jesus Christ.
e 17:16 From the Aramaic text.
f 17:20 Or "When will God's kingdom be established?"

obeying principles[a] or by waiting for signs. [21]The kingdom is not discovered in one place or another, for the kingdom realm of God is already expanding within some of you."[b]

[22]Later, Jesus addressed this again with his apostles, saying, **"The time is coming when a great passion will be awakened within you to see me again. Yes, you will long to see the beginning of the days of the Son of Man, but you won't be able to find me. [23]You will hear reports from some who will say, 'Look, he has returned,' 'He's over here,' or, 'He's over there!' Don't believe it or run after them, for their claims will be false.[c] [24]The day of the Son of Man will burst forth with the brightness of a lightning strike that shines from one end of the sky to the other, illuminating the earth.**

[25]**"But before this takes place, the Son of Man must pass through great suffering and rejection from this generation. [26]The same things that happened in the days of Noah will take place in the days of the Son of Man. [27]The people lived their lives thinking that nothing had changed. They got married and raised families, not realizing what was coming until the day Noah boarded the ark and the devastating flood came and swept them all away.**

[28-30]**"The days of the Son of Man can also be compared to the days of Lot. The people of that time lived their lives as normal. They got married, raised families, built homes and businesses, yet they were totally unaware of what was coming until the day Lot departed from Sodom. The sky opened up and rained fire and burning sulfur upon them, destroying everyone and everything they had built. So it will be on the day of the unveiling of the Son of Man.**

[31]**"In the day of my appearing, if one is out working in the yard,[d] he won't even have time to go back into the house to gather his belongings. And those toiling in their fields won't have time to run back home. [32]Don't forget the example of Lot's wife and what happened to her when she turned back.[e] [33]All**

---

a 17:20 Implied in the Aramaic text where it states, "observances (of the law)." The same word is found in Galatians 4:10 referring to "observances" of keeping the law.
b 17:21 Translated from the Aramaic text. The implication is that the kingdom of God is a person, Jesus Christ. The reality of God's kingdom appears when Jesus lives within us by faith.
c 17:23 Implied in the context.
d 17:31 The Greek text is literally "on the roof."
e 17:32 Genesis 19:26.

who are obsessed with being secure in life will lose it all—including their lives. But those who let go of their lives and surrender them to me will discover true life. ³⁴For in that night there will be two lying in their bed; one will be suddenly swept away while the other will be left alive. ³⁵⁻³⁶There will be two women working together at household duties; one will be suddenly swept away while the other will be left alive."*a*

³⁷His apostles asked, "Lord, where will this judgment*b* happen?"

Jesus responded, **"It will be obvious,***c* **for wherever there are those spiritually dead,***d* **there you will find the eagles circling."***e*

---

a 17:35–36 This Greek word can also refer to being "forgiven of sin." Some later Greek texts add, "Two men will be in the field; one will be taken and the other will be left." "Those who are swept away are taken to judgment; those who are left behind remain to enter into the kingdom glory.".

b 17:37 Implied in the context.

c 17:37 Implied in the context.

d 17:37 The Greek word used here is literally "corpse" and can be a metaphor for those who are spiritually dead.

e 17:37 The Greek word used here is clearly "eagles." Some translations read, "vultures."

Eighteen

Jesus Gives a Parable about Prayer

¹One day Jesus taught the apostles to keep praying and never stop or lose hope. He shared with them this illustration:

²**"In a certain town there was a civil judge, a thick-skinned and godless man who had no fear of others' opinions. ³And there was a poor widow in that town who kept pleading with the judge, 'Grant me justice and protect me against my oppressor!'**

⁴⁻⁵**"He ignored her pleas for quite some time, but she kept asking. Eventually he said to himself, 'This widow keeps annoying me, demanding her rights, and I'm tired of listening to her. Even though I'm not a religious man and don't care about the opinions of others, I'll just get her off my back by answering her claims for justice and I'll rule in her favor. Then she'll leave me alone.'"**

⁶The Lord continued, **"Did you hear what the ungodly judge said—that he would answer her persistent request? ⁷Don't you know that God, the true judge, will grant justice to all of his chosen ones who cry out to him night and day? He will pour out his Spirit upon them.ᵃ He will not delay to answer you and give you what you ask for. ⁸God will give swift justice to those who don't give up. So be ever praying, ever expecting, just like the widow was with the judge. Yet when the Son of Man comes back, will he find this kind of persistent faithfulness in his people?"**

Humility in Prayer

⁹Jesus taught this parable to those who were convinced they were morally upright and those who trusted in their own virtue yet looked down on others with disgust:

---

a 18:7 Translated from the Aramaic text. The Greek text has an unusual verb that means "ever tapping," signifying one who keeps knocking on the door of heaven until he receives what he came for. The nominalized verb becomes the word "chisel."

¹⁰"Once there were two men who went into the temple to pray. One was a proud religious leader, the other a despised tax collector. ¹¹⁻¹²The religious leader stood apart from the others and prayed, 'How I thank you, O God, that I'm not wicked like everyone else. They're cheaters, swindlers, and crooks—like that tax collector over there. God, you know that I never cheat or commit adultery; I fast from food twice a week and I give you a tenth of all I make.'

¹³"The tax collector stood off alone in the corner, away from the Holy Place,ᵃ and covered his face in his hands, feeling that he was unworthy to even look up to God. With brokenness and tears he sobbed, 'God, please, in your mercy and because of the blood sacrifice, forgive me,ᵇ for I am nothing but the most miserable of all sinners!'

¹⁴"Which one of them left for home that day made right with God? It was the humble tax collector and not the religious leader! For everyone who is proud and feels that he is superior to others will one day be humiliated before all, and everyone who humbles himself will one day be lifted up and honored before all."

Jesus Blesses Children

¹⁵The people brought their babies and small childrenᶜ to Jesus so that he might lay his hands on them to bless them. When the disciples saw this, they scolded the parents and told them to stop troubling the Master. ¹⁶But Jesus called for the parents, the children, and his disciples to come and listen to him. Then he told them, **"Never hinder a child from coming to me. Let them all come, for the kingdom realm of God belongs to them as much as it does to anyone else. They demonstrate to you what faith is all about.**ᵈ ¹⁷**Learn this well: unless you receive the revelation of the kingdom realm the same way a little child receives it, you will never be able to enter in."**

---

a 18:13 Implied in the text.
b 18:13 Implied in the text. The Greek text uses a word that implies he was saying to God, "Look at me as you look at the blood-sprinkled mercy seat."
c 18:15 There is a hint in the Greek text that these children may have been sick. Jesus loves and heals children.
d 18:16 Implied in the context, added for clarity.

Jesus Speaks with a Young, Wealthy Official

[18]One day a wealthy Jewish nobleman of high standing posed this question to Jesus: "Wonderful Teacher, what must I do to be saved and receive eternal life?"

[19]Jesus answered, **"Why would you call me wonderful when there is only one who is wonderful—and that is God alone.**[a] **[20]You already know what is right and what the commandments teach: 'Do not commit adultery, do not murder, do not steal, do not lie, and respectfully honor your father and your mother.'"**

[21]The wealthy leader replied, "These are the very things I've been doing for as long as I can remember."

[22]**"Ah,"** Jesus said. **"But there's still one thing you're missing in your life."**

"What is that?" asked the man.

"You must go and sell everything you own and give all the proceeds to the poor so you will have eternal treasures. Then come and follow me."[b]

[23]When the rich leader heard these words, he was devastated, for he was extremely wealthy.

[24]Jesus saw his disappointment, and looking right at him he said, **"It is next to impossible for those who have everything to enter into the kingdom realm of God. [25]Nothing could be harder! It could be compared to trying to stuff a rope through the eye of a needle."**[c]

[26]Those who heard this said, "Then who can be saved?"

[27]Jesus responded, **"What appears humanly impossible is more than possible with God. For God can do what man cannot."**

[28]Peter said, "Lord, see how we've left all that we have, our houses and our careers, to follow you."

[29-30]Jesus replied, **"Listen to my words: anyone who leaves his home behind and chooses the kingdom of God over wife, children, parents, and**

a 18:19 Jesus is implying that if we call him "wonderful," we are calling him "God."
b 18:22 This does not teach us that salvation can be earned by giving away our possessions to the poor. Jesus was showing the young, wealthy man that he couldn't truly be a disciple until there was no competition in his heart in following Jesus.
c 18:25 As translated from the Aramaic. The Greek is "to stuff a camel through the eye of a needle." The Aramaic word for "rope" and for "camel" is the homonym *gamla*. This could be an instance of the Aramaic text being misread by the Greek translators as "camel" instead of "rope." Regardless, this becomes a metaphor for something impossible. It would be like saying, "It's as hard as making pigs fly!"

family, it will come back to him many more times in this lifetime,[a] and in the age to come, he will inherit even more than that—he will inherit eternal life!"

Jesus Prophesies His Death and Resurrection

[31]Jesus took the Twelve aside in private and told them, **"We are going to Jerusalem so that everything prophesied about the Son of Man will be fulfilled. [32]They will betray him and hand him over to the people, and they will mock him, insult him, and spit in his face. [33]And after they have abused[b] and flogged the Son of Man, they will kill him. But in three days he will rise again."**

[34]The disciples didn't have a clue what he was saying, for his words were a mystery that was hidden from them.

Jesus Heals a Blind Beggar

[35]As Jesus and his followers arrived at Jericho, there was a blind beggar sitting on the roadside. [36]When he heard the crowd approaching, he asked, "What's all this commotion about?"

[37]"It's Jesus!" they said. "Jesus the Nazarene is passing by."

[38]The blind beggar shouted, "Jesus, Son of David,[c] have pity and show me mercy!"

[39]Those who were in the front of the crowd scolded him and warned him to be quiet. But the blind beggar screamed out even louder, "Jesus, Son of David, show me mercy!"

[40]Suddenly Jesus stopped. He told those nearby, **"Bring the man over to me."** When they brought him before Jesus, he asked the man, [41]**"What is it you want me to do for you?"**

"Lord," he said, "please, I want to see again."

[42]Jesus said, **"Now you will see. Receive your sight this moment. For your faith in me has given you sight and new life."**[d]

[43]Instantly he could see again. His eyes popped opened, and he saw Jesus. He shouted loud praises to God and he followed Jesus. And when the crowd saw what happened, they too erupted with shouts of praise to God.

---

a 18:29–30 The Mark account of this passage adds, "with persecutions." See Mark 10:29.

b 18:33 The word translated "abused" is powerful. It occurs in the Greek text in verse 32 but in the Aramaic text in verse 33.

c 18:38 The term "Son of David" was used for the Messiah. The blind man believed Jesus was the Messiah.

d 18:42 Translated from the Aramaic. The Greek word signifies both healing and salvation.

Nineteen

Jesus and Zacchaeus

[1-3]In the city of Jericho there lived a very wealthy man named Zacchaeus,[a] who was the supervisor over all the tax collectors. As Jesus made his way through the city, Zacchaeus was eager to see Jesus. He kept trying to get a look at him, but the crowd around Jesus was massive. Zacchaeus was a very short man and couldn't see over the heads of the people. [4]So he ran on ahead of everyone and climbed up a blossoming fig tree[b] so he could get a glimpse of Jesus as he passed by.

[5]When Jesus got to that place, he looked up into the tree and said, **"Zacchaeus, hurry on down, for I am appointed to stay[c] at your house today!"**

[6]So he scurried down the tree and came face-to-face with Jesus.

[7]As Jesus left to go with Zacchaeus, many in the crowd complained, "Look at this! Of all the people to have dinner[d] with, he's going to eat in the house of a crook."

[8]Zacchaeus joyously welcomed Jesus[e] and was amazed over Jesus' gracious visit to his home. Zacchaeus stood in front of the Lord and said, "Half of all that I own I will give to the poor. And Lord, if I have cheated anyone, I promise to pay back four times as much as I stole."

[9-10]Jesus said to him, "This shows that today life[f] has come to you and your household, for you are a true son of Abraham. The Son of Man has come to seek out and to give life to those who are lost."[g]

The Parable of a Prince and His Servants

[11]At this time Jesus was getting close to entering Jerusalem. The crowds that followed him were convinced that the kingdom of God would fully manifest when Jesus established it in Jerusalem. [12]So he told them this story to change their perspective:

"Once there was a wealthy prince who left his province to travel to a distant land, where he would be crowned king and then return. [13]Before he departed he summoned his ten servants together and said, 'I am entrusting each of you with fifty thousand dollars[a] to trade with while I am away. Invest it and put the money to work until I return.'

[14]"Some of his countrymen despised the prince and sent a delegation after him to declare before the royals, 'We refuse to let this man rule over us! He will not be our king!'

[15]"Nevertheless, he was crowned king and returned to his land. Then he summoned his ten servants to see how much each one had earned and what their profits came to.

[16]"The first one came forward and said, 'Master, I took what you gave me and invested it, and it multiplied ten times.'

[17]"'Splendid! You have done well, my excellent servant. Because you have shown that you can be trusted in this small matter, I now grant you authority to rule over ten fortress cities.'

[18]"The second came and said, 'Master, what you left with me has multiplied five times.'

[19]"His master said, 'I also grant you authority in my kingdom over five fortress cities.'

[20]"Another came before the king and said, 'Master, here is the money you entrusted to me. I hid it for safekeeping. [21]You see, I live in fear of you, for everyone knows you are a strict master and impossible to please. You push us for a high return on all that you own, and you always want to gain from someone else's efforts.'[b]

---

a 19:13 Literally, "ten minas."
b 19:21 The text is literally "You pick up what you didn't lay down and reap where you didn't sow." This statement is obviously not true. The opposite can be found in how the master shared his kingdom with the other more faithful servants. Today, many likewise have a misconception of the true heart of our Master. Our Master makes servants into rulers.

²²"The king said, 'You wicked servant! I will judge you using your own words. If what you said about me is true, that I am a harsh man, pushing you for a high return and wanting gain from others' efforts, ²³why didn't you at least put my money in the bank[a] to earn some interest on what I entrusted to you?'

²⁴"The king said to his other servants, 'Take the money he has and give it to the faithful servant who multiplied my money ten times over.'

²⁵"'But master,' the other servants objected, 'why give it to him? He already has so much!'

²⁶"'Yes,' replied the king. 'But to all who have been faithful, even more will be given them. And for the ones who have nothing, even the little they seem to have will be taken from them. ²⁷Now, bring all those rebellious enemies of mine who rejected me as their king—bring them here before me and execute them!"

²⁸After saying all of this, Jesus headed straight for Jerusalem. ²⁹When he arrived at the stables of Annia[b] near the Mount of Olives,[c] he sent two of his disciples ahead, saying, ³⁰"When you enter the next village,[d] you will find tethered there a donkey's young colt that has never been ridden. Untie it and bring it to me. ³¹And if anyone stops you and asks, 'What are you doing?' just tell them this: 'It is needed for the Lord of All.'"[e]

³²The two who were sent entered the village and found the colt exactly like Jesus had said. ³³While they were untying the colt, the owners approached them and asked, "What are you doing?"

³⁴The disciples replied, "We need this donkey for the Lord of All."

³⁵⁻³⁶They brought the colt to Jesus. Then they placed their prayer shawls on its back, and Jesus rode it as he descended the Mount of Olives toward Jerusalem.[f] As he rode along, people spontaneously threw their prayer shawls on the path in front of him like a carpet.[g]

³⁷As soon as he got to the bottom of the Mount of Olives, the crowds of his followers shouted with a loud outburst of ecstatic joy over all the mighty

a 19:23 The text is literally "upon a table," a metaphor for where banking transactions took place.
b 19:29 The Greek text includes two small villages, Bethphage and Bethany. The meaning of the names combined means "the stables of Annia." This is how it is translated in the Aramaic.
c 19:29 This was a large hill less than two miles from Jerusalem and about one hundred feet higher.
d 19:30 Literally, "across the valley."
e 19:31 Implied, for the Lord Jesus created all things and therefore owns it all.
f 19:35–36 See Zechariah 9:9.
g 19:35–36 This was done to signify Jesus was King. See 2 Kings 9:13. This is an obvious reference to the coming of the promised Messiah.

wonders of power they had witnessed. [38]They shouted over and over, "Highest praises to God for the one who comes as King in the name of the Lord! Heaven's peace and glory from the highest realm now comes to us!"[a]

[39]Some Jewish religious leaders who stood off from the procession said to Jesus, "Teacher, you must order your followers at once to stop saying these things!"

[40]Jesus responded, **"Listen to me. If my followers were silenced, the very stones would break forth with praises!"**

Jesus Weeps over Jerusalem

[41]When Jesus caught sight of the city, he burst into tears and sobbed over Jerusalem, [42]saying, **"If only you could recognize that this day peace is within your reach! But you cannot see it. [43]For the day is soon coming when your enemies will surround you, pressing you in on every side, and laying siege to you.**[b] **[44]They will crush you to pieces, and your children too! And when they leave, your city will be totally destroyed. Since you would not recognize God's day of visitation, your day of devastation is coming!"**

Jesus Cleanses the Temple Courts

[45]Jesus entered the temple area and forcibly threw out all the merchants from their stalls. [46]He rebuked them, saying, **"The Scriptures declare, 'My Father's house is to be filled with prayer—a house of prayer,**[c] **not a cave of bandits!'"**

[47]From then on Jesus continued teaching in the temple area, but all the while, the high priests, the experts of the law, and the prominent men of the city kept trying to find a way to accuse Jesus, for they wanted him dead. [48]They could find no reason to accuse him, for he was a hero to the people and the crowds were awestruck by every word he spoke.

---

a 19:38 Implied in the text. This is a quotation of Psalm 118:26.
b 19:43 Translated from the Aramaic. The Greek text states, "They will throw up ramparts." See Isaiah 29:3, Jeremiah 6:6, and Ezekiel 4:2. Jesus was the only one weeping while everyone else was rejoicing.
c 19:46 See Isaiah 56:7 and Jeremiah 7:11.

Twenty

A Day of Controversy

¹One day Jesus was teaching in the temple courts and sharing with the people the wonderful news of salvation.ᵃ The high priest and the experts of the law were there with the prominent men of the city. They confronted Jesus and asked him, ²"We want to know right now by what authority you're doing this. Who gave you the authority to teach these things here in the temple?"

³Jesus responded, **"First, let me ask you a question and you tell me right now. ⁴Did John baptize because of a mandate from heaven or merely from men?"**

⁵His interrogators pulled aside to discuss this among themselves. "What should we say? If we say that John's mandate was from heaven, he will ask us, 'Then why didn't you believe him and get baptized?'ᵇ ⁶But if we say, 'John's mandate was merely from men,' then all the people around him will stone us, for they believe John was a prophet of God." ⁷So they answered Jesus, "We cannot tell where John's authority came from."

⁸Jesus said, **"Then neither will I tell you where my authority comes from to do what I do."**

The Story of the Vine Growers

⁹Jesus taught the people this story:

"Once there was a man who planted a vineyard, then leased it out to tenants and left to go abroad and was away for a long time. ¹⁰When the harvest season arrived, the owner sent one of his servants to the tenants to collect the landowner's share of the harvest. But the tenants sent him away, beaten and empty-handed. ¹¹So the owner dispatched another one of his servants to collect his portion. But the tenants treated him the same way. They cursed him,

---

a 20:1 Translated from the Aramaic text.
b 20:5 Implied in the context.

beat him, and sent him away empty-handed. [12]Then the owner sent a third servant, but they brutalized him also with the same treatment. [13]Finally the owner of the vineyard said to his son, 'Perhaps if I send you, my own cherished son, they will be ashamed of what they've done.'[a]

[14]"But when the tenants saw the son coming, they schemed among themselves. 'This is the heir of the vineyard! If we kill him, the inheritance will be ours.' [15]So they threw the son off the property and killed him.

"I ask you, what do you think the owner of the vineyard will do to those who murdered his son? [16]He will come and destroy them and give his vineyard to another."

When the people heard this story, they all agreed, "This should never happen!"

[17]Jesus looked straight at the people and said, **"What do you think this verse means: 'The worthless, rejected stone has become the cornerstone, the most important stone of all'?[b] [18]Everyone who falls in humility[c] upon that stone will be broken. But if that stone falls on you, it will grind you to pieces!"**

[19]When the high priests and experts of the law realized that this story was about them, they wanted to have Jesus arrested that very moment, but they were afraid of all the people.

Paying Taxes

[20]So they sent spies who pretended to be honest seekers, but who watched closely for an opportunity to entangle Jesus by his words. Their plan was to catch him saying something against the government, and then they could hand him over to the jurisdiction of the Roman authorities to be killed.[d]

[21]At the right time they asked him this question: "Teacher, we know that all you say is straightforward and what you teach us is right, giving us the true ways of God. You're one who doesn't show favoritism to anyone's status. So we ask you—[22]is it proper or not to pay taxes to a corrupt government?"[e]

---

a 20:13 Translated from the Aramaic text.
b 20:17 This is a quotation from Psalm 118:22. See also Isaiah 8:14–15 and Isaiah 28:16.
c 20:18 Implied in the context.
d 20:20 Implied from the text regarding their plan and desire that Jesus be killed.
e 20:22 Implied in the context. The Greek text states, "to the emperor."

²³Jesus saw right through their cunning ploy and said, **"Why are you testing me?**ᵃ ²⁴**Show me one of the Roman coins. Whose head is on the coin? Whose title is stamped on it?"**

They answered, "Why, it's Caesar's."

²⁵Jesus said, **"Precisely. The coin**ᵇ **bears the image of the Emperor Caesar, and you should give back to Caesar all that belongs to him. But you bear the image of God. So give back to God all that belongs to him."**

²⁶The imposters were left speechless and amazed in the presence of all the people, unable to trap Jesus with his words.

A Question about the Resurrection

²⁷Some of the Sadducees, a religious group that denies there is a resurrection of the dead, came to ask Jesus this question: ²⁸"Teacher, the law of Mosesᶜ teaches that if a man dies before he has children, his brother should marry the widow and raise up children for his brother's family line. ²⁹But suppose there was a family with seven brothers, and the oldest married and died without children. ³⁰⁻³¹Then his brother married the widow, but he too died with no children. And so it happened, one brother after another brother, until each of the seven had married the widow and died childless. ³²Then finally, the widow died too. So here's our dilemma: ³³Whose wife will the woman be when she's resurrected from the dead? Which of the brothers will be her husband, for all seven were once married to her?"

³⁴Jesus replied, **"Marriage is for the sons of this world only. ³⁵⁻³⁶But those who are worthy of the resurrection from the dead into glory become immortal, like the angels, who never die nor marry. When the dead come to life again, they will be sons of God's life—the sons of the resurrection. ³⁷In fact, it was Moses who taught the resurrection of the dead**ᵈ **when he wrote of the Lord God who was at the burning bush and described him as 'the God of Abraham, Isaac, and Jacob.' ³⁸Don't you agree that God is not the God of the**

---

a 20:23 Although not found in most Greek manuscripts, it is included in the Aramaic text.
b 20:25 Actual coins from that era have been found with the emperor's image and a superscription saying, "Tiberius Caesar Augustus, son of the divine Augustus."
c 20:27 See Deuteronomy 25:5–10.
d 20:37 See Exodus 3:6.

dead, but the God of the living? For in his eyes, Abraham, Jacob, and Isaac are alive forevermore. He must be the God who raises the dead."

[39]The experts of the law[a] chimed in, "Yes, Teacher, you speak the truth beautifully."

[40]From then on, the religious Sadducees never dared to ask Jesus a question again.

The Messiah, Both God and Man

[41]Jesus then posed this question to the people: **"How can the experts of the law[b] say that Christ the Messiah is David's son? [42]Haven't you read in the Psalms where David himself wrote:**

> **The Lord Jehovah said to my Lord,[c]**
> **"Sit near me in the place of authority**
> **[43]Until I subdue all your enemies**
> **Under Your feet!"[d]**

[44]Jesus explained, **"If David calls this one 'my Lord,' how can he merely be his son?"[e]**

Jesus Denounces the Experts of the Law

[45]Within earshot of all the people, Jesus warned his disciples, [46]**"Don't follow the example of these pretentious experts of the law! They love to parade around in their clergy robes so that they are honored wherever they go, sitting right up front in every meeting and pushing for the head table at every banquet. [47]And for appearance' sake they will pray long religious prayers at the homes of widows for an offering,[f] cheating them out of their very livelihood. Beware of them all, for they will one day be stripped of honor, and the judgment they receive will be severe."**

---

a 20:39 Historically, these "experts of the law" (Pharisees) were opposed to, and argued with, the Sadducees over their unbelief of a supernatural resurrection.

b 20:41 Or "scribes," as translated from the Aramaic.

c 20:42 A Hebrew translation of this passage would read, "Yahweh said to my Adonai." Paraphrased it would read, "The Lord (God) said to my protecting Lord (Messiah)."

d 20:43 See Psalm 110:1. Translated from the Aramaic and one Greek manuscript. Most Greek texts have "until all your enemies become a footstool under your feet."

e 20:44 Jesus is challenging them to consider that the Christ will be both God and man (David's son and David's Lord).

f 20:47 Translated from the Aramaic. The implication is that the religious leaders would go and pray at the homes of widows, then intimidate them and ask for offerings.

Twenty-one

The Widow's Offering

[1]Jesus was in the temple,[a] observing all the wealthy wanting to be noticed as they came with their offerings. [2]He noticed a very poor widow dropping two small copper coins in the offering box. [3]**"Listen to me,"** he said. **"This poor widow has given a larger offering than any of the wealthy. [4]For the rich only gave out of their surplus, but she sacrificed out of her poverty and gave to God all that she had to live on."**

The Signs of the End of the Age

[5]Some of the disciples remarked about the beauty of the temple. They pointed out all the lovely adornments and how it was built with excellence from the gifts given to God.

Jesus said, [6]**"The day will come that everything you admire here will be utterly destroyed. It will all become a heap of rubble!"**

[7]"Master, tell us," they asked, "when exactly will this happen? Can you tell us what warning sign to look for when it is about to take place?"

[8]Jesus responded, **"Deception will run rampant with many who will appear on the scene, saying I have sent them, or saying about themselves, 'I am the Messiah!'[b] And the doomsday deceivers will say, 'The end of the age is now here!' But listen to me. Don't be fooled by these imposters.**

[9]**"There will also be many wars and revolutions on every side, with rumors of more wars to come. Don't panic or give in to your fears, for these things are bound to happen. This is still not the end yet."**

---

a 21:1 This would have been in the courtyard of the temple, where men and women came to deposit their contributions to the temple treasury. Historians say there were thirteen trumpet-mouthed boxes used in the courtyard for offerings.
b 21:8 Translated from the Aramaic, it literally states, "I Am! The Messiah!"

[10]Jesus continued, "There will be upheavals of every kind.[a] Nations will go to war against each other and kingdom against kingdom—[11]and there will be terrible earthquakes, seismic events of epic proportion, resulting in famines in one place after another. There will be horrible plagues and epidemics, cataclysmic storms[b] on the earth, and astonishing signs and cosmic disturbances in the heavens. But before all of this happens, you will be hunted down and arrested, persecuted by both civil and religious authorities, and thrown into prison. [12-13]And because you follow me, you will be on trial before kings and governmental leaders as an opportunity to testify to them in my name. [14-15]Yet determine in your hearts not to prepare for your own defense. Simply speak with the words of wisdom that I will give you that moment, and none of your persecutors will be able to withstand the grace and wisdom that comes from your mouths.

[16]"You can expect betrayal even by your parents, your brothers, your relatives and friends—and yes, some of you will die as martyrs. [17]You will be hated by all because of my life in you.[c] [18]But don't worry. My grace will never desert you or depart from your life.[d] [19]And by standing firm with patient endurance you will find your souls' deliverance."

The Destruction of Jerusalem

[20]"When you see Jerusalem being surrounded by armies, you will know for sure that its devastation is imminent.[e] [21]At that time all who are living in Judea must flee to the mountains. Those who live inside the city gates, go out and flee, and those who live outside the city must not enter it seeking refuge. [22]For these are the days of God's vengeance to fulfill what has been written[f] against Jerusalem. [23]It will be horrible for pregnant women and for those nursing little ones in that day, for there will be great persecution and wrath against this nation. [24]Many will be cut down by the sword or scattered as prisoners in

a 21:10 A summary statement implied by the context.
b 21:11 As translated from the Aramaic. Only one Greek manuscript adds, "great storms."
c 21:17 Implied in the text. The Greek says, "because of my name."
d 21:18 Although quite different from the Greek manuscripts, this is the literal translation of the Aramaic figure of speech "Grace will not leave your head."
e 21:20 This was fulfilled in AD 70 when Jerusalem was left desolate by Roman armies. Some historians estimate that more than one million Jews were slaughtered at this time and up to one hundred thousand were taken captive to other nations.
f 21:22 See 1 Kings 9:6–9, Daniel 9:26, Hosea 9:7, and Micah 3:12.

many countries. And Jerusalem shall be trampled down by nations until the days of world empires come to an end."

The Coming of the Son of Man

²⁵"Expect to witness amazing and perplexing signs throughout the universe with the sun, the moon, and the stars.[a] The raging of the sea will bring desperation and turmoil to many nations. ²⁶Earthquakes[b] will bring panic and disaster. What men see coming to the earth will cause the fear of doom to grip their hearts, for they will even see the powers of the heavenly realm shaken!

²⁷⁻²⁸"And at last, when you see how the Son of Man[c] comes—surrounded with a cloud, with great power and miracles, in the radiance of his splendor, and with great glory and praises[d]—it will make you jump for joy! For the day of your full transformation[e] has arrived."

The Lesson of the Fig Tree

²⁹⁻³⁰Jesus gave his disciples this parable:

"Haven't you observed the fig tree, or any tree, that when it buds and blooms you realize that the season is changing and summer is near? ³¹In the same way, when you see these prophetic signs occurring, you realize the earth is yielding to the fullness of the kingdom realm of God. ³²I assure you, the end of this age will not come until all I have spoken comes to pass. ³³Earth and sky will wear out and fade away before one word I speak loses its power or fails to accomplish its purpose."

Guard Your Hearts

³⁴"Be careful that you never allow your hearts to grow cold. Remain passionate[f] and free from anxiety and the worries of this life. Then you will not be caught off guard by what happens. Don't let me come and find you drunk or careless

---

a 21:25 See Isaiah 13:10, Ezekiel 32:7–8, and Joel 2:10.

b 21:26 The word "earthquakes" is found only in Aramaic manuscripts.

c 21:27–28 The title "Son of Man" was used frequently when Jesus spoke of himself. Note that he is not the "son of a man," but the Son of God who became a man.

d 21:27–28 "Praises" is only found in Aramaic manuscripts.

e 21:27–28 The Greek word is "redemption" or "liberation." It speaks of the total transformation of our body, soul, and spirit when we see him as he is.

f 21:34 The Aramaic text says, "Beware that your hearts never grow cold."

in living like everyone else. [35]For that day will come as a shocking surprise to all, like a downpour[a] that drenches everyone, catching many unaware and unprepared. [36]Keep a constant watch over your soul, and pray for the courage and grace to prevail over these things that are destined to occur and that you will stand before the presence of the Son of Man with a clear conscience."[b]

[37]Each day, Jesus taught in the temple, and he spent his nights on the Mount of Olives. [38]And all the people came early to the temple courts to listen to the Manifestation of the word[c] he taught.

---

a 21:35 Greek manuscripts have "like a snare." The Aramaic text states, "like a downpour."
b 21:36 Implied in the context.
c 21:38 The Greek text is *logos*. The Aramaic is literally "Manifestation."

Twenty-two

Satan Entered into Judas

[1-2]As the celebration of the Passover Lamb[a] was approaching, the Jewish religious leaders and scholars of the law continually schemed to find a way to murder Jesus without starting a riot—for they feared the crowds.

[3]At that time Satan himself entered into Judas the locksmith,[b] who was one of the twelve apostles. [4]He secretly went to the religious hierarchy and the captains of the temple guards to discuss with them how he could betray Jesus and turn him over to their hands. [5]The religious hierarchy was elated over Judas's treachery, and they agreed to give him a sum of money in exchange for Jesus' betrayal. [6]Judas vowed that he would find them a suitable opportunity to betray Jesus when he was away from the crowds.

Jesus Prophesies the Location of the Last Supper

[7-8]On the day the sacrifice of the Passover lambs was to take place, Jesus sent for Peter and John and instructed them, **"Go and prepare the Passover supper so we can eat it together."**

[9]They asked him, "Where do we make the preparations to eat the meal?"

[10]Jesus gave them this sign: **"When you enter the city, you will find a man[c] carrying a jug of water. Follow him home [11]and say to the owner of the house, 'The Teacher told us to ask you, "Where is the room I may use to have the Passover meal with my disciples?"' [12]He will then take you to a large, fully furnished upstairs room. Make the preparations for us there."**

[13]They went and found everything to be exactly like Jesus had prophesied, and they prepared the Passover meal.

---

a 22:1-2 The Passover celebration was known as the "Feast of Bread without Yeast." The Jewish people commemorate their exodus from Egypt to this day with a weeklong Passover feast. See Exodus 12:1-20 and Deuteronomy 16:1-8.
b 22:3 See footnote on Luke 6:14-16.
c 22:10 Carrying water was a task given to women; it would have been easy to spot a man carrying the water jug.

Jesus and His Disciples Eat the Last Supper

[14]When Jesus arrived at the upper room, he took his place at the table along with all the apostles. [15]Then he told them, **"I have longed with passion and desire to eat this Passover lamb with you before I endure my sufferings. [16]I promise you that the next time we eat this, we will be together in the banquet of the kingdom realm of God."**

[17]Then he raised a cup and gave thanks to God and said to them, **"Take this and pass it on to one another and drink. [18]I promise you that the next time we drink this wine, we will be together in the feasting of the kingdom realm of God."**[a]

[19]Then he lifted up a loaf, and after praying a prayer of thanksgiving to God, he gave each of his apostles a piece of bread, saying, **"This loaf is my body,**[b] **which is now being offered to you. Always eat it to remember me."**

[20]After supper was over, he lifted the cup again and said, **"This cup is my blood of the new covenant**[c] **I make with you, and it will be poured out soon for all of you. [21]But I want you to know that the hands of the one who delivers me to be the sacrifice are with mine on the table this very moment. [22]The Son of Man must now go where he will be sacrificed. But there will be great and unending doom for the man who betrays me. "**

[23]The apostles questioned among themselves which one of them was about to do this.

Apostles Argue over Which of Them Will Be the Greatest

[24]The disciples bickered over which one of them would be considered the greatest[d] in the kingdom. [25]Jesus interrupted their argument, saying, **"The kings and men of authority in this world rule oppressively over their subjects, claiming that they do it for the good of the people. They are obsessed with how others see them.**[e] **[26]But this is not your calling. You will lead by a different model. The greatest one among you will live as one called to serve others**

---

a 22:18 Verses 17–18 are not found in most Aramaic texts. Most Greek texts and a fifth-century Aramaic manuscript known as "the Palestinian Syriac" include them in the narrative.

b 22:19 From here to the end of verse 20 is considered the most highly debated passage in Luke's gospel because of a few reliable Greek manuscripts that do not have it. Yet there is ample internal evidence to argue for its inclusion.

c 22:20 The Aramaic word used here is literally "new testament."

d 22:24 This took place at the Lord's Passover table. Their discussion of who was the worst among them led them to argue over who was the greatest. Jesus was only hours away from the horrible death of crucifixion while his apostles argued.

e 22:25 The Aramaic is actually "They want to be called 'servants of goodness.'"

without honor.[a] The greatest honor and authority is reserved for the one who has a servant heart. [27]The leaders who are served are the most important in your eyes, but in the kingdom, it is the servants who lead. Am I not here with you as one who serves you?

[28]"Because you have stood with me through all my trials and ordeals, [29]I give you your destiny:[b] I am promising you the kingdom realm that the Father has promised me. [30]We will celebrate in this kingdom and you will feast with me at my table. And each of you will be given a throne, twelve thrones in all, and you will be made rulers on thrones to judge the tribes of Israel."

Jesus Prophesies of Peter's Denial

[31]"Peter, my dear friend, listen to what I'm about to tell you. Satan has demanded to come and sift you like wheat and test your faith. [32]But I have prayed for you, Peter, that you would stay faithful to me no matter what comes. Remember this: after you have turned back to me and have been restored, make it your life mission to strengthen the faith of your brothers."

[33]"But Lord," Peter replied, "I am ready to stand with you to the very end, even if it means prison or death!"

[34]Jesus looked at him and prophesied, **"Before the rooster crows in the morning, you will deny[c] three times that you even know me."**

[35]Then he said to all of them, **"When I sent you out empty-handed, did you lack anything?"**

"Not a thing," they answered. "God provided all we needed."

Jesus said, **"But now I say to you: Take what you need. [36]If you have money, take it[d]—and a knapsack and a sword.[e] Danger is imminent.[f] [37]For the prophetic Scripture about me 'He will be accused of being a criminal'[g] will now come to pass. All that was prophesied of me will be fulfilled."**

---

a 22:26 The Greek text uses the word here for "youngest," and the Aramaic is "small one." In Hebrew culture in the days of Jesus, the firstborn of the household had honor, while the youngest accepted the role of menial service to all the others of the house.

b 22:29 Implied in the context.

c 22:34 The Aramaic text says, "blasphemed."

d 22:36 Now the disciples were to take needed items with them, including money, for they were to be a source of blessing to others with their generosity.

e 22:36 It is possible that Jesus was using symbolic speech, for we take with us the sword of the Spirit, which is the Word of God. See Ephesians 6:17.

f 22:36 The text here is a Hebraic figure of speech: "If you don't have a sword, you'd better sell something and buy one," which implies that danger is imminent.

g 22:37 See Isaiah 53:8-9

³⁸The disciples told him, "Lord, we already have two swords!"

"You still don't understand,"ᵃ Jesus responded.

The Garden of Gethsemane

³⁹Jesus left the upper room with his disciplesᵇ and, as was his habit, went to the Mount of Olives, his place of secret prayer.ᶜ ⁴⁰There he told the apostles, **"Keep praying for strength to be spared from the severe test of your faith that is about to come."**

⁴¹Then he withdrew from them a short distanceᵈ to be alone. Kneeling down, he prayed, ⁴²**"Father, if you are willing, take this cup of agony away from me.ᵉ But no matter what, your will must be mine."**

⁴³Jesus calledᶠ for an angel of glory to strengthen him, and the angel appeared. ⁴⁴He prayed even more passionately, like one being sacrificed,ᵍ until he was in such intense agony of spirit that his sweat became drops of blood, dripping onto the ground.ʰ

⁴⁵When Jesus finished praying, he got up and went to his disciples and found them all asleep, for they were exhausted and overwhelmed with sorrow. ⁴⁶**"Why are you sleeping?"** he asked them. **"You need to be alert and pray for the strength to endure the great temptation."**

Judas Betrays Jesus

⁴⁷No sooner had he finished speaking when suddenly a mob approached, and right in front of the mob was his disciple Judas. He walked up close to Jesus and greeted him with a kiss. For he had agreed to give the religious leaders a sign, saying, "The one I kiss is the one to seize."ⁱ

---

a 22:38 Or "That will be enough." Jesus is saying, "Never mind. You still don't get it." He corrected their thinking about taking swords and using violent means in verses 50–51.

b 22:39 That is, with the exception of Judas. See verse 47.

c 22:39 Implied in the context.

d 22:41 Literally, "a stone's throw away."

e 22:42 Jesus asked the Father to be spared from death in the garden so that he could go all the way to the cross. His prayer was answered. The blood that dripped in the garden would not redeem. Jesus had to carry the cross and fulfill all that was written of him. See Hebrews 5:7.

f 22:43 Translated from the Aramaic text. The Greek manuscripts state it passively: "An angel from heaven appeared."

g 22:44 The Aramaic text is literally "He prayed sacrificially."

h 22:44 Although verses 43–44 are found in the Aramaic manuscript, many Greek texts omit them. Most of the early church fathers included them in their translations and commentaries. Though very rare, the phenomenon of hematidrosis, sweating blood, is well documented. Under great emotional stress, tiny capillaries in the sweat glands can break, thus mixing blood with sweat. This process could have marked weakness and possibly shock.

i 22:47 Nearly every Greek manuscript leaves out this information. The Aramaic text includes it.

⁴⁸Jesus looked at him with sorrow and said, **"A kiss, Judas? Are you really going to betray the Son of Man with a kiss?"**

⁴⁹When the other disciples understood what was happening, they asked, "Lord, shall we fight them with our swords?"

⁵⁰Just then, one of the disciples[a] swung his sword at the high priest's servant and slashed off his right ear.

⁵¹Jesus stopped the incident from escalating any further by shouting, **"Stop! That's enough of this!"** Then he touched the right side of the injured man's head and the ear grew back[b]—he was healed!

⁵²Jesus turned to those who had come to seize him—the ruling priests, the officers of the temple police, and the religious leaders—and said, **"Am I a criminal that you come to capture me with clubs and swords? Wasn't I with you day after day, teaching in the temple courts? ⁵³You could have seized me at any time. But in the darkness of night you have now found your time, for it belongs to you and to the prince of darkness."**[c]

Peter Denies He Knew Jesus

⁵⁴The religious leaders seized Jesus and led him away, but Peter followed from a safe distance. They brought him to the home of the high priest, where people were already gathered out in the courtyard. ⁵⁵Someone had built a fire, so Peter inched closer and sat down among them to stay warm.

⁵⁶A girl noticed Peter sitting in the firelight. Staring at him, she pointed him out and said, "This man is one of Jesus' disciples!"

⁵⁷Peter flatly denied it, saying, "What are you talking about, girl? I don't know him!"

⁵⁸A little while later, someone else spotted Peter and said, "I recognize you. You're one of his, I know it!"

Peter again said, "I'm not one of his disciples."

⁵⁹About an hour later, someone else identified Peter and insisted he was a

---

a 22:50 The unnamed disciple was Peter; the servant's name was Malchus. See John 18:10.

b 22:51 Implied in the context of this miracle. Jesus, the Creator, re-created his ear.

c 22:53 The "prince of darkness" is Satan. This phrase is found only in the Aramaic manuscripts. The Greek text states, "the powers of darkness."

disciple of Jesus, saying, "Look at him! He's from Galilee,[a] just like Jesus. I know he's one of them."

[60]But Peter was adamant. "Listen, I don't know what you're talking about. Don't you understand? I don't even know him." While the words were still in his mouth, the rooster crowed.

[61]At that moment, the Lord, who was being led through the courtyard by his captors,[b] turned around and gazed at Peter. All at once Peter remembered the words Jesus had prophesied over him, **"Before the rooster crows in the morning, you will deny three times that you even know me."** [62]Peter burst into tears,[c] ran off from the crowd, and wept bitterly.

Jesus Is Mocked and Severely Beaten

[63]Those who were guarding Jesus mocked and beat him severely. [64]They also made fun of him, blindfolding him and slapping his face and saying, "Prove that you are a prophet and tell us which one of us hit you!" [65]They blasphemed and heaped insult after insult upon him.

Jesus Before the Jewish Council

[66]At daybreak the high priests, the experts of the law, and the top religious leaders convened and had Jesus brought before their council. [67]They asked him point blank, "Tell us, are you the Christ, the Messiah, or not?"

Jesus responded, **"If I tell you the truth, you won't believe me. [68]And if I question you, you will not answer me or release me.[d] [69]But from today on, the Son of Man will be enthroned in the place of honor, power, and authority with Almighty God."**

[70]They all shouted, "Then you do claim to be the Son of God?"

He said to them, **"You are the ones who say I AM!"**

[71]They all shouted, "We've heard it from his very lips! What further proof do we need?"

---

a 22:59 Peter's accent gave him away as being a Galilean. See also Mark 14:70.
b 22:61 Implied by the context, necessary for proper understanding of the narrative.
c 22:62 It is not just our sin that causes us to weep. It is seeing the Savior whom we have sinned against that brings our tears.
d 22:68 The phrase "or release me" is found only in the Aramaic text.

Twenty-three

Jesus before Pilate

¹The entire council stood at once and took Jesus to Pilate, the Roman governor. ²They accused him with false testimony before the governor, saying, "This man tells us we're not to pay our taxes to Caesar. And he proclaims himself to be Christ the King and Messiah. He's a deceiver of our nation."

³Pilate asked Jesus, "Is this true? Are you their king and Messiah?"

Jesus answered, **"It is true."**

⁴Pilate turned to the high priests and to the gathered crowd and said, "This man has committed no crime. I find nothing wrong with him."

⁵But they yelled and demanded that Pilate do something, saying, "He has stirred up our nation, misleading people from the moment he began teaching in Galilee until he has come here to Jerusalem!"

Jesus before Herod

⁶⁻⁷When Pilate heard the word Galilee, he asked if Jesus was a Galilean, as he knew that Antipas, son of Herod, was the ruler over Galilee. When they told him yes, Pilate saw a way out of his problem. Herod happened to be in Jerusalem at that time, so Pilate sent Jesus to Antipas.

⁸When Antipas saw Jesus, he was elated, for he had heard a great deal about his ministry and wanted Jesus to perform a miracle in front of him. ⁹Antipas questioned him at length, but Jesus wouldn't even answer him.

¹⁰⁻¹¹All the while the high priests and religious leaders stood by, hatefully accusing Jesus of wrongdoing, so that Antipas and his soldiers treated him with scorn and mocking. Antipas put an elegant purple robe on Jesus and sent him back to Pilate. ¹²That day, Antipas, son of Herod, and Pilate healed the rift between themselves due to old hostilities and they became good friends.

Jesus Sentenced to Death

¹³⁻¹⁴Pilate gathered the people together with the high priests and all the religious leaders of the nation[a] and told them, "You have presented this man to me and charged him with stirring a rebellion among the people. But I say to you that I have examined him here in your presence and have put him on trial. My verdict is that none of the charges you have brought against him are true. I find no fault in him.[b] ¹⁵⁻¹⁶And I sent him to Antipas, son of Herod, who also, after questioning him, has found him not guilty. Since he has done nothing deserving of death, I have decided to punish him with a severe flogging and release him to go."¹⁷ For it was Pilate's custom to honor the Jewish holiday by releasing a prisoner.[c]

¹⁸When the crowd heard this, they went wild. Erupting with anger, they cried out, "No! Take this one away and release Barabbas!"[d] ¹⁹For Barabbas had been thrown in prison for robbery[e] and murder.

²⁰Pilate, wanting to release Jesus, tried to convince them it was best to let Jesus go. ²¹But they cried out over and over, "Crucify him! Crucify him!"[f]

²²A third time, Pilate asked the crowd, "What evil crime has this man committed that I should have him crucified? I haven't found one thing that warrants a death sentence! I will have him flogged severely and then release him and let him go."

²³But the people and the high priests, shouting like a mob, screamed out at the top of their lungs, "No! Crucify him! Crucify him!"

Finally their shouts and screams succeeded. ²⁴Pilate caved in to the crowd and ordered that the will of the people be done. ²⁵Then he released the guilty murderer Barabbas, as they had insisted, and handed Jesus over to be crucified.

---

a 23:13-14 This group of religious leaders was known as the Jewish council of the Sanhedrin.
b 23:13-14 The phrase "I find no fault in him" is found in the Aramaic text.
c 23:17 Although many Greek manuscripts do not have this verse in the text, it is found in the Aramaic text.
d 23:18 There were two men, two sons. Barabbas means "son of a father." Jesus was the Son of our heavenly Father. One was a son of Adam; the other was the Son of God.
e 23:19 Most Greek manuscripts have "for insurrection." The Aramaic states, "for robbery."
f 23:20 Crucifixion was the cruelest form of execution, reserved for only the worst of criminals.

The Crucifixion of Jesus

²⁶As the guards led Jesus to be crucified, there was an African man[a] in the crowd named Simon, from Libya.[b] He had just arrived from a rural village to keep the Feast of the Passover.[c] The guards laid Jesus' cross on Simon's shoulders[d] and forced him to walk behind Jesus and carry his cross.²⁷

Massive crowds gathered to follow Jesus, including a number of women, who were wailing with sorrow over him. ²⁸Jesus turned to them and said, **"Daughters of Jerusalem, do not weep for me. You should be weeping for yourselves and your children. ²⁹For the day is coming when it will not be the women with children who are blessed but the childless. Then you will say, 'The barren women are the most fortunate! Those who have never given birth and never nursed a child—they are more fortunate than we are, for they will never see their children put to death!'[e] ³⁰And the people will cry out for the mountains and hills to fall on top of them to hide them from all that is to come.[f] ³¹For if this is what they do to the Living Branch,[g] what will they do with the dead ones?"**

³²Two criminals were led away with Jesus, and all three were to be executed together. ³³When they came to the place that is known as The Skull, the guards crucified Jesus, nailing him on the center cross between the two criminals.³⁴ While they were nailing Jesus to the cross, he prayed over and over, **"Father, forgive them,[h] for they don't know what they're doing."**

The soldiers, after they crucified him, gambled over his clothing.[i]

³⁵A great crowd gathered to watch what was happening. The religious leaders sneered at Jesus and mocked him, saying, "Look at this man! What kind of

a 23:26 Implied in the text.
b 23:26 The text is literally "from Cyrene," which is present-day Tripoli, Libya.
c 23:26 Implied in the text.
d 23:26 By this time Jesus had been severely beaten and flogged, had gone days without sleep, and was carrying a heavy load. Presumably this is why Simon was compelled to carry the cross for him.
e 23:29 Implied in the context to convey the meaning of the text.
f 23:30 See Hosea 10:8.
g 23:31 The Aramaic is literally "a green tree." This could be a figure of speech for "an innocent man." The "dead" could be a figure of speech for "an evil man."
h 23:34 The Greek text implies a repetitive action. He did not pray, "Forgive me," but "Forgive them." As the centurion crushed him to the ground and tied his arms to the crossbeam, Jesus prayed, "Father, forgive them." When the spikes tore through each quivering palm, he prayed again, "Father, forgive them." And when the soldiers parted his garments and gambled for the seamless robe, again Jesus prayed, "Father, forgive them." Only heaven knows how many times that prayer was spoken.
i 23:34 Many Greek manuscripts have omitted verse 34.

'chosen Messiah' is this? He pretended to save others, but he can't even save himself!"

³⁶The soldiers joined in the mockery by offering Jesus a drink of vinegar.ª

³⁷⁻³⁸Over Jesus' head on the cross was written an inscription in Greek, Latin, and Aramaic:ᵇ "This man is the king of all the Jews." And all the soldiers laughed and scoffed at him, saying, "Hey! If you're the king of Jews, why don't you save yourself?"

³⁹One of the criminals hanging on the cross next to Jesus kept ridiculing him, saying, "What kind of Messiah are you? Save yourself and save us from this death!"

⁴⁰The criminal hanging on the other cross rebuked the man, saying, "Don't you fear God? You're about to die! ⁴¹We deserve to be condemned, for we're just being repaid for what we've done. But this man—he's done nothing wrong!"

⁴²Then he said, "I beg of you, my Lord Jesus, show me grace and take me with you into your everlastingᶜ kingdom!"

⁴³Jesus responded, **"I promise you—this very day you will enter Paradise with me."**

The Death of the Savior

⁴⁴It was now only midday, yet the whole world became dark for three hours as the light of the sun faded away.ᵈ ⁴⁵And suddenly in the temple the thick veil hanging in the Holy Place was ripped in two! ⁴⁶Then Jesus cried out with a loud voice, "Father, I surrender my Spirit into your hands."ᵉ And he took his last breath and died.

⁴⁷When the Roman captain overseeing the crucifixion witnessed all that took place, he was awestruck and glorified God. Acknowledging what they had done, he said, "I have no doubt; we just killed the Righteous One."ᶠ

⁴⁸The crowds that had gathered to observe this spectacle went back to

---

a 23:36 See Psalm 69:21. It was likely Jesus had had nothing to drink since the night before.
b 23:37-38 Many Greek texts omit the mention of these three languages.
c 23:42 Implied in the context.
d 23:44 This indicates the "day of the Lord" has now come. See Joel 2:10 and Amos 8:9.
e 23:45 See Psalms 22:1 and 31:5.
f 23:47 As translated from the Aramaic.

their homes, overcome with deep sorrow[a] and devastated by what they had witnessed. [49]But standing off at a distance were some who truly knew Jesus, and the women who had followed him all the way from Galilee were keeping vigil.

[50-51]There was also a member of the Jewish council named Joseph, from the city of Aramathea, a good-hearted, honorable man who was eager for the appearing of the kingdom realm of God. He had strongly disagreed with the decision of the council to crucify Jesus.[b] [52]He came before Pilate and asked permission to take the body of Jesus and give him a proper burial, and Pilate granted his request.[c] [53]So he took the body from the cross and wrapped it in a winding sheet of linen and placed it in a new, unused tomb chiseled out of solid rock. [54]It was Preparation Day, and the Sabbath was fast approaching.

[55]The women who had been companions of Jesus from the beginning saw all this take place and watched as the body was laid in the tomb. [56]Afterward they returned home and prepared fragrant spices and ointments and were planning to anoint his body after the Sabbath was completed, according to the commandments of the law.

---

a 23:48 Literally, "beating their breasts," which is a figure of speech for deep sorrow.
b 23:51 One ancient Syriac manuscript adds here, "This man was one who did not take part with the mind of the Devil."
c 23:52 Implied in the text.

Twenty-four

The Resurrection of Jesus

¹Very early that Sunday morning, the women made their way to the tomb, carrying the spices they had prepared. Among them were Mary Magdalene, Joanna, and Mary, Jesus' mother.ᵃ ²Arriving at the tomb they discovered that the huge stone covering the entrance had been rolled aside, ³so they went in to look. But the tomb was empty. The body of Jesus was gone!

⁴They stood there, stunned and perplexed. Suddenly two men in dazzling white robes shining like lightning appeared above them.ᵇ ⁵Terrified, the women fell to the ground on their faces.

The men in white said to them, "Why would you look for the Living One in a tomb?ᶜ He is not here, for he has risen! ⁶Have you forgotten what he said to you while he was still in Galilee: ⁷'The Son of Man is destined to be handed over to sinful men to be nailed to a cross, and on the third day he will rise again'?"

⁸All at once they remembered his words. ⁹Leaving the tomb, they went to break the news to the Eleven and to all the others of what they had seen and heard.ᵈ

¹¹When the disciples heard the testimony of the women, it made no sense, and they were unable to believe what they heard. ¹²But Peter jumped up and ran the entire distance to the tomb to see for himself. Stooping down, he looked inside and discovered it was empty! There was only the linen sheet lying there. Staggered by this, he walked away, wondering what it meant.

---

a 24:1 For the sake of the English narrative, the information found in verse 10 is placed here.
b 24:4 "Above them" is found only in the Aramaic text.
c 24:5 The Aramaic text is literally "The Life."
d 24:10 For the sake of the English narrative, the information of verse 10 is included in verse 1.

Jesus Walks to Emmaus

[13]Later that Sunday, two of Jesus' disciples were walking from Jerusalem to Emmaus,[a] a journey of about seven miles. [14-15]They were in the midst of a discussion about all the events of the last few days when Jesus walked up and accompanied them in their journey. [16]They were unaware that it was Jesus walking alongside them, for God prevented them from recognizing him.

[17-18]Jesus said to them, **"You seem to be in a deep discussion about something. What are you talking about, so sad and gloomy?"**

They stopped, and the one named Cleopas[b] answered, "Haven't you heard? Are you the only one in Jerusalem unaware of the things that have happened over the last few days?"

[19]Jesus asked, **"What things?"**

"The things about Jesus, the Man from Nazareth," they replied. "He was a mighty prophet of God who performed miracles and wonders. His words were powerful and he had great favor with God and the people. [20-21]But three days ago the high priest and the rulers of the people sentenced him to death and had him crucified. We all hoped that he was the one who would redeem and rescue Israel. [22]Early this morning, some of the women informed us of something amazing. [23]They said they went to the tomb and found it empty. They claimed two angels appeared and told them that Jesus is now alive. [24]Some of us went to see for ourselves and found the tomb exactly like the women said. But no one has seen him."

[25]Jesus said to them, **"Why are you so thick-headed? Why do you find it so hard to believe every word the prophets have spoken? [26]Wasn't it necessary for Christ, the Messiah, to experience all these sufferings and then afterward to enter into his glory?"**

[27]Then he carefully unveiled to them the revelation of himself throughout the Scripture. He started from the beginning and explained the writings of Moses and all the prophets, showing how they wrote of him and revealed the truth about himself.

---

a 24:13 Emmaus was a village about seven miles northwest of Jerusalem. The word *Emmaus* is taken from a Hebrew root that means "the burning place."

b 24:17–18 Cleopas means "from a renowned father." Some scholars believe this could be the Clopas mentioned in John 19:25. *Cleopas* is a Hebrew feminine word and thus a woman's name. Some have speculated that Cleopas was Peter's wife.

²⁸As they approached the village, Jesus walked on ahead, telling the men he was going on to a distant place. ²⁹They urged him to remain there and pleaded, "Stay with us. It will be dark soon." So Jesus went with them into the village.

³⁰Joining them at the table for supper, he took bread and blessed it and broke it, then gave it to them. ³¹All at once their eyes were opened and they realized it was Jesus! Then suddenly, in a flash, Jesus vanished from before their eyes!

³²Stunned, the men looked at each other and said, "Why didn't we recognize it was him? Didn't our hearts burn with the flames of holy passion[a] while we walked beside him? He unveiled for us such profound revelation from the Scriptures!"

³³They left at once and hurried back to Jerusalem to tell the other disciples. When they found the Eleven and the other disciples all together, ³⁴they overheard them saying, "It's really true! The Lord has risen from the dead. He even appeared to Peter!" ³⁵Then the two disciples told the others what had happened to them on the road to Emmaus and how Jesus had unveiled himself as he broke bread with them.[b]

Jesus Appears to the Disciples

³⁶⁻³⁷While they were still discussing all of this, Jesus suddenly manifested right in front of their eyes! Startled and terrified, the disciples were convinced they were seeing a ghost. Standing there among them he said, **"Be at peace. I am the living God. Don't be afraid.**[c] ³⁸**Why would you be so frightened? Don't let doubt or fear**[d] **enter your hearts, for I AM!** ³⁹**Come and gaze upon my pierced hands and feet. See for yourselves, it is I, standing here alive. Touch me and know that my wounds are real. See that I have a body of flesh and bone."** ⁴⁰He showed them his pierced hands and feet and let them touch his wounds.[e]

---

a 24:32 As translated from the Greek text. The Aramaic manuscript reads, "Were not our hearts dull as he taught us?" This is also the translation of the Latin text. The Aramaic words for "burning" and "dull" are almost identical.

b 24:35 Luke's gospel begins and ends with a similar story. In the beginning of Jesus' life we have the story of his parents walking off from Jerusalem and leaving him in the temple (Luke 2:41–52), unaware that they had left Jesus behind. Luke ends with the story of Jesus walking alongside two disciples and they weren't aware of who was walking next to them. Both accounts were after the "Feast." In both stories they were leaving Jerusalem. And both the Jewish scholars in the temple (Luke 2) and the two Emmaus road disciples (Luke 24) were astounded at what Jesus taught them.

c 24:37 The words "I am the living God. Don't be afraid" are only found in the Aramaic text and the Latin Vulgate. The Greek text omits this sentence.

d 24:38 The Aramaic reads, "imaginations."

e 24:40 Verse 40 is missing in some manuscripts.

⁴¹The disciples were ecstatic yet dumbfounded, unable to fully comprehend it.

Knowing that they were still wondering if he was real, Jesus said, **"Here, let me show you. Give me something to eat."**

⁴²⁻⁴³They handed him a piece of broiled fish and some honeycomb. And they watched him eat it.

⁴⁴Then he said to them, **"Don't you remember the words that I spoke to you when I was still with you? I told you that everything written about me would be fulfilled, including all the prophecies from the law of Moses through the Psalms and the writings of the prophets—that they would all find their fulfillment in what has happened."**

⁴⁵He supernaturally unlocked their understanding[a] to receive the revelation of the Scriptures, ⁴⁶then said to them, **"Everything that has happened fulfills what was prophesied of me. Christ, the Messiah, was destined to suffer and rise from the dead on the third day. ⁴⁷Now you must go into all the nations and preach salvation's grace[b] and forgiveness of sins so that they will turn to me. Start right here in Jerusalem. ⁴⁸For you are my witnesses and have seen for yourselves all that has transpired. ⁴⁹And I will send the fulfillment of the Father's promise[c] to you. So stay here in the city until the mighty power of heaven falls upon you and wraps around you."**

The Ascension of Jesus

⁵⁰Jesus led his disciples out to Bethany. He lifted his hands over them and blessed them in his love. ⁵¹While he was still speaking out words of love and blessing, he floated off the ground into the sky,[d] ascending into heaven before their very eyes! ⁵²And all they could do was worship him.

Overwhelmed and ecstatic with joy, they made their way back to Jerusalem. ⁵³Every day they went to the temple, praising and worshipping God.[e]

---

a   24:45 Implied in the text.
b   24:47 The Aramaic reads, "grace" or "conversion."
c   24:49 The Aramaic reads, "the kingdom" or "rule." The Father's promise would be the coming of the Holy Spirit to live in them and empower them. See Acts 2:1–12.
d   24:51 Implied in the text.
e   24:53 So ends the glorious gospel of Luke. The one who walked with his friends on the way to Emmaus wants to walk with us. May we never walk in sadness or unbelief, for Jesus has risen from the grave and lives victorious as the living God in resurrection life! May you pause here and rejoice, believing that Jesus is the Christ, the Son of the living God and the only one who will bring us to the Father. Trust in him alone to save you, and you will spend eternity with him.

Acts

Translator's Introduction to Acts

The book of Acts provides us with the startling details of how the church of Jesus Christ began. We see the pillar of fire that led Israel through her wilderness years appearing in the upper room and splitting into 120 personal pillars of fire over the heads of the lovers of God. This inspired account of church history will awaken your soul with transforming power and give you courage to be a witness for Christ wherever he sends you!

Both Luke and Acts were written by a physician named Luke. The material in Luke and Acts covers a period of about sixty years, from the birth of Christ to the birth of the church and the early years of the expansion of the kingdom of God on the earth. You could consider Acts to be "Luke Volume 2," since he wrote them both for the lovers of God.

Although many consider this book to be the "Acts of the Apostles," there are only two apostles who are predominantly mentioned in Acts: Peter and Paul. It would be more accurate to call it the "Acts of the Holy Spirit." God indeed uses men and women to fulfill his purpose—those who are empowered, filled, anointed, and overflowing with the Holy Spirit.

Acts takes up the story where Luke left off. We begin with 120 disciples who had been in a ten-day prayer meeting. It explains the explosive beginning of the outpouring of the Holy Spirit that resulted in tongues, prophecy, miracles, salvations, and the birthing of countless churches. Acts provides us with the story of Paul's three missionary journeys, with many Gentile nations hearing the gospel and believers being added to the church. Acts demonstrates the healing miracles of Peter, Paul, and the apostles. We see miracles in answer to prayers, including signs and wonders, and many deliverances. To remove the supernatural activity of God from the book of Acts would be futile. God will do what only God can do—and he is still working in power today through his yielded lovers.

Luke wrote both of his books to someone named Theophilus. This man has never been found, nor is it likely that he will be, for his name means "lover of God." *You* are meant to be the recipient of Luke and Acts, for he wrote them to you, the lover of God. You are the most excellent and favored one. Luke wrote his books for you!

We learn much about the Spirit of God in Acts. Without him there would be no church, no evangelistic impact, no miracles, and no expression of the power of God. For it is not by human means, human power, or human might, but by the limitless power of the Holy Spirit that the kingdom of God advances on the earth. Christ builds his church through the Holy Spirit.

The book of Acts reveals how God is moving on the earth today. Jump into this book heart first, and you'll experience the same fire that burned in the lives of his messengers two thousand years ago!

—Dr. Brian Simmons

One

---

¹To the lover of God,

I write to you again, my dear friend,[a] to give you further details[b] about the life of our Lord Jesus and all the things that he did and taught.[c]

²Just before he ascended into heaven, he left instructions[d] for the apostles he had chosen by the Holy Spirit.[e] ³After the sufferings of his cross, Jesus appeared alive many times[f] to these same apostles over a forty-day period.[g] Jesus proved to them with many convincing signs that he had been resurrected.[h] During these encounters, he taught them the truths of the kingdom of God ⁴and shared meals with them.[i]

Jesus instructed them, **"Don't leave Jerusalem, but wait here until you receive the gift I told you about, the gift the Father has promised. ⁵For John baptized you in water, but in a few days from now you will be baptized in the Holy Spirit!"[j]**

⁶Every time they were gathered together, they asked Jesus, "Lord, is it the time now for you to free Israel and restore our kingdom?"

---

a   1:1 Or "Theophilus." This is most likely not written to one individual. When the meaning of his name is translated, the sentence reads, "I wrote to you before, O lover of God." Both Luke and Acts were written to every lover of God.

b   1:1 Implied in the text. This gospel was written by Luke, the human author of Acts. The title Lord Jesus is found only in the Aramaic. The Greek is simply "Jesus."

c   1:1 Although Jesus' work of redemption has been completed for us, there is still the unfinished work of preparing and beautifying his eternal partner, the bride of Christ. With gifts of power his church is continuing what Jesus began to do and teach through evangelism and discipleship. See Ephesians 4:11–13, Matthew 28:19-20, and John 21:25.

d   1:2 Or "commands."

e   1:2 As translated from the Aramaic. The Greek implies that the instructions (commands) he gave them were "by the Holy Spirit."

f   1:3 Implied in the text. Jesus appeared to his followers at least eleven times and taught them the mysteries of the kingdom of God. See also Matthew 13:11.

g   1:3 The number forty is significant, for it speaks of transformation and completeness through testing. Jesus was tempted for forty days, the deluge during Noah's day lasted forty days and nights, Moses met with God for forty days on Sinai, Israel wandered for forty years, and Elijah fasted for forty days. Jesus spent forty days appearing to his disciples to teach them that a day of completeness and transformation had arrived. It took them forty days to comprehend that Christ's kingdom was spiritual, not merely political.

h   1:3 The world is still waiting to see "many convincing signs" from our lives signifying that we too have been raised from the dead. Spiritual fruit and spiritual power provide these signs.

i   1:4 As translated from the Aramaic.

j   1:5 The Aramaic implies that they would be the ones who would do the baptizing. "John baptized you in water, but you will baptize (others) in the Holy Spirit."

[7]He answered, **"The Father is the one who sets the fixed dates and the times of their fulfillment. You are not permitted to know the timing of all that he has prepared by his own authority. [8]But I promise you this—the Holy Spirit will come upon you and you will be filled with power.**[a] **And you will be my messengers**[b] **to Jerusalem, throughout Judea, the distant provinces**[c]**—even to the remotest places on earth!"**[d]

[9]Right after he spoke those words, the disciples saw Jesus lifted into the sky and disappear into a cloud![e] [10]As they stared into the sky, watching Jesus ascend, two men in white robes suddenly appeared beside them. [11]They told the startled disciples, "Galileans, why are you staring up into the sky? Jesus has been taken from you into heaven, but he will come back the same way that you saw him ascend."

A New Apostle Is Chosen

[12]The disciples left the Mount of Olives and returned to Jerusalem, about a mile away.[f] [13]Arriving there, they went into a large second-floor room to pray.[g] Those present were Peter, John, James, Andrew, Phillip, Thomas, Bartholomew, Matthew, James (the son of Alpheus), Simon (the zealot), Judas (the son of James), and a number of women, including Mary, Jesus' mother. His brothers[h] were there as well. [14]All of them were united in prayer, gripped with one passion,[i] interceding night and day.

[15]During this time Peter stood up among the 120 believers who were gathered and said, [16]"Fellow believers,[j] the Scripture David prophesied by the Holy

a 1:8 Or "You will seize power," or "You will be seized with power."
b 1:8 Or "witnesses." The Greek word can also be translated "martyrs."
c 1:8 Or "Samaria," a term used for a distant province populated by another people group.
d 1:8 See Matthew 24:14.
e 1:9 Or "A cloud came under him and took him up from their sight." The Aramaic is "A cloud accepted him and covered him from their eyes."
f 1:12 The Aramaic is "seven stadia (furlongs)." A furlong is about one eighth of a mile. The Greek uses a phrase not found in the Septuagint or elsewhere in the Greek New Testament or in any Greek literature: "of a Sabbath having away." It is rendered in most modern translations "a Sabbath's journey."
g 1:13 Implied in the context. The Greek uses the definite article "the upstairs room." This was where they had met before to have the Last Supper with Jesus. In Mark's gospel, after the disciples returned from witnessing the ascension, they preached, for Mark is the gospel of ministry. In Luke, after Jesus' ascension, they praised, and here in Acts they prayed.
h 1:13 Or "siblings." Jesus' four brothers are named in Matthew 13:55 and Mark 6:3 as James, Joses (or Joseph), Simon, and Judas. Even though John 7:5 records that early in Jesus' ministry his own brothers did not believe in him, they obviously later repented and received the revelation of the resurrected Christ, their own brother, and believed in him.
i 1:14 The Aramaic is "They prayed with one soul."
j 1:16 Or "brothers."

Spirit concerning Judas must be fulfilled.[a] Judas betrayed our Lord Jesus and led the mob to the garden to arrest him. [17]He was one of us, and he was chosen to be an apostle just as we were.[b] [18]He earned the wages of his sin,[c] for he fell headfirst, and his belly split open, spilling his intestines on the ground. [19]Everyone in Jerusalem knows what happened to him. That's why the field where he died is called in Aramaic[d] 'Haqel Dama;' that is, 'The Bloody Field.' [20]For it is written in the Psalms:

> **Let his house be deserted and become a wasteland.**
> **No one will live there.[e]**

"And also:

> **Let another take his ministry.[f]**

[21]"So then, we must choose his replacement from among those who have been with us from the very beginning.[g] [22]He must be one who was baptized by John and has walked with our Lord Jesus from then to his ascension. And, like us, he must be a witness of Jesus' resurrection."

[23]They proposed two candidates: Joseph, who is also called Barsabbas the Just, and Matthias.[h] [24]They all prayed, "Lord Yahweh,[i] you know the heart of every man.[j] Please give us clear revelation to know which of these two men you have chosen [25]to be an apostle and take Judas's place because he renounced his apostleship to go where he belonged."[k] [26]They cast lots[l] and determined that Matthias was the Lord's choice, so he was added to the eleven apostles.

---

a 1:16 That is, replacing Judas with another to complete the Twelve. See verse 20.

b 1:17 As translated from the Aramaic.

c 1:18 As translated from the Aramaic. The Greek is "He acquired a field with the reward of his wickedness." Judas would have had no time between his betrayal and his suicide to purchase land. This plot of land was likely purchased by the Jewish authorities. They could not use the returned blood money for temple purposes, so instead they purchased a small burial plot for Judas.

d 1:19 Or "in the language of the region." The Greek text is clear that the Jews of Jesus' day spoke Aramaic, the language that Jesus and his apostles taught in. The Greek text transliterates the name of the field into a Greek equivalent for a Greek audience.

e 1:20 See Psalm 69:25.

f 1:20 See Psalm 109:8.

g 1:21 Or "that our Lord Jesus went in and out among us."

h 1:23 Barsabbas means "son of promise." Matthias means "gift of YHWH."

i 1:24 As translated from the Aramaic. The Greek is simply "Lord."

j 1:24 The Greek is "Lord, you are the Heart Knower of all."

k 1:25 The Aramaic is "go to his place." The Greek is "departed from this life," a euphemism for death.

l 1:26 This was similar to rolling dice. Casting lots is not mentioned again in the New Testament after the Holy Spirit was poured out. The Aramaic reads, "They raised up a shaking-free and elevated Matthias," which indicates they shook free from Judas's claim to apostleship and appointed Matthias.

Two

The Holy Spirit Comes at Pentecost

¹On the day Pentecost was being fulfilled,ᵃ all the disciples were gathered in one place. ²Suddenly they heard the sound of a violent blast of windᵇ rushing into the house from out of the heavenly realm. The roar of the wind was so overpowering it was all anyone could bear!ᶜ Then all at once a pillar of fire appeared before their eyes.ᵈ ³It separated into tongues of fire that engulfedᵉ each one of them. ⁴They were all filled and equippedᶠ with the Holy Spirit and were inspiredᵍ to speak in tongues—empowered by the Spirit to speak in languages they had never learned!

⁵Now, at that time there were Jewish worshippersʰ who had emigrated from many different lands to live in Jerusalem. ⁶When the peopleⁱ of the city heard the roaring sound, crowds came running to where it was coming from, stunned over what was happening, because each one could hear the disciples

a   2:1 Or "came to be fulfilled." The Greek word means "to fill completely (to be fulfilled)." Pentecost was one of the main feasts of Israel. The name is derived from *pentekostos*, which means "fiftieth," since it was held on the fiftieth day after the Passover Sabbath. It was also known as the Feast of Harvest.

b   2:2 The Aramaic can also be translated "like the roar of a groaning spirit." This mighty wind is for power; the breath of Jesus breathed into his disciples in John 20:22 was for life.

c   2:2 Or "It filled the house." Although most believe this was in an upper room, it is possible to conclude from the Aramaic that it was the House of the Lord (the temple), where they all gathered to celebrate Pentecost. See also Luke 24:53.

d   2:2 Implied in the text. This was the pillar of fire that led Israel from bondage into the Promised Land. The same pillar of fire manifested here to initiate a new beginning from dead religious structures into the powerful life of the Spirit. Each believer received an overpowering flame of fire, signified by the shaft of light that engulfed them. It was as though each one received his own personal pillar of fire that would empower him and lead him throughout his life. This was the promise Jesus gave to his disciples of "the Redeemer, the one like me," who would be sent by the Father and never leave them. Today every believer is indwelt by the Spirit of Christ (Romans 8:9). This was the birthday of the church of Jesus Christ.

e   2:3 Or "rested over them."

f   2:4 There are two Greek words used here for "filled." In verse 2, it is *pleroo*, which means "filled inwardly." In verse 4 it is *pletho*, which means "filled outwardly" or "furnished and equipped." This was the anointing of the Spirit for ministry. Every believer needs the filling of the Spirit both inwardly for life and outwardly for ministry.

g   2:4 The Greek word *apotheggomai* literally means "to ring out (like a bell)." It can also mean "carried along" or "inspired."

h   2:5 Or "devout Jewish men."

i   2:6 The Greek word *andres* implies respect, such as "Ladies and gentlemen."

speaking in his or her own language. [7]Bewildered, they said to one another, "Aren't these all Galileans?[a] [8]So how is it that we hear them speaking in our own languages? [9]We are northeastern Iranians,[b] northwestern Iranians,[c] Elamites,[d] and those from Mesopotamia,[e] Judea, east central Turkey,[f] the coastal areas of the Black Sea,[g] Asia,[h] [10]north central Turkey,[i] southern Turkey, Egypt, Libyans who are neighbors of Cyrene, visitors from all over the Roman Empire, both Jews and converts to Judaism, Cretans and Arabs. [11]Yet we hear them speaking of God's mighty wonders in our own dialects!"[j] [12]They all stood there, dumbfounded and astonished, saying to one another, "What is this phenomenon?"[k]

[13]But others poked fun at them and said, "They're just drunk on new wine."

Peter's Pentecost Sermon

[14]Peter stood up with the eleven apostles[l] and shouted[m] to the crowd. "Listen carefully, my fellow Jews[n] and residents of Jerusalem. You need to clearly understand what's happening here. [15]These people are not drunk like you think they are, for it is only nine o'clock in the morning.[o] [16]This is the fulfillment[p] of what was prophesied through the prophet Joel, for God says:[q]

---

a 2:7 It is likely they knew they were Galileans by their Aramaic dialect common in Galilee.
b 2:9 Or "Parthians."
c 2:9 Or "Medes."
d 2:9 This area is now Khuzestan and the Ilam Province, including a small part of southern Iraq.
e 2:9 The Aramaic is Beth-Nahrin, which means "land of the rivers." This would include Iraq, parts of Syria, southeastern Turkey, and southwestern Iran. The Assyrians also consider themselves to be natives of Beth-Nahrin (Mesopotamia).
f 2:9 Or "Cappadocia."
g 2:9 Or "Pontus," which is northeastern Turkey. Pontus means "sea."
h 2:9 Or "Orientals."
i 2:10 Or "Phrygia."
j 2:11 This is the universal remedy of the curse of Babel, where human beings were divided by languages (Genesis 11:9). Now, in Christ, the language of the Spirit unifies us all in him.
k 2:12 As translated from the Aramaic.
l 2:14 All of the Twelve standing there would prove that they were not drunk. They stood before this massive crowd, most likely in the courts of the temple. There were three thousand converted and baptized that day, so the crowd was most likely much larger than that.
m 2:14 See footnote for verse 4 above. Peter was speaking under the anointing of the Holy Spirit. The tongues being spoken, along with the sound of the wind, drew the crowd. Peter would have spoken to them in the common language of Aramaic. Even with the Galilean and Judean dialects, nearly all of the Jewish people present would understand his words.
n 2:14 Or "you Jewish men." This is also used in 2:22, 3:12, 5:35, 13:16, and 21:28.
o 2:15 Or "the third hour," the time for Jewish morning prayer.
p 2:16 Implied in the context.
q 2:17 See Joel 2:28–32.

[17]"This is what I will do in the last days[a]—I will pour out[b] my Spirit on everybody and cause your sons and daughters to prophesy, and your young men will see visions,[c] and your old men will experience dreams from God.[d] [18]The Holy Spirit will come upon all my servants, men and women alike, and they will prophesy. [19]I will reveal startling signs and wonders in the sky above and mighty miracles on the earth below. Blood and fire and pillars of clouds[e] will appear. [20]For the sun will be turned dark[f] and the moon blood-red before that great and awesome appearance[g] of the day of the Lord. [21]But everyone who calls on the name of the Lord[h] will be saved."

[22]Peter continued, "People of Israel, listen to the facts.[i] Jesus, the Victorious,[j] was a Man on a divine mission[k] whose authority was clearly proven. For you know how God performed many powerful miracles, signs, and wonders through him. [23]This Man's destiny was prearranged, for God knew that Jesus would be handed over to you to be crucified and that you would execute him on a cross by the hands of lawless men. Yet it was all part of his predetermined plan. [24]God destroyed the cords of death[l] and raised him up, because it was impossible for death's power to hold him prisoner. [25]This is the very thing David

---

a 2:17 The New Testament term "the last days" began at Pentecost and extends until the return of Christ. We have technically been in "the last days" for over two thousand years.

b 2:17 Or "gush forth," or "run greedily." The Aramaic can be translated "I will be splashing my Spirit-Wind over all flesh (humanity)."

c 2:17 Or "divinely appointed appearances." The Greek word for "visions," *horasis*, can also mean "our eyes opened to have divine encounters and see into the spiritual realm." These are not daydreams but visions of the heavenly realm. See Strong's concordance 3700 and 3706.

d 2:17 Implied in the text. This verse can be translated from the Aramaic as "Your grandparents shall see visions and your priests shall dream dreams."

e 2:19 Or "columns (plumes) of smoke." The Aramaic can be translated "the sweet smell of burning incense."

f 2:20 This could be a figure of speech similar to "Lights out on the old order." The Aramaic is "The sun will be in mourning." Perhaps this prophecy was fulfilled when Christ was crucified.

g 2:20 This is the Greek word for "epiphany," and it occurs only here in the New Testament. The Aramaic is "the great and feared day of the Lord." The Aramaic is "until the Lord's Day arrives in glory and power."

h 2:21 The Aramaic can be translated "Whoever calls on the name of Jesus as the Messiah will receive life."

i 2:22 Peter wisely begins his sermon with a recounting of Jewish history, keeping the main point of his sermon until the end. A great transformation had taken place in Peter, who had denied Christ three times only six weeks ago. Now he preaches with power and authority. This is the difference the Holy Spirit makes in the life of a believer.

j 2:22 Or "Jesus the Nazarene (the Branch)." The Aramaic word used here also implies the title of an heir of a powerful family, or one who is victorious ("Jesus the Victorious").

k 2:22 The Aramaic is "the Man from God," which may be an idiomatic saying for "the Man born of God."

l 2:24 As translated from the Aramaic, which can also be translated "God destroyed death's destruction." The Greek is "God freed him from the travails of death." The Greek word translated "travails" is commonly used for the labor pains of childbirth.

prophesied about him:[a]

> I continually see the Lord[b] in front of me—
> He's at my right hand, and I am never shaken.[c]
> [26]No wonder my heart is glad and my glory celebrates![d]
> My mouth is filled with his praises,
> And I have hope that my body will live[e]
> [27]Because you will not leave my soul among the dead,[f]
> Nor will you allow your sacred one to experience decay.
> [28]For you have revealed to me the pathways to life,
> And seeing your face fills me with euphoria![g]

[29]"My fellow Jews, I can tell you there is no doubt that our noted patriarch has both died and been buried in his tomb, which remains to this day. So you can see that he was not referring to himself with those words.[h] [30]But as a prophet, he knew God's faithful promise, made with God's unbreakable oath, that one of his descendants would take his throne.[i] [31]So when peering into the future, David prophesied[j] of the Messiah's resurrection. And God revealed to him[k] that the Messiah would not be abandoned to the realm of death, nor would his body experience decay.

[32]"Can't you see it? God has resurrected Jesus, and we all have seen him![l]

[33]"Then God exalted him to his right hand upon the throne of highest honor. And the Father gave him the authority to send the promised Holy Spirit, which is being poured out[m] upon us today. This is what you're seeing and hearing!

[34]"David wasn't the one who ascended into heaven, but the one who

---

a 2:25 See Psalm 16:8–11.
b 2:25 The Hebrew-Aramaic word is *Yahweh*.
c 2:25 As translated from the Aramaic. The Greek is "so that I will not be shaken."
d 2:26 As translated from the Aramaic.
e 2:26 The Greek word for "live" (*kataskenosei*) is always used for "pitch a tent." Or "My body will pitch its tent in hope (expectation)." The Aramaic is "Even my body he will restore to hope."
f 2:27 The Aramaic is "Sheol"; the Greek is "Hades." Both refer to the realm of death.
g 2:28 This Greek word (*euphrosune*) occurs only here and in Acts 14:17. It is the spirit of joy, an ecstasy that comes from God. The Aramaic is "You will fill me, O Sweetness, with your presence."
h 2:29 Made explicit from what is implied by Peter's statements.
i 2:30 See Psalm 132:11 and Luke 1:32.
j 2:31 The Aramaic can be translated "David rose up after seeing a vision and he saw."
k 2:31 Implied in the context.
l 2:32 Or "of whom we are witnesses," which implies that they all had seen the resurrected Jesus.
m 2:33 The Aramaic is "splashed out the gift of the Holy Spirit."

prophesied:

> The Lord Jehovah[a] said to my Lord,
> I honor you by enthroning you beside me,[b]
> [35]Until I make your enemies
> A footstool beneath your feet.[c]

[36]"Now everyone in Israel[d] can know for certain[e] that Jesus, whom you crucified, is the one God has made[f] both Lord[g] and the Messiah."

The Crowd Responds to Peter's Words

[37]When they heard this they were crushed and realized what they had done to Jesus.[h] Deeply moved, they said to Peter and the other apostles, "What do we need to do to become your brothers?"[i]

[38]Peter replied, "Repent and return to God,[j] and each one of you must be baptized in the name of Jesus, the Anointed One,[k] to have your sins removed. Then you may take hold of the gift of the Holy Spirit. [39]For God's promise of the Holy Spirit is for you[l] and your families, for those yet to be born[m] and for everyone whom the Lord our God calls to himself."

---

a 2:34 As translated from the Aramaic.

b 2:34 Or "at my right hand."

c 2:35 See Psalm 110:1, which is the most frequently quoted Old Testament verse found in the New Testament. This shows there is a continuing work of defeating Christ's enemies as his kingdom increases on earth as it is in heaven.

d 2:36 Or "all the house of Israel."

e 2:36 Or "inescapably," for no one can escape the claims of Christ.

f 2:36 The Aramaic is "Lord Yahweh made him (from birth) to be both Elohim and Messiah." The Greek verb used for "made" can also mean "brought forth." This is a clear statement of both Jesus' humanity (God brought him forth by human birth) and his deity.

g 2:36 Y'shua (Jesus) is now Lord of a new creation company, a new heaven, and a new earth—he is Lord of all. The Greek word kurios is not necessarily a divine title. The Aramaic text uses a clear title of Jesus' deity.

h 2:37 This Greek verb indicates the deepest sorrow and emotional agitation. It is taken from a root word that means "mortally wounded" and is found only here in all the New Testament.

i 2:37 As translated from the idiomatic figure of speech in the Aramaic.

j 2:38 The Greek word translated "repent" means both "to change the mind and direction of your life" and "to turn back to God."

k 2:38 Peter was likely saying these words from the steps of the temple. Below him were dozens of mikveh (immersion pools used for ceremonial cleanings of Jewish worshippers). Peter was pointing them to the cleansing that comes through the name and authority of Jesus Christ. The Aramaic is startling: "Be immersed in the name of Lord Yahweh Y'shua." Peter is clearly saying that Lord Yahweh and Jesus are one and the same.

l 2:39 The Aramaic can be translated "This outpouring is for you."

m 2:39 Or "for those who are far away (Gentiles)."

⁴⁰Peter preached to them and warned them with these words: "Be rescued from the wayward and perverse culture of this world!"ᵃ

⁴¹Those who believed the word that day numbered three thousand. They were all baptized and added to the church.ᵇ

The Community of Believers

⁴²Every believer was faithfully devoted to following the teachingsᶜ of the apostles. Their hearts were mutually linked to one another,ᵈ sharing communionᵉ and coming together regularly for prayer.ᶠ ⁴³A deep sense of holy aweᵍ swept over everyone, and the apostles performed many miraculous signs and wonders.ʰ ⁴⁴All the believers were in fellowship as one body,ⁱ and they shared with one another whatever they had. ⁴⁵Out of generosityʲ they even sold their assets to distribute the proceeds to those among them who in need. ⁴⁶Daily they met together in the temple courts and in one another's homes to celebrate communion. They shared meals together with joyful hearts and tender humility. ⁴⁷They were continually filled with praises to God, enjoying the favor of all the people. And the Lord kept adding to their number daily those who were being saved.ᵏ

---

a 2:40 Or "Be free from and preserved from this crooked people!"
b 2:41 Although the word "church" is not in the text, it is implied. They were converted by the message of Peter and brought into the fellowship of the believers.
c 2:42 The Greek word *didache* means "skilled instruction and training."
d 2:42 Or "They became partners."
e 2:42 Or "breaking of bread." This was more than sharing meals, but participating together in observing the Lord's Table. The Aramaic, which can be translated "the Eucharist" or "holy communion," makes it even more explicit.
f 2:42 Or "(all kinds of) prayers."
g 2:43 Or "Fear (of God) came upon every person."
h 2:43 The Aramaic adds, "in Jerusalem," which is missing in the Greek.
i 2:44 Or "added into one body."
j 2:45 Implied in the context.
k 2:47 The Aramaic is "daily adding to the church those who were coming to life." The Aramaic word for "church" is the joining of "meet" and "come." This word is an invitation to enter into fellowship with Christ and his people. The Greek word for "church" is *ekklesia*, which is "called-out ones." (See footnote on Matthew 16:16.)

Three

Healing at the Beautiful Gate

[1]One afternoon Peter and John went to the temple for the three o'clock prayer.[a] [2]As they came to the entrance called the Beautiful Gate,[b] they were captured by the sight of a man crippled from birth being carried and placed at the entrance to the temple. He was often brought there to beg for money from those going in to worship. [3]When he noticed Peter and John going into the temple, he begged them for money.

[4]Peter and John, looking straight into the eyes of the crippled man, said, "Look at us!" [5]Expecting a gift, he readily gave them his attention. [6]Then Peter said, "I don't have money, but I'll give you this—by the power of the name of Jesus Christ of Nazareth, stand up and walk!"

[7-8]Peter held out his right hand to the crippled man. As he pulled the man to his feet, suddenly power surged into his crippled feet and ankles. The man jumped up, stood there for a moment stunned, and then began to walk around! As he went into the temple courts with Peter and John, he leapt for joy and shouted praises to God.

[9]When all the people saw him jumping up and down and heard him glorifying God, [10]they realized it was the crippled beggar they had passed by in front of the Beautiful Gate. Astonishment swept over the crowd, for they were amazed over what had happened to him.

---

a 3:1 Daily sacrifices were made in the temple at sunrise and about three o'clock every afternoon.

b 3:2 Or "the gate called Wonderful" (in Aramaic). It is difficult to ascertain which of the many gates of the temple this might have been, and there is varying speculation with no certain conclusion. However, this Beautiful Gate points to Jesus Christ, who is the gate or entrance into the sheepfold of God. Furthermore, it hints of Ezekiel's temple (Ezekiel 47), which has a river flowing out from the threshold through the gateway of the temple. This river was first measured to be ankle deep. This man, lame in his ankles, was healed by the spiritual "river" that flowed out the "Beautiful Gate" of Christ. The gateway opened up and the river poured out of Peter and John, bringing healing to the lame.

Peter Preaches to the Crowd

[11]Dumbfounded over what they were witnessing, the crowd ran over to Peter and John, who were standing under the covered walkway called Solomon's Porch. Standing there also was the healed beggar, clinging to Peter and John.[a]

[12]With the crowd surrounding him, Peter said to them all, "People of Israel,[b] listen to me! Why are you so amazed by this healing? Why do you stare at us? We didn't make this crippled man walk by our own power or authority.[c] [13]The God of our ancestors, Abraham, Isaac, and Jacob,[d] has done this.[e] For he has glorified his Servant[f] Jesus, the one you denied to Pilate's face when he decided to release him—and you insisted that he be crucified. [14]You rejected the one who is holy and righteous, and instead begged for a murderer to be released. [15]You killed the Prince of Life![g] But God raised him from the dead, and we stand here as witnesses to that fact. [16]Faith in Jesus' name has healed this man standing before you. It is the faith that comes through believing in Jesus' name that has made the crippled man walk right in front of your eyes!

[17]"My fellow Jews, I realize that neither you nor your leaders realize the grave mistake you made. [18]But in spite of what you've done, God has fulfilled what he foretold through the prophets long ago about the sufferings of his Anointed One. [19]And now you must repent and turn back to God so that your sins will be removed,[h] and so that times of refreshing[i] will stream from the Lord's presence. [20]And he will send you Jesus, the Messiah, the chosen one for you.[j] [21]For he must remain in heaven until the restoration of all things has taken place,[k] fulfilling everything that God said long ago through his holy prophets.[l]

---

a 3:11 What an amazing picture this makes. This scene transpired at Solomon's Porch. Lessons of wisdom, greater than the wisdom of Solomon, were uncovered by this miracle to those who had hearts of understanding.

b 3:12 The Aramaic could be translated "protectors of Israel."

c 3:12 As translated from the Aramaic. The Greek is "piety."

d 3:13 See Exodus 3:6.

e 3:13 Implied in the text.

f 3:13 See Isaiah 52:13.

g 3:15 Or "Originator of Life."

h 3:19 The Greek word used here, exaleipho, means "obliterated" or "canceled."

i 3:19 Or "cooling breeze," which occurs only here in the New Testament. This hints of the time when God walked with Adam in the cooling breeze of the day. The work of the cross begins the restoration of Paradise within the hearts of Christ's followers.

j 3:20 The Aramaic can be translated "He will send you all that has been already prepared for you through Jesus, the Anointed One."

k 3:21 Or "This one the heavens must receive until the times of universal restoration." Luke's choice of the Greek word found only here in the New Testament is noteworthy. It is a medical term that means "restoration of perfect health." It has also been found on an ancient Greek inscription as "the restoration of boundaries." See ancient Greek inscription I.Eph.VII, 2.3513.

l 3:21 Implied in the text.

²²"For has not Moses told us:ª

> **The Lord your God will raise up**
> **A prophet from among you who is like me.**
> **Listen to him and follow everything he tells you.**
> **²³Every person who disobeys that prophet**
> **Will be cut off and completely destroyed.**

²⁴"In fact, every prophet from the time of Samuel onward has prophesied of these very days! ²⁵And you are heirs of their propheciesᵇ and of the covenants God made with your fathers when he promised Abraham,ᶜ 'Your descendantᵈ will bring blessing to all the people on the earth.'

²⁶"Now that God raised up his Son,ᵉ he has chosen to send him first to you that he might bless you by turning each one of youᶠ from your wickedness."ᵍ

a 3:22 See Deuteronomy 18:15, 19 and Leviticus 23:29.
b 3:25 Or "sons of the prophets."
c 3:25 See Genesis 22:18, 26:4.
d 3:25 Or "seed (descendants)."
e 3:26 The Greek word *pais* can mean either "servant" or "son." See Strong's concordance 3816. The Aramaic is clearly "son." Notice how many times in the book of Acts that the followers of Christ preached the resurrection. The power and virtue of the cross can never be diminished; however, it is the resurrection of Christ that became the apostolic center of their preaching in the book of Acts.
f 3:26 The Aramaic uses the conditional clause "if you turn and repent from your evils."
g 3:26 The Greek is plural, "wickednesses" or "evil ways."

$$\mathcal{Four}$$

Peter and John Arrested

¹⁻²The teaching and preaching of Peter and John angered the priests, the captain of the temple police, and representatives of the Jewish sect of the Sadducees.ᵃ They were furious that the people were being taught that in Jesus there is a resurrection from the dead. So while Peter and John were still speaking, the Jewish authorities came to the temple courts to oppose them. ³They had them arrested, and since it was already evening they kept them in custody until the next day. ⁴Yet there were many in the crowd who believed the message,ᵇ bringing the total number of men who believedᶜ to nearly five thousand!

⁵The next day many Jewish leaders, religious scholars, and elders of the people convened a meeting in Jerusalem. ⁶Annas the high priest was there with Caiaphas, John, Alexander,ᵈ and others who were members of the high priest's family. ⁷They made Peter and John stand in front of the council as they questioned them, saying, "Tell us, by what power and authority have you done these things?"ᵉ

⁸Peter, filled with the Holy Spirit, answered, "Respected elders and leaders of the people, listen. ⁹Are we being put on trial today for doing an act of kindness by healing a frail, crippled man? Well then, ¹⁰you and everyone else in Israel should know that it is by the power of the name of Jesus that the crippled man stands here today completely healed! You crucified Jesus Christ of

---

a 4:1 Of the three major sects of Judaism of that day (Pharisees, Essenes, and Sadducees), the Sadducees were a small but influential group that philosophically denied the supernatural and gravitated instead toward political control of the people. Their denial of the resurrection is what prompted their actions here.

b 4:4 Or "the Word (logos)."

c 4:4 Although the cultural way of numbering the Jewish crowd is technically "adult males," the usage of the Greek term ton andron is consistently found throughout Greek literature as an inclusive and formal term of respect, similar to "ladies and gentlemen." Including women and children, the early church swelled rapidly into tens of thousands.

d 4:6 There is little known about John (or Jonathan) and Alexander. It is possible that John was the son of Caiaphas, who would one day be the high priest. Or John and Alexander could have been the leaders of the Sadducees.

e 4:7 Or "In whose name did you do this?"

Nazareth,[a] but God raised him from the dead. [11]This Jesus is **'the stone that you, the builders, have rejected, and now he has become the cornerstone!'**[b] [12]There is no one else[c] who has the power to save us, for there is only one name to whom God has given authority to release to us the experience of salvation:[d] the name of Jesus."[e]

[13]The council members were astonished as they witnessed the bold courage[f] of Peter and John, especially when they discovered that they were just ordinary men who had never had religious training.[g] Then they began to understand the effect Jesus had on them simply by spending time with him. [14]Standing there with them was the healed man, and there was nothing further they could say.

[15]So they ordered them to leave the room while they discussed the matter. Among themselves, they said, [16]"What should we do with these men? Everyone in Jerusalem can clearly see that they've performed a notable sign and wonder—we can't deny that. [17]But to keep this propaganda from spreading any further among the people, let's threaten them severely and warn them to never speak to anyone in this name again."

[18]So they had them brought back in before the council, and they commanded them to never teach the people or speak again using the name of Jesus. [19]But Peter and John replied, "You can judge for yourselves—is it better to listen to you or to God? [20]It's impossible for us to stop speaking about all the things we've seen and heard!"

[21]Since the members of the council couldn't come up with a crime they could punish them for, they threatened them once more and let them go. All the people praised God, thrilled over the miraculous healing of the crippled man.[h] [22]And the man who received this miracle sign of healing was over forty years old.[i]

---

a 4:10 Or "the Nazarene."
b 4:11 See Psalm 118:22.
c 4:12 Peter insisted there was no man who could claim to be the Messiah other than Jesus.
d 4:12 The Aramaic is "We must experience the Life Giver" or "We must receive the covenant of life."
e 4:12 Implied in the text.
f 4:13 The Aramaic is "hearing the bold words of Peter and John."
g 4:13 The Aramaic is "They did not know the scrolls." The Greek is "uneducated."
h 4:21 Made explicit from the text, "over what had happened."
i 4:22 For the significance of the number forty, see footnote on 1:3.

The Church Prays

[23]As soon as they were released from custody, Peter and John went to the other believers and explained all that had happened with the high priest and the elders. [24]When the believers heard their report, they raised their voices in unity and prayed, "Lord Yahweh,[a] you are the Lord of all! You created the universe—the earth, the sky, the sea, and everything that is in them.[b] [25]And you spoke by the Holy Spirit through your servant David, our forefather, saying:

> How dare the nations plan a rebellion,
> Ranting and raging against the Lord Most High?
> Their foolish plots are futile!
> [26]Look at how the kings of the earth take their stand,
> With the rulers scheming and conspiring together
> Against God[c] and his anointed Messiah![d]

[27]"In fact, Herod and Pontius Pilate, along with Jews and non-Jews, met together to take their stand against your holy servant, Jesus the Messiah. [28]They did to him all that your purpose and will had determined, according to the destiny you had marked out for him. [29]So now, Lord, listen to their threats to harm us and empower us, as your servants, to speak the word of God freely and courageously. [30]Stretch out your hand of power through us[e] to heal, and to move in signs and wonders by the name of your holy Son, Jesus!"[f]

[31]At that moment the earth shook beneath them, causing the building they were in to tremble.[g] Each one of them was filled with the Holy Spirit, and they proclaimed the word of God with unrestrained boldness.[h]

---

a 4:24 As translated from the Aramaic.
b 4:24 See Exodus 20:11 and Psalm 146:6.
c 4:26 The Aramaic is "Lord Yahweh," and the Greek is "Lord (kurios)."
d 4:26 See Psalm 2:1–2.
e 4:30 Implied in the text.
f 4:30 As translated from the Aramaic. The Greek is "your holy servant, Jesus."
g 4:31 The Aramaic is "an earthquake."
h 4:31 The Greek word is parresia. This involves more than confidence; it was a free-flowing, unrestrained boldness. It can also mean "freedom of speech." Parresia carries nuances that are not easily brought over into English. The person who speaks with parresia will say everything that is on his mind with no restraint, flowing out of his heart with confidence. It involves being frank and honest, hiding nothing and speaking directly to the heart. Most often it is a word used for public speaking. It refers to speech that is not tailored to make everyone happy but to speak the truth, in spite of what that may cost. It is the courage to speak truth into the ears of others. This was reserved for only the highest rank of Greek citizens, not people of other lands or slaves. The right to speak freely was an essential aspect of Athenian democracy. Although it is sometimes associated with negative speech, in this context parresia refers to an unrestrained boldness. There was a Greek idiom that said essentially, "If you tell me the truth no matter what that truth

³²All the believers were one in mind and heart. Selfishness was not a part of their community, for they shared everything they had with one another. ³³The apostles gave powerful testimonies about the resurrection of the Lord Jesus, and great measures of grace rested upon them all. ³⁴⁻³⁵Some who owned houses or land sold them and brought the proceeds before the apostles to distribute to those without. Not a single person among them was needy.

³⁶⁻³⁷For example, there was a Levite from Cyprus named Joseph, who sold his farmland and placed the proceeds at the feet of the apostles. They nicknamed him Barnabas (or "Encourager") because of his kind generosity.^a

---

turns out to be, I will not punish you." This was known as the Parresiastic Contract. See M. Foucault, "Discourse and Truth: The Problematization of Parresia," six lectures given at the University of California at Berkeley, 1983, ed. by Joseph Pearson in 1985. *Parresia* is found also in Mark 8:32; John 7:4, 13, 26; 10:24; 11:14, 54; 2 Corinthians 3:12; 7:4; Ephesians 3:12; 6:19; Philippians 1:20, and numerous other places.

a 4:36–37 Implied in the text. This was the Barnabas who traveled with Paul as an apostle.

Five
—

The Judgment of Ananias and Sapphira

[1]Now, a man named Ananias and his wife, Sapphira,[a] likewise sold their farm. [2]They conspired to secretly keep back for themselves a portion of the proceeds. So when Ananias brought the money to the apostles, it was only a portion of the entire sale. [3]God revealed their secret to Peter,[b] so he said to him, "Ananias, why did you let Satan fill your heart and make you think you could lie to the Holy Spirit? You only pretended to give it all, yet you hid back part of the proceeds from the sale of your property to keep for yourselves. [4]Before you sold it, wasn't it yours to sell or to keep? And after you sold it, wasn't the money entirely at your disposal? How could you plot such a thing in your heart? You haven't lied to people; you've lied to God!"[c]

[5]The moment Ananias heard those words, he fell over dead. Everyone was terrified when they heard what had happened. [6]Some young men came in and removed the body and buried him.

[7]Three hours later, his wife came into the room, with no clue what had happened to her husband.

[8]Peter said to her, "Tell me, were the two of you paid this amount for the sale of your land?"

Sapphira said, "Yes, that's how much it was."

[9]Peter told her, "Why have you agreed together to test the Spirit of the Lord?[d] I hear the footsteps of those who buried your husband at the door—

---

a 5:1 The Aramaic can be translated "Ananias, together with his wife, who was famous for her beauty." The Aramaic name Shapeera means "beauty."

b 5:3 Implied in the text. With supernatural discernment, God revealed to Peter what had happened. The words "pretended to give it all" are not in the text, but supplied because of the inference of the words "lie to the Holy Spirit." The true sin was more than simply telling Peter a lie, but lying to the Holy Spirit.

c 5:4 The Aramaic can be translated "You are not a phony with just men, but with God."

d 5:9 The Aramaic is "the Spirit of the Lord Yahweh."

they're coming here to bury you too!" [10]At that moment she dropped dead at Peter's feet.

When the young men came in, she was already dead, so they carried her out and buried her next to her husband. [11]The entire church was seized with a powerful sense of the fear of God,[a] which came over all who heard what had happened.

The Apostles Perform Miracles, Signs, and Wonders

[12]The apostles performed many signs, wonders, and miracles among the people. [13]And the believers were wonderfully united as they met regularly in the temple courts in the area known as Solomon's Porch. No one dared harm them,[b] for everyone held them in high regard.

[14]Continually more and more people believed in the Lord[c] and were added to their number—great crowds of both men and women. [15]In fact, when people knew Peter was going to walk by, they carried the sick out to the streets and laid them down on cots and mats, knowing the incredible power emanating from him would overshadow them and heal them.[d] [16]Great numbers of people swarmed into Jerusalem from the nearby villages. They brought with them the sick and those troubled by demons—and everyone was healed!

The Apostles Persecuted

[17]The high priest and his officials, who formed the party of the Sadducees, became extremely jealous over all that was happening. [18]So they had the apostles arrested, placed in chains,[e] and thrown into jail. [19]But during the night, the Lord[f] sent an angel who appeared before them.[g] He supernaturally opened their prison doors and brought the apostles outside. [20]"Go," the angel told

---

a 5:11 Or "mega-fear fell on the church."
b 5:13 As translated from the Aramaic. The Greek is "No one else dared join them," which is somewhat confusing because of the next verse.
c 5:14 The Aramaic is "the Lord Yahweh."
d 5:15 Implied in the context. The Greek word translated "overshadow" is *episkiazo*, which is used exclusively for the power of the Almighty "overshadowing," such as Mary, who conceived a child supernaturally by God. It is also used for the cloud that overshadowed Jesus on the Mount of Transfiguration. See Matthew 17:5, Mark 9:7, and Luke 1:35. This was not a natural shadow created by the light of the sun, but the supernatural overshadowing of God's power coming upon the sick to bring healing.
e 5:18 As translated from the Aramaic.
f 5:19 The Aramaic is "Lord Yahweh."
g 5:19 Implied in the text.

them. "Stand in the temple courts and preach the words that bring life!" ²¹So early that morning they entered the temple courts and taught the people.

The high priest and his officials, unaware of their supernatural release from prison,ᵃ convened the members of the supreme council.ᵇ They sent for the apostles to be brought to them from prison. ²²But when the officers came to the prison cell, it was empty! They returned to the council and informed them, ²³"We found the jail securely locked and the guards standing by their cell, but when we opened the door, there was no one inside!"

²⁴When the captain of the temple guard and the leading priests heard this report, they were perplexed and at a loss over what to make of it.

²⁵Someone came and informed them, "The men you put in prison are out there standing in the temple courts, teaching the people!"

²⁶So the captain of the temple guard and his officers went to arrest them once again, but without using force, for they were afraid the people would stone them.

²⁷When they brought them before the council, the high priest demanded an explanation, ²⁸saying, "Didn't we strictly warn you that you were to never again teach in this name? But instead you have now filled all of Jerusalem with this doctrine and are committed to holding us responsible for this man's death!"ᶜ

²⁹Peter and the apostles replied, "We must listen to and obey God more than pleasing religious leaders. ³⁰You had Jesus arrested and killed by crucifixion,ᵈ but the God of our forefathersᵉ has raised him up. ³¹He's the one God has exalted and seated at his right hand as our Savior and Champion.ᶠ He is the provider of grace as the Redeemer of Israel.ᵍ ³²We are witnesses of these things,ʰ and so is the Holy Spirit, whom God freely gives to all who believe in him."ⁱ

³³When they heard this, they were infuriated and determined to murder them. ³⁴But a Pharisee named Gamaliel, a noted religious professor who was

a 5:21 Implied in the context.
b 5:21 Or "the Sanhedrin."
c 5:28 Or "bringing (the guilt of) this Man's blood on us."
d 5:30 Or "by hanging him on a tree," an Aramaic idiom for crucifixion. See Deuteronomy 21:22–23.
e 5:30 See Exodus 3:15.
f 5:31 Or "Prince."
g 5:31 As translated from the Aramaic. The Greek is "He gives repentance and removal of sins to Israel."
h 5:32 Or "words." This is the Greek word *rhema*.
i 5:32 As translated from the Aramaic. The Greek is "to those who hear and obey him."

highly respected by all, stood up. He gave orders to send the apostles outside. [35]Then he said to the council, "Men of Israel, you need to be very careful about how you deal with these men. [36]Some time ago there was a man named Theudas who rose up claiming to be somebody. He had a following of about four hundred men, but when he was killed, all of his followers were scattered, and nothing came of it.

[37]"After him, in the days of the census,[a] another man rose up, Judas the Galilean, who got people to follow him in a revolt. He too perished, and all those who followed him were scattered. [38]So in this situation, you should just leave these men to themselves. For if this plan or undertaking originates with men, it will fade away and come to nothing. [39]But if this movement is of God, you won't be able to stop it. And you might discover that you were fighting God all along!"

Gamaliel's words convinced the council. [40]So they brought the apostles back in and had them severely beaten. They ordered them never again to speak in the name of Jesus and then let them go.

[41]The apostles left there rejoicing, thrilled that God had considered them worthy to suffer disgrace for the name of Jesus. [42]And nothing stopped them! They kept preaching every day in the temple courts and went from house to house, preaching the gospel of Jesus, God's Anointed One!

---

a 5:37 Or "registration for the Roman tax."

$\mathcal{S}ix$

_____

Servant Leaders

[1]During those days the number of Jesus' followers kept multiplying greatly. But a complaint was brought against those who spoke Aramaic[a] by the Greek-speaking Jews,[b] who felt their widows were being overlooked during the daily distribution of food.

[2]The twelve apostles called a meeting of all the believers and told them, "It is not advantageous for us to be pulled away from the word of God to wait on tables. [3]We want you to carefully select[c] from among yourselves seven godly men. Make sure they are honorable, full of the Holy Spirit and wisdom, and we will give them the responsibility of this crucial ministry of serving. [4]That will enable us to give our full attention to prayer and preaching the word of God."

[5]Everyone in the church loved this idea.[d] So they chose seven men. One of them was Stephen,[e] who was known as a man full of faith and overflowing with the Holy Spirit. Along with him they chose Philip, Prochorus, Nicanor, Timon, Parmenas, and Nicholas from Antioch,[f] who had converted to Judaism. [6]All

a 6:1 Or "the Hebrews (converts from orthodox Judaism)." There was one dominant language in Israel: Aramaic. However, the issue between the two groups was more than merely a language difference. Those who spoke Aramaic were natives, while the Greek-speaking minority were most likely Jews from other nations.

b 6:1 Or "Hellenists." These were Jewish converts who sought to maintain a Greek language and culture and were predominantly Alexandrian Jews. These may have been Jews who were scattered throughout the Roman Empire, including Greece and Alexandria, Egypt.

c 6:3 The Aramaic is "select with awe"; that is, in the presence of the Lord.

d 6:5 The Aramaic can be translated "This proposal appeared beautiful."

e 6:5 It is most likely that Stephen was not a Gentile but a Jewish believer. His Hebrew name, Tzephania, is transliterated into Greek as Astaphanos (Stephen in English). Tzephania is the name of the prophet Zephaniah. Zephaniah means "Yah has treasured (him)." Stephen was not a Gentile proselyte to Judaism but a Greek-speaking Hebrew. He spoke in Acts 7 and addressed his hearers as "fellow Jews and fathers." Although he was a powerful minister of the word, Stephen was not so proud that he wouldn't accept the task of serving.

f 6:5 The Aramaic can be translated "Nicholas, the hero of Antioch."

seven stood before the apostles, who laid their hands on them and prayed for them, commissioning them to this ministry.[a]

[7]God's word reigned supreme[b] and kept spreading. The number of Jesus' followers in Jerusalem quickly grew and increased by the day. Even a great number of Jewish priests became believers and were obedient to the faith!

[8]Stephen, who was a man full of grace and supernatural power, performed many astonishing signs and wonders and mighty miracles among the people.[c] [9]This upset some men belonging to a cult who called themselves the Men Set Free.[d] They were Libyans,[e] Egyptians,[f] and Turks.[g]

They all confronted Stephen to argue[h] with him. [10]But the Holy Spirit gave Stephen remarkable wisdom to answer them. His words were prompted by the Holy Spirit, and they could not refute what he said. [11]So the Men Set Free conspired in secret to find those who would bring false accusations against Stephen and lie about him by saying, "We heard this man speak blasphemy against Moses and God."[i]

[12]The Men Set Free agitated the crowd, the elders, and the religious scholars,[j] then seized Stephen and forcefully took him before the supreme council. [13]One after another, false witnesses stepped forward and accused Stephen, saying, "This man never stops denigrating our temple and our Jewish law. [14]For

a 6:6 Implied in the purpose of laying hands on them. The practice of laying on of hands indicates approval, impartation of authority, commissioning, and ordaining. As the Old Testament priest laid hands on a sacrifice and transferred the guilt of sins upon the animal, the New Testament apostles laid their hands on men and appointed them to ministry. See Leviticus 16:21–22 and Numbers 27:18–20.
b 6:7 As translated from the Aramaic.
c 6:8 Stephen was not an apostle, yet he worked miracles of power through his ministry. The miraculous is not for the few, but for the many.
d 6:9 Although some expositors view these as former Hebrew slaves, the Aramaic is Libertines. These were pagan cult members who followed a Roman mythical hero named Liber. From this word we get the English word liberty. They emphasized drunkenness and promiscuity. They boasted in their freedom from all moral laws as the Men Set Free to do whatever they desired. They were so hedonistic that even other pagans viewed them as wicked. These Libertines were the antithesis to the true freedom that comes through Christ (John 8:36).
e 6:9 Or "Cyrene," a region of eastern Libya.
f 6:9 Or "Alexandria," a large Egyptian city on the Mediterranean.
g 6:9 Or "Cilicia" (southeastern coastal area of Turkey) and "the province of Asia" (that is, Asia Minor, comprised of western and southwestern Turkey). Both regions are included in the word Turks.
h 6:9 The Aramaic is "word wrestle."
i 6:11 How ironic that these Men Set Free were bound to the past and resisted the Holy Spirit's wisdom pouring out of Stephen. They placed Moses before God in their accusations. The penalty for speaking against God was death by stoning. See Leviticus 24:15–16.
j 6:12 Or "scribes." These were considered the experts in the law of Moses.

we have heard him teach that Jesus of Nazareth will destroy the temple and change the traditions and customs that Moses handed down to us."[a]

[15]Every member of the supreme council focused his gaze on Stephen, for right in front of their eyes, while being falsely accused,[b] his face glowed as though he had the face of an angel![c]

---

a 6:14 The Aramaic is "We heard him teach that Jesus the Nazarene is the one who freed our nation and changes the feasts that Moses observed."

b 7:15 Implied in the context.

c 7:15 As he faced persecution and martyrdom, Stephen's face lit up with heaven's light, shining as an angelic messenger. What manifests in your life when you are opposed and falsely accused?

$$\mathscr{Seven}$$

Stephen's Sermon

[1]The high priest asked, "Are these accusations true?"

[2]Stephen replied, "My fellow Jews and fathers, listen to me. The God of glory appeared[a] to our ancestor Abraham while he was living in Iraq[b] and before he moved to Haran[c] in Syria. [3]God said to him, 'Go! Leave behind your country and your relatives. Begin your journey and come to the land that I will show you.'[d]

[4]"So Abraham left southeastern Iraq[e] and began his journey. He settled in Haran in Syria and stayed there until his father passed away. Then God had him move to the land of Israel with only a promise. [5]Although God gave him no parcel of land he could call his own, not even a footprint,[f] yet he promised Abraham that he and his descendants would one day have it all. And even though as yet Abraham had no child, [6]God spoke with him and gave him this promise:

> **Your descendants will live in a foreign land with a people**
> **Who will make slaves of them**
> **And oppress them for four hundred years.[g]**
> **[7]But I will judge the nation that enslaves them,**

---

a 7:2 The entire Hebrew family, and consequently the life of believers today, all began with a divine encounter as the God of glory appeared before Abraham. It is this same glory that calls people to faith in Christ. We, like Abraham, have been captured by the God of glory. See 2 Peter 1:3.

b 7:2 Or "Mesopotamia," or "the land between two rivers (Euphrates and Tigris)."

c 7:2 This is the city to which Abraham migrated on his way to the Promised Land. Haran was also the son of Caleb who claimed a mountain. Haran means "mountain climber."

d 7:3 See Genesis 12:1.

e 7:4 Or "the land of Chaldeans."

f 7:5 See Deuteronomy 2:5.

g 7:6 See Genesis 15:13–14, Exodus 2:22, and 12:40.

> And your descendants will be set free
> To return to this land to serve and worship me.[a]

⁸"Then God entered into covenant with Abraham, which included the requirement of circumcision. So when he became the father of Isaac, he circumcised him eight days after his birth.

⁹"Isaac then became the father of Jacob, who was the father of our twelve patriarchs. Jacob's sons became jealous of their brother Joseph and sold him to be a slave in Egypt. But God's favor and blessing rested upon Joseph, and in time, ¹⁰God rescued him from all his oppression and granted him extraordinary favor before Pharaoh, the king of Egypt. Pharaoh appointed him as the overseer of his nation and even of his own palace.[b]

¹¹"Then a devastating famine came over all of Egypt and Canaan, bringing great misery to the people, including our ancestors, who couldn't find food.[c] ¹²But when Jacob learned that there was food in Egypt, he sent his sons, our ancestors, on their first trip to purchase grain for their family. ¹³On their second trip to Egypt, Joseph revealed his identity to his brothers,[d] and because of this, Pharaoh learned about Joseph's family and where he came from.

¹⁴"Joseph sent for his father, Jacob, and his entire family, a total of seventy-five people, to come and reside in Egypt. ¹⁵Eventually, Jacob died there, along with all of his sons, our forefathers. ¹⁶Their bones[e] were later carried back to the Promised Land and buried in Shechem, in the tomb Abraham had purchased for a sum of money from the sons of Hamor.

¹⁷"The time drew near for God to fulfill the prophetic promise he had made to Abraham. Our Jewish people had increased greatly in number, multiplying many times over while in Egypt.

¹⁸"Another[f] king arose to rule over Egypt, who had forgotten how Joseph made their nation great.[g] ¹⁹He was an abusive king who exploited our people

---

a 7:7 See Exodus 3:12.
b 7:10 See Genesis 41:37–44.
c 7:11 See Genesis 41:54 and 42:5.
d 7:13 See Genesis 45:1.
e 7:16 The Aramaic is "his (Jacob's) bones," while every Greek manuscript is "their bones." Jacob was buried in Abraham's tomb according to Genesis 50:1–14. Joseph was buried in a plot purchased in Shechem for one hundred pieces of silver (Genesis 33:18–20; Joshua 24:32).
f 7:18 The Greek is "another of a different kind (character)."
g 7:18 Implied in the context of the account of Joseph. See Exodus 1:7–8.

with his smooth talk. With cruelty he forced our ancestors to give up their infant boys as he committed infanticide![a]

[20]"Then Moses came on the scene—a child of divine beauty.[b] His parents hid him from Pharaoh as long as they could to spare his life.[c] After three months they could conceal him no longer, [21]so they had to abandon him to his fate. But God arranged that Pharaoh's daughter would find him, take him home, and raise him as her own son. [22]So Moses was fully trained in the royal courts and educated in the highest wisdom Egypt had to offer, until he arose as a powerful prince and an eloquent orator.[d]

[23]"When Moses turned forty, his heart was stirred for his people, the Israelites. [24]One day he saw one of our people being violently mistreated, so he came to his rescue, and with his own hands Moses murdered the abusive Egyptian. [25]Moses hoped that when the people realized how he had rescued one of their own, they would recognize him as their deliverer. How wrong he was! [26]The next day he came upon two of our people engaged in a fist fight, and he tried to break it up by saying, 'Men, you are brothers! Why would you want to hurt each other?'

[27]"But the perpetrator pushed Moses aside and said, 'Who do you think you are? Who appointed you to be our ruler and judge? [28]Are you going to kill me like you did the Egyptian yesterday?'[e]

[29]"Shaken by this, Moses fled Egypt[f] and lived as an exile in the land of Midian, where he became the father of two sons. [30]After forty years had

---

a 7:19 The Aramaic can also be translated "forced them to abort their children."
b 7:20 Or "beautiful (well pleasing) in the eyes of God." The Aramaic is "He was loved by God." Ancient Hebrew scholars believed Moses may have had a shining of glory on his countenance when he was born, distinguishing him as a special servant of the Lord God. This shining face would later mark him as one who dwelt in the presence of the Lord (Exodus 34:29). Moses was a type or picture of the Lord Jesus Christ. No one was fairer than he. No one was more extraordinary than our Lord. We learn from Exodus 6:20 that Moses's father was Amram and his mother was Jochebed. Amram means "family of the Lofty One" and Jochebed means "Yah makes great." The sister of Moses was Miriam (the Hebrew name for Mary), which comes from the root word for "myrrh," meaning "aromatic, fragrant, or bitter." The name Moses means "rescued out of the water."
c 7:20 See Hebrews 11:23.
d 7:22 Jewish tradition is that Pharaoh's daughter had no child of her own and she herself was an only child. Moses stood in line to receive the throne of Egypt, the great world power. God was going to prepare a servant who would do his pleasure. All the education and culture of this world dynasty with its unlimited resources was placed before Moses. See Psalm 113:7–8.
e 7:28 See Exodus 2:14. Moses missed the timing. To know God's will doesn't mean you know God's timing. God made Moses a ruler and a judge, but it took forty years to prepare him. Moses wanted the position forty years before he was ready. No one can make himself ruler and judge—only God has authority to set leaders in place. We cannot raise ourselves up with ministry responsibilities until God releases us. See also Proverbs 8:16.
f 7:29 See Hebrews 11:24–27.

passed, while he was in the desert near Mount Sinai, the Messenger of Yahweh[a] appeared to him in the midst of a flaming thorn bush.[b] [31]Moses was astonished and stunned by what he was seeing, so he drew closer to observe this marvel. Then the Lord Yahweh spoke to him out of the flames:

> [32]I am the living God,[c] the God of your ancestors.
> I am the God of Abraham, Isaac, and Jacob.

"Trembling in God's presence and overwhelmed with awe, Moses didn't even dare to look into the fire.

[33]"Out of the flames the Lord Yahweh said to him:

> Take the sandals off your feet,[d]
> For you are standing in the realm of holiness.[e]
> [34]I have watched and seen how my people
> Have been mistreated[f] in Egypt.
> I have heard their painful groaning,
> And now I have come down to set them free.
> So come to me, Moses,
> For I am sending you to Egypt to represent me.[g]

[35]"So God sent back to Egypt the man our people rejected and refused to recognize by saying, 'Who appointed you to be our ruler and judge?' God sent this man back to be their ruler and deliverer, commissioned with the power of the messenger who appeared to him in the flaming thorn bush. [36]This man brought the people out from their Egyptian bondage with many astonishing wonders and miracle signs—miracles in Egypt, miracles at the Red Sea, and miracles during their forty-year journey through the wilderness. [37]This is the same Moses who said to our ancestors, 'The Lord God[h] will raise up one from

---

a 7:30 As translated from the Aramaic.
b 7:30 See Exodus 3:2.
c 7:32 As translated from the Aramaic.
d 7:33 Removing one's shoes indicated the highest reverence. It is symbolic of removing earthly matters from our minds and hearts in readiness to accept spiritual realities.
e 7:33 Or "You are standing on ground that is set apart (sacred)."
f 7:34 The Aramaic is "I have seen their torment."
g 7:34 See Exodus 3:6–10.
h 7:37 As translated from the Aramaic.

among you who will be a prophet to you, like I have been. Listen to everything he will say!'[a]

[38]"Moses led the congregation in the wilderness[b] and he spoke face-to-face[c] with the angel who spoke with him on the top of Mount Sinai. Along with our ancestors, he received the living oracles of God that were passed down to us. [39]But our forefathers refused to obey. They pushed him away, and their hearts longed to return to Egypt.

[40]"While Moses was on the mountain, our forefathers said to Aaron, 'Make us gods to lead us, because we don't know what has become of this Moses who brought us out of Egypt.'[d]

[41]"So they made a god, an idol in the form of a bull calf. They offered sacrifices to it and celebrated with delight what their own hands had made.[e]

[42]"When God saw what they had done, he turned away from them and handed them over to the worship of the stars of heaven,[f] as recorded in the prophetic writings:[g]

> **People of Israel, you failed to worship me**
> **When you offered animal sacrifices**
> **For forty years in the wilderness.**
> **[43]Instead you worshipped the god Moloch,[h]**
> **And you carried his tabernacle, not mine.**
> **You worshipped your star-god, Rephan.[i]**
> **You made idols with your hands**
> **And worshipped them instead of me.**
> **So now I will cast you into exile beyond Babylon.**

[44]"God gave Moses the revelation of the pattern of the tabernacle of the testimony. By God's command, he made it exactly according to the specifications

---

a 7:37 As translated from the Aramaic. See Deuteronomy 18:15.
b 7:38 Or "Moses is the one who was in the church in the wilderness."
c 7:38 Implied in the context.
d 7:40 The Aramaic is "We don't know who this Moses is." See Exodus 32:1 and 23.
e 7:41 Or "They had a party in honor of what their own hands had made."
f 7:42 This was in violation of Deuteronomy 4:19 and 17:2–5.
g 7:42 See Amos 5:25–27.
h 7:43 This was the Canaanite god of the sun and sky.
i 7:43 Or "Derphan," or "Remphan." This is the Assyrian deity also referred to as Saturn.

given to him for our ancestors in the wilderness. ⁴⁵The next generation received possession of it, and under Joshua's[a] leadership they took possession of the land of the nations, which God drove out in front of them. The tabernacle was carried about until ⁴⁶David found loving favor with God and prayed for a dwelling place for the God of Jacob, ⁴⁷but it was[b] Solomon who built him a house.

⁴⁸"However, the Most High God does not live in temples made by human hands, as the prophet said:[c]

> ⁴⁹"Heaven is my throne room and the earth
> Is but a footstool for my feet.
> How could you possibly build a house
> That could contain me?" says the Lord Yahweh.
> "And where could you find a place
> Where I could live?
> ⁵⁰Don't you know that it is my hands
> That have built my house,[d] not yours?"[e]

⁵¹"Why would you be so stubborn as to close your hearts and your ears to me? You are always opposing the Holy Spirit, just like your forefathers! ⁵²Which prophet was not persecuted and murdered by your ancestors? Name just one! They killed them all—even the ones who prophesied long ago of the coming of the Righteous One! Now you follow in their steps and have become his betrayers and murderers. ⁵³You have been given the law by the visitation[f] of angels, but you have not obeyed it."

Stephen Is Stoned to Death

⁵⁴When they heard these things, they were overtaken with violent rage filling their souls, and they gnashed their teeth at him. ⁵⁵But Stephen, overtaken with great faith,[g] was full of the Holy Spirit. He fixed his gaze into the heavenly realm

---

a 7:45 In Aramaic-Hebrew, the spelling of Joshua and Jesus is the same: Yeshua.
b 7:47 See 2 Chronicles 5:5.
c 7:48 See Isaiah 66:1–2.
d 7:50 Or "all these things."
e 7:50 Implied in the context.
f 7:53 As translated from the Aramaic. The Greek is "by angelic decrees."
g 7:55 As translated from the Aramaic.

and saw the glory and splendor of God—and Jesus, who stood up at the right hand of God.

[56]"Look!" Stephen said. "I can see the heavens opening and the Son of Man standing at the right hand of God to welcome me home!"[a]

[57]His accusers covered their ears with their hands and screamed at the top of their lungs to drown out his voice. [58]Then they pounced on him and threw him outside the city walls to stone him. His accusers, one by one, placed their outer garments at the feet of a young man named Saul of Tarsus.[b]

[59]As they hurled stone after stone at him, Stephen prayed, "Our Lord Jesus, accept my spirit into your presence." [60]Then he crumpled to his knees and shouted in a loud voice, "Our Lord, don't hold this sin against them."[c] And then he died.

a 7:56 Implied in the text. Jesus sits at the right hand of God, but when he saw Stephen give his last breath for the gospel, he stood to welcome his martyr into his eternal reward.
b 7:58 That is, Saul, who would be converted and become Paul the apostle. Stephen's graduation was Paul's initiation.
c 7:60 See Luke 23:34 and 46.

Eight

Saul Persecutes the Believers

¹Now, Saul agreed to be an accomplice to Stephen's stoning and participated in his execution. From that day on, a great persecution of the church in Jerusalem began. All the believers scattered into the countryside of Judea and among the Samaritans, except the apostles who remained behind in Jerusalem. ²God-fearing men gave Stephen a proper burial and mourned greatly over his death.

³Then Saul mercilessly persecuted the church of God, going from house to house into the homes of believers to arrest both men and women and drag them off to prison.

The Gospel Spreads to Samaria

⁴Although the believers were scattered by persecution, they preached the wonderful news of the word of God wherever they went. ⁵Philip traveled to a Samaritan city[a] and preached to them the wonderful news of the Anointed One. ⁶The crowds were eager to receive[b] Philip's message and were persuaded by the many miracles and wonders he performed. ⁷Many demon-possessed people were set free and delivered as evil spirits came out of them with loud screams and shrieks, and many who were lame and paralyzed were also healed.[c] ⁸This resulted in an uncontainable joy filling the city!

Simon the Sorcerer Converted

⁹Now, there was a man who lived there who was steeped in sorcery. For some time he had astounded the people of Samaria with his magic, boasting to be

---

a 8:5 Or "the main city of Samaria." Many believe this was the Samaritan city of Sebaste.
b 8:6 As translated from the Aramaic, which indicates they did more than just hear the good news; they silenced those who said anything against Philip's message.
c 8:7 Healings, miracles, and deliverances were being accomplished through others, not just the apostles.

someone great.[a] [10]Everyone, from the least to the greatest among them, was dazzled by his sorcery,[b] saying, "This man is the greatest wizard of all! The divine power of God walks among us!" [11]For many years everyone was in awe of him because of his astonishing displays of the magic arts.

[12]But as Philip preached the wonderful news of the kingdom realm of God, and the name of Jesus the Anointed One, many believed his message and were baptized, both men and women. [13]Even Simon believed and was baptized! Wherever Philip went, Simon was right by his side, astounded by all the miracles, signs, and enormous displays of power that he witnessed.

[14]When the apostles in Jerusalem heard that the Samaritans had accepted God's message of life, they sent Peter and John [15]to pray over them so that they would receive[c] the Holy Spirit. [16]For they had only been baptized into the name of the Lord Jesus and were yet to have the Holy Spirit fall upon them. [17]As soon as Peter and John arrived, they laid their hands on the Samaritan believers, one after another, and the Holy Spirit fell and filled each one of them![d]

[18]When Simon saw how the Holy Spirit was released through the laying on of the apostles' hands, he approached them and offered them money, [19]saying, "I want this power too. I'm willing to pay you for the anointing[e] that you have, so that I also can lay my hands on everyone to receive the Holy Spirit."

[20]Peter rebuked him and said, "Your money will go with you to destruction! How could you even think that you could purchase God's supernatural gift with money? [21]You will never have this gift or take part in this ministry,[f] for your heart is not right with God. [22]Repent this moment for allowing such wickedness to fill you. Plead with the Lord that perhaps he would forgive you the treachery of your heart. [23]For I discern that jealous envy[g] has poisoned you and binds you as a captive to sin."

[24]Simon begged, "Peter, please pray to God for me. Plead with him so that nothing you just said over me may come to pass!"

a 8:9 The Aramaic is "He boasted of himself, saying, 'I am the great god!'"
b 8:10 The Aramaic is "They were all praying to him" or "bowing down to him."
c 8:15 Or "take hold of the Holy Spirit."
d 8:17 Implied in the text. The Greek is "They took hold of the Holy Spirit." That is, the power of the Holy Spirit came upon them and filled them.
e 8:19 Or "authority."
f 8:21 Or "You have no part with us in this word (logos)." The Aramaic is "You have no portion in this faith."
g 8:23 Or "bitter anger."

Philip and the Ethiopian

²⁵After Peter and John had testified and taught the word of God in that city, they returned to Jerusalem, stopping at many Samaritan villages along the way to preach the hope of the gospel.ᵃ

²⁶Then the Lord's angel said to Philip, "Now go south from Jerusalem on the desert road to Gaza." ²⁷He left immediately on his assignment.

Along the way he encountered an Ethiopian who believed in the God of the Jews,ᵇ who was the minister of finance for Candace, queen of Ethiopia. He was on his way home from worshipping God in Jerusalem. ²⁸As he rode along in his chariot, he was reading from the scroll of Isaiah.

²⁹The Holy Spirit said to Philip, **"Go and walk alongside the chariot."**

³⁰So Philip ran to catch up. As he drew closer he overheard the man reading from the scroll of Isaiah the prophet. Philip asked him, "Sir, do you understand what you're reading?"

³¹The man answered, "How can I possibly make sense of this without someone explaining it to me?"ᶜ So he invited Philip up into his chariot to sit with him.

³²The portion from Isaiah he was reading was this:

> He was led away to the slaughter
> Like a lamb to be offered.
> He was like a lamb that is silent
> Before those who sheared him—
> He never even opened his mouth.
> ³³In his lowliness justice was stripped away from him.ᵈ
> And who could fully express his struggles?
> For his life was taken from the earth.ᵉ

³⁴The Ethiopian asked Philip, "Please, can you tell me who the prophet is speaking of? Is it himself or another man?"

---

a 8:25 As translated from the Aramaic.

b 8:27 Implied by the Aramaic word *mhymna*, a homonym that can mean "believer" or "eunuch." It is difficult to understand why a minister of finance would need to become a eunuch.

c 8:31 Or "unless someone guide me."

d 8:33 Which means he had no one there to defend him and stand up for justice.

e 8:33 As translated from the Aramaic. Both the Greek and the Aramaic are difficult to translate. The Greek is "Who can describe his posterity?" or "Who could describe the (evil) people of his time?" The Aramaic word for "struggles" (sufferings) and "generation" is the homonym *darreh*. See Isaiah 53:7–8.

³⁵Philip started with this passage and shared with him the wonderful message of Jesus.

³⁶As they were traveling down the road, the man said, "Look, here's a pool of water. Why don't I get baptized right now?"

³⁷Philip replied, "If you believe with all your heart, I'll baptize you."

The man answered, "I believe that Jesus is the Anointed One, the Son of God."[a]

³⁸The Ethiopian stopped his chariot, and they went down into the water[b] and Philip baptized him. ³⁹⁻⁴⁰When they came up out of the water, Philip was suddenly snatched up by the Spirit of the Lord and instantly carried away to the city of Ashdod,[c] where he reappeared, preaching the gospel in that city.

The man never saw Philip again. He returned to Ethiopia full of great joy. Philip, however, traveled on to all of the towns of that region, bringing them the good news, until he arrived at Caesarea.[d]

---

a 8:37 Although there is little manuscript evidence to include verse 37, it is found in one of the oldest Aramaic texts (Harklean Syriac Version, AD 616) and one Greek uncial from the eighth century. There is widespread consensus among scholars of both Greek and Aramaic texts that verse 37 was added as an ancient Christian confession of faith.

b 8:38 There was no need to go down into the water if it was a baptism of sprinkling. Phillip immersed the believing Ethiopian man in baptism.

c 8:39–40 Or "Azotus." This translation of Philip was an amazing miracle, as the city of Ashdod would have been fifteen miles or more from the desert road to Gaza. This miracle of being translated also took place with Ezekiel. See Ezekiel 3:12–15.

d 8:39–40 This prominent Roman city was also known as Caesarea by the Sea.

Nine

Saul Encounters Jesus

[1]During those days, Saul, full of angry threats and rage,[a] wanted to murder the disciples of the Lord Jesus. So he went to ask the high priest [2]and requested a letter of authorization he could take to the Jewish leaders in Damascus,[b] requesting their cooperation in finding and arresting any who were followers of the Way.[c] Saul wanted to capture all of the believers he found, both men and women, and drag them as prisoners back to Jerusalem. [3]So he obtained the authorization[d] and left for Damascus.

Just outside the city, a brilliant light flashing from heaven suddenly exploded all around him. [4]Falling to the ground, he heard a booming voice say to him, **"Saul, Saul, why are you persecuting me?"**[e]

[5-7]The men accompanying Saul were stunned and speechless, for they heard a heavenly voice but could see no one.

Saul replied, "Who are you, Lord?"

"I am Jesus, the Victorious,[f] **the one you are persecuting.**[g] **Now, get up and go into the city, where you will be told what you are to do."**

[8]Saul stood to his feet, and even though his eyes were open he could see nothing—he was blind. So the men had to take him by the hand and lead him into Damascus. [9]For three days he didn't eat or drink and couldn't see a thing.

---

a 9:1 As translated from the Aramaic.

b 9:2 Or "synagogues of Damascus."

c 9:2 The "Way" is Jesus Christ, the way that God dispenses himself into human beings. He lives inside of those who believe in him. See John 14:6.

d 9:3 Implied in the text.

e 9:4 To persecute the church is to persecute Jesus. He is one with his beloved church. See Zechariah 2:8.

f 9:5-7 As translated from the Aramaic, which uses the word *scion*. Although *scion* is often translated "branch (Nazarene)," it can also be mean "victorious" or "heir of a mighty family."

g 9:5-7 The Aramaic adds a line here that can be translated "Is it hard for you to rear up against a scorpion's stinger (or goads)?"

[10]Living in Damascus was a believer named Ananias. The Lord spoke to him in a vision, calling his name. **"Ananias."**

"Yes, Lord," Ananias answered.

[11-12]The Lord said, **"Go at once to the street called Abundance**[a] **and look for a man from Tarsus**[b] **named Saul. You will find him at Judah's house.**[c] **While he was praying,**[d] **he saw in a supernatural vision a man named Ananias**[e] **coming to lay hands upon him to restore his sight."**[f]

[13]"But Lord," Ananias replied, "many have told me about his terrible persecution of those in Jerusalem who are devoted to you.[g] [14]In fact, the high priest has authorized him to seize and imprison all those in Damascus who call on your name."

[15]The Lord Yahweh[h] answered him, **"Arise and go! I have chosen this man to be my special messenger.**[i] **He will be brought before kings, before many nations, and before the Jewish people to give them the revelation of who I am. **[16]**And I will show him how much he is destined to suffer**[j] **because of his passion for me."**

[17]Ananias left and found the house where Saul was staying. He went inside and laid hands on him, saying, "Saul, my brother, the Lord Jesus, who appeared to you on the road, has sent me to pray for you so that you might see again and be filled to overflowing with the Holy Spirit."

[18]All at once, the crusty substance that was over Saul's eyes disappeared

---

a 9:11-12 As translated from the Aramaic, or "Fat Street." The Greek is "Straight Street." As the straightest street in the city, this is the main east-west thoroughfare in Damascus, which is known today as Suk Meihat Pasha. Damascus, only 190 miles northeast of Jerusalem, currently has a population of twelve million and is considered to be the oldest continually inhabited city in the world. Many remnants of the Roman occupation, including two thirds of the walls of the city, can still be seen today. The conversion of Saul the legalist into Paul the grace preacher has a significant lesson for us. We can be amazingly wrong while thinking we are doing right. The Holy Spirit awakens our hearts to feast on Christ, our righteousness. Religion has a soporific effect on our hearts. Like Saul, we have to fall off our "high horse" and bite the dust before our blinded eyes can see.

b 9:11-12 Tarsus, or Cilicia, is in southeastern Turkey. Tarsus means "a basket." See verse 25.

c 9:11-12 Or "Judah's house." (Judah's house is the house of praise).

d 9:11-12 Made explicit from the text.

e 9:11-12 Ananias means "the Lord's gracious gift." He truly was the Lord's gracious gift to Paul, who was healed by God's gracious gift. The word *grace* is found 125 times in the New Testament, and Paul uses the word 120 times.

f 9:12 Ananias means "Yah is merciful." This is a wonderful play on words in the Aramaic, for God is about to show mercy to Saul and is asking Ananias to live up to his name.

g 9:13 Or "your holy ones."

h 9:15 As translated from the Aramaic word for Yahweh, *MarYah.*

i 9:15 Or "tool."

j 9:16 Or "experience."

and he could see perfectly. Immediately, he got up and was baptized. [19]After eating a meal,[a] his strength returned.[b]

[20]Within the hour[c] he was in the Jewish meeting houses, preaching about Jesus and proclaiming, "Jesus is the Son of God!"[d] [21]Those who heard him were astonished, saying among themselves, "Isn't this the Saul who furiously persecuted those in Jerusalem who called on the name of Jesus? Didn't he come here with permission from the high priest to drag them off and take them as prisoners?"

[22]Saul's power increased greatly as he became more and more proficient in proving that Jesus was the anointed Messiah. Saul remained there for several days with the disciples, even though it agitated the Jews of Damascus.

Saul Escapes from Damascus

[23]As time passed, the Jews plotted together to kill Saul, [24]but it was revealed to him what they were about to do. They closely guarded the gates of the city and tracked his every movement so they could kill him. [25]But during the night, some of Saul's converts helped him escape by lowering him down through an opening in the wall, hiding him in a woven basket.[e]

Saul Returns to Jerusalem

[26]When Saul arrived in Jerusalem, he attempted to introduce himself to the fellowship of the believers, but everyone was afraid of him because they doubted he was a true disciple. [27]Barnabas[f] came to his defense and brought him before the apostles. Saul shared with them his supernatural experience of seeing the Lord, who spoke with him on the road to Damascus. Barnabas also told them how boldly Saul preached throughout the city in Jesus' mighty name.

[28]Then they accepted him as a brother and he remained with them, joining them wherever they went in Jerusalem, boldly preaching in the power

a 9:19 Some Aramaic manuscripts add, "He accepted the message of salvation," or "He received the hope (of the kingdom)."
b 9:19 The clause "He remained with the disciples for several days" has been moved to verse 23 as a concluding statement of the narrative.
c 9:20 As translated from the Aramaic.
d 9:20 Or "This Man is the Son of God."
e 9:25 See 2 Corinthians 11:33.
f 9:27 See Acts 4:36–37.

and authority of Jesus.[a] [29]He openly debated with some of the Jews who had adopted the Greek culture,[b] yet they were secretly plotting to murder him. [30]When the believers discovered their scheme, they smuggled him out of the city and took him to Caesarea and then sent him on to Tarsus.[c]

[31]After this, the church all over Judea, Galilee, and Samaria experienced a season of peace. [d] The congregations grew larger and larger, with the believers being empowered and encouraged by the Holy Spirit. They worshipped God in wonder and awe,[e] and walked in the fear of the Lord.

Peter Heals Aeneas

[32]As Peter was ministering[f] from place to place, he visited God's devoted ones in the village of Lydda.[g] [33]He met a man there named Aeneas[h] who had been paralyzed and bedridden for eight years. [34]Peter said to him, "Aeneas, Jesus the Anointed One instantly and divinely heals you. Now, get up and make your bed."

[35]All at once he stood to his feet. And when all the people of Lydda and Sharon saw him, they became believers in the Lord.[i]

Peter Raises the Dead

[36]Now, there was a follower of Jesus who lived in Joppa. Her Aramaic name, Tabitha, means "gazelle."[j] She lived her life doing kind things for others and serving the poor. [37]But then she became very ill and died. After the disciples prepared her body for burial,[k] they laid her in an upstairs room.

---

a 9:28 Or "in the name of Jesus."
b 9:29 Or "Hellenist Jews." These were Jews who had adopted the Greek culture and language, as opposed to the orthodox Jews, who were strictly following Hebrew culture. The respected historian Josephus writes in AD 44, in his book of Jewish wars, that Greek was not the predominant language spoken in Israel. (See Antiquities xx, xi, 2.) The Hellenists were Jewish immigrants who had lived in Alexandria, Greece, and in Rome. They would have learned Greek culture and language as well as Hebrew.
c 9:30 Tarsus was a city in south-central Turkey, about ten miles from the Mediterranean coast. Saul's family originated from Tarsus, but he grew up in Jerusalem as an orthodox Jew.
d 9:31 The "church" in a region is mentioned here, "Judea, Galilee, and Samaria." Even though great cultural distinctions existed between them, the Holy Spirit had made them one church.
e 9:31 Implied in the Hebraic concept of "the fear of the Lord," which means more than just dread or terror. It also includes "to worship with awe."
f 9:32 Or "traveling."
g 9:32 Lydda (Aramaic, Lod) means "strife."
h 9:33 Aeneas means "praise." Praise had been paralyzed for eight years. Eight is the number of a new beginning.
i 9:35 Or "They turned to the Lord."
j 9:36 Or "Dorcas," which is the Greek word for "deer." The name Dorcas is also found in verse 39.
k 9:37 Or "washed her body." By implication they prepared her for burial.

³⁸When the believers heard that Peter was nearby in Lydda, they sent two men with an urgent message for him to come without delay. ³⁹So Peter went with them back to Joppa, and upon arriving they led him to the upper room.

There were many widows standing next to Peter, weeping. One after another showed him the tunics and other garments that Tabitha had made to bless others. ⁴⁰Peter made them all leave the room.^a Then he knelt down and prayed. Turning to the dead body, he said, "Gazelle, rise up!"

At once she opened her eyes, and seeing Peter, she sat up. ⁴¹He took her by the hand and helped her to her feet. Then he called for the believers and all the widows to come and see that she was alive!

⁴²The news spread all over the city of Joppa, and many believed in the Lord. ⁴³Peter remained in Joppa for several more days as a guest at the house of Simon the tanner.^b

---

a 9:40 The Greek word used here is *ekballo*, a strong word that can mean "drive out" or "cast out."
b 9:43 Or "Simon Berseus."

An Angel Comes to Cornelius

¹At that time there was a Roman military officer, Cornelius, who was in charge of one hundred men stationed in Caesarea. He was the captain of the Italian regiment,ᵃ ²a devout man of extraordinary character who worshipped God and prayed regularly, together with all his family. He also had a heart for the poor and gave generously to help them.

³One afternoon about three o'clock, he had an open vision and saw the angel of God appear right in front of him, calling out his name, "Cornelius!"

⁴Startled, he was overcome with fear by the sight of the angel. He asked, "What do you want, Lord?"

The angel said, "All of your prayers and your generosity to the poor have ascended before God as an eternal offering.ᵇ ⁵Now, send some men to Joppa at once. Have them find a man named Simon the Rock,ᶜ ⁶who is staying as a guest in the home of Simon the tanner, whose house is by the sea."

⁷After the angel left, Cornelius called for two of his servants and a trusted, godly soldier who was his personal attaché. ⁸He explained to them everything that had just happened and sent them off to Joppa.

Peter's Trance

⁹The next day around noon, as Cornelius's men were approaching Joppa, Peter went up to the flat roofᵈ of the house to pray. ¹⁰He was hungry and wanted to eat, but while lunch was being prepared he fell into a trance and entered

---

a 10:1 Cornelius was a centurion who was in charge of a sixth of a cohort of six hundred men. It seems likely that Cornelius was a Gentile who had converted to Judaism.
b 10:4 Or "as an offering that he remembers."
c 10:5 Or "Simon, who is also called Peter (Rock)."
d 10:9 This was common when the house was filled with smoke from the cooking fires.

into another realm.[a] [11]As the heavenly realm opened up, he saw something resembling a large linen tablecloth that descended from above, being let down to the earth by its four corners. [12]As it floated down he saw that it held many kinds of four-footed animals, reptiles, and wild birds.

[13]A voice said to him, **"Peter, go and prepare them to be eaten."**

[14]Peter replied, "There's no way I could do that, Lord, for I've never eaten anything forbidden or impure according to our Jewish laws."[b]

[15]The voice spoke again. **"Nothing is unclean if God declares it to be clean."**[c]

[16]The vision was repeated three times.[d] Then suddenly the linen sheet was snatched back up into heaven.

[17]Peter was so stunned by the vision that he couldn't stop wondering about what all it meant.

Meanwhile, Cornelius's men had learned where Peter was staying and at that same moment were standing outside the gate.

[18]They called out to those in the house, "Is this where Simon, the Rock, is staying?"[e]

[19-20]As Peter was in deep thought, trying to interpret the vision, the Spirit said to him, **"Go downstairs now, for three men are looking for you. Don't hesitate to go with them,**[f] **because I have sent them."**

[21]Peter went downstairs to the men and said, "I believe I'm the one you're looking for. What brings you here?"

[22]They answered, "We serve Cornelius, a Roman military captain, who sent us to find you. He is a devout man of the highest integrity who worships[g] God and is respected throughout the Jewish community. He was divinely instructed

---

a 10:10 The Greek word for "trance" (ekstasis, from which we get the word ecstasy) literally means "to be taken to another place (state or realm)." See Strong's concordance 1611. He was actually taken into another realm as a trance came over him.

b 10:14 Implied in the context.

c 10:15 Or "purified." The meaning of this spiritual vision is this: God has declared every human being to be of special worth and dignity. The entire world needs the gospel. The four corners of the large tablecloth represent the four corners of the earth. The clean animals represent God's people, the Jews, and the unclean speak of the non-Jewish nations. This encounter helped Peter understand that God was about to send him off with the men who were at the door of the house, even though their religion had been labeled "unclean."

d 10:16 Peter's history contains a number of threes. Peter denied he knew Jesus three times, the Lord restored Peter by challenging his love three times, and here we have the vision repeated three times.

e 10:18 Or "Peter."

f 10:20 Or "Don't let prejudice keep you from going with them." The Aramaic is literally "Don't be divided (in your soul)."

g 10:22 Or "fears God."

through the appearance of an angel to summon you to his home and to listen to the message that you would bring him."

²³Peter invited them to stay for the night as his guests. The next morning they departed, accompanied by some of the believers from Joppa.

²⁴The next day they arrived in Caesarea, where Cornelius was waiting anxiously for them and had gathered together all of his relatives and close friends. ²⁵The moment Peter walked in the door, Cornelius fell at his feet to worship him. ²⁶But Peter pulled him to his feet and said, "Stand up, for I'm only a man and no different from you."

²⁷They talked together and then went inside, where Peter found a large gathering waiting to hear his words.[a]

²⁸Peter said to them, "You all know that it is against the Jewish laws for me to associate with or even visit the home of one who is not a Jew. Yet God has shown me that I should never view anyone as inferior[b] or ritually unclean. ²⁹So when you sent for me, I came without objection.[c] Now, may I ask why you sent for me?"

³⁰Cornelius replied, "Four days ago I was fasting[d] and praying here in my home at this very hour, three o'clock in the afternoon, when a man in glistening clothing suddenly appeared in front of my eyes. ³¹He said, 'Cornelius, God has heard your prayers. Your generosity to the poor[e] has been recorded and remembered in God's presence. ³²However, you must send for a man named Simon, the Rock, who is staying in Joppa as a guest of Simon the tanner, who lives by the sea.' ³³So I immediately sent my men to bring you here—and you were kind enough to come. And now, here we are, all of us in God's presence, anxious to hear the message that God has put into your heart to share with us."

³⁴Peter said, "Now I know for certain that God doesn't show favoritism with people[f] but treats everyone on the same basis.[g] ³⁵It makes no difference

---

a 10:27 Implied in the context.
b 10:28 Or "forbidden."
c 10:29 The Aramaic is "I was destined to come to you."
d 10:30 As translated from the Aramaic. The Greek has no mention of Cornelius fasting.
e 10:31 The Aramaic is "Your acts of righteousness are offerings before God."
f 10:34 The Aramaic is "God is not the God of hypocrites."
g 10:34 Implied in the text. The Greek is "God is not one who receives masks (faces)." God doesn't treat us according to externalities but according to what is in our hearts.

what race of people one belongs to. If they show deep reverence for God, and are committed to doing what's right, they are acceptable before him. ³⁶God sent his word to the Jewish people first,ᵃ announcing the wonderful news of hope and peaceᵇ through Jesus, the Anointed One, the Lord of all.ᶜ ³⁷You are well aware of all that began in Galilee and spread throughout the land of Israel immediately after John preached his message of baptism.

³⁸"Jesus of Nazareth was anointed by God with the Holy Spirit and with great power. He did wonderful things for others and divinely healed all who were under the tyranny of the Devil,ᵈ for God's manifest presence rested upon him.ᵉ ³⁹We apostles were eyewitnesses to all the miraclesᶠ that he performed throughout the land of Israel. Finally, in Jerusalem, he was crucified on a cross,ᵍ ⁴⁰but God raised him from the dead three days later, allowing him to be seen openly.ʰ ⁴¹He didn't appear to everyone, but he appeared to us, his chosen witnesses. He actually ate and drank with usⁱ after he rose from the dead!ʲ

⁴²"Jesus ordered us to preach and warn the peopleᵏ that God had appointed him to be the judge of the living and the dead. ⁴³And not only us,ˡ but all of the prophets agree in their writings that everyone who believes in him receives complete forgivenessᵐ of sins through the power of his name."

The Holy Spirit Falls

⁴⁴While Peter was speaking, the Holy Spirit cascaded over all those listening to his message. ⁴⁵The Jewish brothers who had accompanied Peter were astounded that the gift of the Holy Spirit was poured out on people who

---

a 10:36 The Aramaic is "For the Manifestation [Living Expression] was the inheritance of the Jewish people."
b 10:36 Or by inference, "peace with God through Jesus Christ." Only the Aramaic has "hope and peace."
c 10:36 The Aramaic is "who is Master Yahweh of all." That is, Jesus is Lord, not just for the Jewish people but for all people groups. The Aramaic is "who is Master Yahweh of all."
d 10:38 The Greek word for "Devil" can also be translated "slanderer-liar."
e 10:38 The Aramaic is "God was within him."
f 10:39 Or "things." By inference, the miracles of healing and deliverance.
g 10:39 Or "hung him on a tree and killed him." See Deuteronomy 21:23.
h 10:40 As translated from the Aramaic.
i 10:41 The word sumpino means "to drink together" and can be used figuratively. It is used only here in the New Testament and refers to being refreshed by drinking the after-dinner wine together. Jesus celebrated with his disciples after his resurrection. He still longs to celebrate with us today.
j 10:41 See Luke 24:35–49.
k 10:42 Or "He commanded us to tell everyone the command."
l 10:43 Implied in the text.
m 10:43 Or "cancellation."

weren't Jews, [46]for they heard them speaking in supernaturally given languages and passionately praising God.[a]

[47]Peter said, "How could anyone object to these people being baptized? For they have received the Holy Spirit just as we have." [48]So he instructed them to be baptized in the power of the name of Jesus, the Anointed One.

After their baptism, they asked Peter to stay with them for a few more days.[b]

---

a 10:46 This is the Gentile Pentecost as the Holy Spirit fell on Gentile believers for the first time, imparting to them the gift of tongues.
b 10:48 At last the gospel broke through and penetrated into the non-Jewish cultures and people groups. The Holy Spirit was now uniting Jewish believers and non-Jewish believers into one mystical body of Christ on the earth. Because of this there would no longer be a distinction between Jew and non-Jew, but one family of believers is formed by faith in Jesus Christ. See Galatians 3:26–29. The three conversions of the Ethiopian dignitary in chapter 8, Saul of Tarsus in chapter 9, and the Roman officer Cornelius in chapter 10 prove the power of the gospel of God. These three represent all of the sons of Noah: Ham (Ethiopian), Shem (Saul), and Japheth (the Roman Cornelius). A black man, a Jew, and a Gentile were converted!

Eleven

Ethnic Barriers Broken

[1]The news traveled fast and soon reached the apostles and the believers living in Judea that non-Jewish people were also receiving God's message of new life.[a] [2]When Peter finally arrived in Jerusalem, the Jewish believers called him to task, saying, [3]"Why did you stay in the home of people who aren't Jewish? You even ate your meals with them!"

[4]Peter explained what had happened, saying, [5]"One day when I was in the city of Joppa, while I was praying I fell into an ecstatic trance and I went into another realm.[b] I saw in a vision something like a linen tablecloth descending out of heaven, being let down by its four corners, and it got close to me. [6]As I examined it I saw many four-footed animals, wild animals, reptiles, and wild birds. [7]Then I heard a voice say to me, **'Get up, Peter. Kill and eat them.'**

[8]"I said, 'I can't do that, Lord! For I've never eaten anything that is forbidden or impure according to our Jewish laws.'

[9]"The voice spoke to me again, saying, **'Nothing is unclean if God declares it to be clean.'**

[10]"The vision repeated itself three times. Then suddenly the linen sheet was snatched back up into heaven. [11]At that moment three men from Caesarea, who had been sent for me, approached the house where I was staying. [12]The Spirit told me to accompany them with no questions asked. These six brothers here with me made the trip, and we entered into the home of the man who had sent for me. [13]He shared with us about the angel who appeared to him and told him to send messengers to Joppa to find Simon, the Rock. The angel had told him, [14]'He will tell you and your family the message of how you can be saved!'

a   11:1 Implied in the text.
b   11:5 See footnote on 10:10.

[15]"Shortly after I began to speak, the Holy Spirit was poured out upon them, just like what happened to us at the beginning. [16]And I remembered the words the Lord had told us: **'John immersed you in water, but you will be immersed in the Holy Spirit.'** [17]So I concluded that if God is pleased to give them the same gift of the Holy Spirit that he gave us after they believed in the Lord Jesus Christ, who am I to stand in the way of God?"

[18]When they heard this, their objections were put to rest and they all glorified God, saying, "Look what God has done! He's giving the gift of repentance that leads to life to people who aren't even Jews."

The Church at Antioch

[19]Because of the persecution triggered by Stephen's death in Jerusalem, many of the believers were scattered. Some reached as far as the coast of Lebanon,[a] the island of Cyprus, and Antioch of Syria, but they were still only preaching the word to Jews. [20]However, some of the believers from Cyprus and Cyrene,[b] who had come to Antioch in Syria,[c] preached to the non-Jews living there, proclaiming the message of salvation in the Lord Jesus.[d] [21]The mighty power of the Lord was with them as they ministered, and a large number of people believed and turned their hearts to the Lord.

[22]News of what was happening in Antioch reached the church of Jerusalem, so the apostles sent Barnabas to Antioch as their emissary. [23]When he got there and witnessed for himself God's marvelous grace, he was enthused and overjoyed. He encouraged[e] the believers to remain faithful and cling to the Lord with passionate hearts.[f] [24]Barnabas was a good man,[g] full of the Spirit

---

a 11:19 Or "Phoenicia."
b 11:20 A city on the coast of Libya.
c 11:20 Antioch was important from both a commercial and a military point of view. It was the seat of the Roman governor-general, with large garrisons and military supplies stored there. It was also a center of art and culture, known for its beauty and recognized as the capital of the Syrian kingdom. The church prospered greatly in Antioch, and it became a Christian hub and headquarters for the apostles. For many centuries in church history, Antioch remained a strong witness for evangelization, sending missionaries into Persia and throughout the Roman Empire.
d 11:20 In the early days of the church, every believer was a missionary. There was a great cost involved with following Christ. They laid their lives down to serve him and to make him known among the nations. Not just the apostles, but all of the believers did their part in spreading the teachings of Jesus wherever they went.
e 11:23 Barnabas was given the nickname "Encourager." See Acts 4:36–37.
f 11:23 The Aramaic is "He begged them to imitate the Lord with all their hearts."
g 11:24 The Aramaic is "He was a blessed man."

of holiness, and he exuded a life of faith. Because of his ministry even more crowds of people were brought to the Lord!

²⁵Barnabas left for Tarsus to find Saul and bring him back to Antioch. ²⁶Together Saul and Barnabas ministered there for a full year, equipping the growing church and teaching the vast number of new converts. It was in Antioch that the followers of Jesus were first revealed as "anointed ones."ᵃ

Agabus Prophesies a Coming Famine

²⁷At that time there were prophets in the church of Jerusalem, and some of them came to Antioch. ²⁸One of them, named Agabus, stood up in one of the meetings and prophesied by the Holy Spirit that a severe famine was about to come over Israel. (This prophecy was fulfilled during the reign of Claudius Caesar.)ᵇ ²⁹So they determined that each believer, according to his or her ability, would give an offering to send as relief to the brothers living in Judea. ³⁰They set aside the gifts and entrusted the funds to Barnabas and Saul to take to the eldersᶜ of the church in Jerusalem.ᵈ

---

a 11:26 Or "Christians." The Greek word *chrematizo* means "supernaturally revealed (imparted)," more than simply "called." It was first in Antioch that the revelation came that the believers were anointed ones. See also Matthew 2:12, where the term is used as God giving revelation in a dream.

b 11:28 This would have been about AD 45–46.

c 11:30 The Aramaic is "priests."

d 11:30 Upon hearing the prophecy of a famine coming, the church of Antioch determined to receive an offering for the Judean believers, for the gospel came to them from Jerusalem. They gave back to the place where the gospel was sent to them.

$$Twelve$$

Peter's Miraculous Escape from Prison

[1]During this period King Herod[a] incited persecution against the church, causing great harm to the believers. [2]He even had the apostle James,[b] John's brother, beheaded.[c] [3-4]When Herod realized how much this pleased the Jewish leaders, he had Peter arrested and thrown into prison during the Feast of Passover.[d] Sixteen soldiers were assigned to guard him until Herod could bring him to public trial, immediately after the Passover celebrations were over. [5]The church went into a season of intense intercession,[e] asking God to free him.

[6]The night before Herod planned to bring him to trial, he made sure that Peter was securely bound with two chains. Peter was sound asleep between two soldiers, with additional guards stationed outside his cell door, [7]when all at once an angel of the Lord appeared, filling his prison cell with a brilliant light. The angel struck Peter on the side[f] to awaken him and said, "Hurry up! Let's go!" Instantly the chains fell off his wrists. [8]The angel told him, "Get dressed. Put on your sandals, bring your cloak, and follow me."

[9]Peter quickly left the cell and followed the angel, even though he thought it was only a dream or a vision, for it seemed unreal—he couldn't believe it was really happening! [10]They walked unseen past the first guard post and then the second before coming to the iron gate that leads to the city—and the gate swung open all by itself right in front of them!

They went out into the city and were walking down a narrow street when

---

a 12:1 Or "King Herod Agrippa."
b 12:2 According to the Gospels, James and John were the first two disciples of Jesus, and James was the first apostle to be martyred.
c 12:2 Or "executed by the sword."
d 12:4 These events most likely took place in AD 42 or 43.
e 12:5 The Greek phrase used here for intense intercession means "to stretch tightly in prayer."
f 12:7 The word translated "struck" is the same Greek word used for Jesus being "struck" for our sins (Matthew 26:31). Jesus was pierced in his side to awaken hearts to God. Peter was awakened from his sleep by an angel who struck him on his side.

all of a sudden the angel disappeared. [11]That's when Peter realized that he wasn't having a dream! He said to himself, "This is really happening! The Lord sent his angel to rescue me from the clutches of Herod and from what the Jewish leaders planned to do to me."

[12]When he realized this, he decided to go to the home of Mary[a] and her son John Mark. The house was filled with people praying. [13]When he knocked on the door to the courtyard, a young servant girl named Rose[b] got up to see who it was. [14]When she recognized Peter's voice, she was so excited that she forgot to open the door, but ran back inside the house to announce, "Peter is standing outside!"

[15]"Are you crazy?" they said to her. But when she kept insisting, they answered, "Well, it must be his angel."

[16]Meanwhile, Peter was still outside, knocking on the door. When they finally opened it, they were shocked to find Peter standing there.

[17]He signaled for them to be quiet as he shared with them the miraculous way the Lord brought him out of prison. Before he left he said, "Make sure you let James[c] and all of the other believers know what has happened."

[18]At the first sign of daylight, the prison guards were in a tremendous uproar because of Peter's disappearance.[d] Herod ordered a thorough search for him, but no one could find him. [19]After he interrogated the guards, he ordered them executed. Then Herod left the province of Judea for Caesarea and stayed there for a period of time.

[20]Now, during those days, Herod was engaged in a violent dispute with the people of Tyre and Sidon.[e] So they sent a united delegation to Caesarea to appeal to him and reconcile their differences[f] with the king, for Herod controlled their food supply. First they enlisted the support of his trusted personal assistant, Blastus, who secured them an appointment with the king.

[21]On the chosen day, Herod came before them, arrayed in his regal robes. Sitting on his elevated throne, he delivered a stirring public address to

---

a 12:12 This Mary was the sister of Barnabas. See Colossians 4:10.

b 12:13 Or "Rhoda."

c 12:17 This was James, the brother of Jesus.

d 12:18 This is the last mention of Peter in the book of Acts. The remaining chapters focus on the ministry of Paul.

e 12:20 Tyre and Sidon are coastal cities in Lebanon, north of Israel.

f 12:20 The Aramaic can also be translated "They wanted cultivated land," which makes sense if their food supply was running out.

the people. [22]At its conclusion the people gave him a round of applause. The crowd shouted, "These are the words of a god, not a man!"

[23]Immediately, an angel of the Lord struck Herod with a sickness, an infestation of worms, because he accepted the people's worship and didn't give the glory to God, and he died. [24]But the hope of God's kingdom[a] kept spreading and multiplying everywhere!

[25]After Barnabas and Saul had delivered the charitable offering for relief,[b] they left Jerusalem, bringing with them a disciple named Mark (who was also known as John).[c]

---

a 12:24 As translated from the Aramaic. The Greek is "the word."
b 12:25 Implied in the context.
c 12:25 This is the Mark who wrote the second gospel included in our New Testament. John (or Yochanan) was his Jewish name; Marcus was his Roman name. Because he once abandoned Paul during a missionary journey, Paul refused to take him with him again. But later, Mark and Paul were fully restored in their ministry together. See 2 Timothy 4:11.

Thirteen

Saul and Barnabas Sent Out as Apostles

¹In the church at Antioch there were a number of prophets and teachers of the word, including Barnabas, Simeon from Niger,[a] Lucius the Libyan, Manean (the childhood companion of King Herod Antipas),[b] and Saul. ²While they were worshipping as priests[c] before the Lord in prayer and fasting, the Holy Spirit said,[d] **"I have called Barnabas and Saul to do an important work for me. Now, release them[e] to go and fulfill it."** ³So after they had fasted and prayed, they laid hands on them and sent them off.[f]

⁴⁻⁵So Saul and Barnabas, and their assistant Mark (known as John), were directed by the Holy Spirit to go to Seleucia,[g] and from there they sailed to Cyprus.[h] When they arrived at Salamis,[i] they went to the Jewish meeting houses and preached the manifestation of our Lord.[j] ⁶From there they crossed the island as far as Paphos,[k] where they encountered a Jewish false prophet, a sorcerer named Elymas,[l] who also went by name of "son of Jesus."[m] ⁷He

---

a 13:1 The Aramaic word *Niger* means "someone who works with wood, a carpenter." The Latin word *Niger* means "black."

b 13:1 Or "who was like a brother to Herod the tetrarch."

c 13:2 Or "serving the Lord." The Greek word used here is also used for priestly duties.

d 13:2 Here we see the Lord of the Harvest, the Holy Spirit, sending out laborers into the harvest field. The Holy Spirit speaks in many different ways. Perhaps he spoke a prophecy through one of the prophets in the church, or a divine voice may have interrupted their worship. God's Spirit still speaks today in any way he chooses.

e 13:2 Or "appoint them." The Greek word used here is found in the Septuagint of Numbers 8:11 for consecrating Levites for God's service as priests.

f 13:3 Or "dispatched them" (a military term). This was the commissioning of Barnabas and Saul as apostles. The word *apostle* means "sent one." They were sent by the Holy Spirit and by the church and released as missionaries. The New Testament shows there were many other apostles besides the Twelve. See also Ephesians 4:11–13.

g 13:4-5 Implied in the text. Seleucia (modern-day Samandag) was a coastal city in Syria from which Paul and Barnabas left with John Mark for their first missionary journey in AD 49. Seleucia means "white light."

h 13:4-5 Cyprus was the home of Barnabas.

i 13:4-5 Salamis is a city on the southeastern coast of Cyprus. Salamis means "in the middle of salty water."

j 13:4–5 As translated from the Aramaic. The Greek is "the word of God."

k 13:6 Paphos is a city on the southwestern coast of Cyprus. *Paphos* means "boiling hot."

l 13:6 Or "spiritual advisor." The Greek word *magos* is often translated "astrologer." Although the text does not give us his name, Elymas, until verse 8, it is included here for the sake of the English narrative.

m 13:6 Or "Bar-Jesus" (son of Joshua). The Aramaic is "Bar-Shuma."

had gained influence as the spiritual advisor to the regional governor, Sergius Paulus, considered by many to be a wise and intelligent leader. The governor requested a meeting with Barnabas and Saul because he wanted to hear the message of God's word.[a] [8]But Elymas, whose name means "sorcerer,"[b] stood up against them and tried to prevent the governor from believing their message.

[9]Saul, also known as Paul,[c] stared into his eyes and rebuked him. Filled with the Holy Spirit, he said, [10]"You son of the Devil![d] You are full of every form of fraud and deceit and an enemy of all that is right. When will you stop perverting the truth of God into lies? [11]At this very moment the hand of God's judgment comes down upon you and you will be blind—so blind you won't even be able to see the light of the sun."[e]

As Paul spoke these words, a shadowy mist[f] and darkness came over the sorcerer, leaving him blind and groping about, begging someone to lead him around by the hand. [12]When the governor witnessed this, he believed and was awestruck by the power of the message of the Lord.

Paul and Barnabas at Antioch in Turkey

[13]Paul and his companions sailed from the Cyprus port of Paphos to Perga in southern Turkey.[g] John left them[h] there and returned to Jerusalem [14]as they journeyed on to the city of Antioch in the region of Pisidia.[i]

On the Sabbath they went into the Jewish meeting house and took their seats. [15]After the reading from the scrolls of the books of Moses and the prophets, the leader of the meeting[j] sent Paul and Barnabas a message, saying,

---

a 13:7 The Aramaic can be translated "the Manifestation of God."
b 13:8 The Aramaic name Elymas means "magician or sorcerer." This would be similar to the Arabic name Alumas, which also means "magician."
c 13:9 From here on in Acts, Saul is only referred to as Paul. Saul means "sought after," and Paul means "little." The name change is descriptive of what happened within Paul, leaving behind greatness in his own eyes and being content to be insignificant. This is the journey every believer must take.
d 13:10 Or "son of the accuser."
e 13:11 The Aramaic is "until the end of the age."
f 13:11 The Aramaic can be translated "gloom."
g 13:13 Or "Pamphylia," which may mean "a place of mingled races." It is a region in southern Turkey.
h 13:13 The sudden departure of John from the team became an issue between Paul and Barnabas. See Acts 15:36–39.
i 13:14 Antioch in the region of Pisidia is situated in the Sultandag Mountains about one hundred miles north of Perga. This would have been an arduous journey from the sea into the mountains. God was directing his missionaries where to go.
j 13:15 Or "president of the synagogue."

"Brothers, do you have a word of encouragement to share with us? If so, please feel free to give it."

¹⁶Paul stood and motioned that he had something to say. He said, "Listen, all of you Jews and non-Jews who worship God. ¹⁷The God of Israel divinely chose our ancestors to be his people. While they were enslaved in Egypt, he made them great, both in numbers and in strength, until he unveiled his mighty power and led them out of bondage.ᵃ ¹⁸For nearly forty years, he nourished them in the wilderness.ᵇ ¹⁹He was the one who destroyed the seven nations inhabiting the land of Canaanᶜ and afterward gave the land to his people as their inheritance. ²⁰This took about four hundred and fifty years.ᵈ

"Then God raised up deliverers for the people until the time of the prophet Samuel. ²¹The people craved for a king, so God gave them one from the tribe of Benjamin: Saul, the son of Kish, who ruled for forty years. ²²After removing him, God raised up David to be king, for God said of him, **'I have found in David, son of Jesse, a man who always pursues my heart**ᵉ **and will accomplish all that I have destined him to do.'**ᶠ

²³"From David's lineage God brought Israel a Savior, just as he promised. ²⁴ So before Jesus appeared, John preached the message of a baptism of repentanceᵍ to prepare all of Israel. ²⁵As John was about to finish his mission, he said repeatedly, 'If you think that I am the one to come, you're mistaken. He will come after me, and I don't even deserve to stoop down and untie his sandals!'

²⁶"Fellow Jews, Abraham's descendants, and all those among you who worship and reverence God, this Manifestation of Lifeʰ has been sent for us all to hear. ²⁷But the people of Jerusalem and their leaders didn't realize who he was, nor did they understand the prophecies written of him. Yet they fulfilled those very prophecies, which they read week after week in their meetings, by condemning him to death. ²⁸Even though they could come up with no legal

a 13:17 See Exodus 6:6 and 12:51.
b 13:18 As translated from the Aramaic and some Greek manuscripts. See also Exodus 16:35 and Numbers 14:34.
c 13:19 See Deuteronomy 7:1.
d 13:20 There is much debate over where this clause fits. It is possible that it would go with the next sentence, "For four hundred and fifty years God raised up deliverers."
e 13:22 See 1 Samuel 13:14 and Psalm 89:19–29.
f 13:22 Or "He will do all my pleasure."
g 13:24 The Aramaic is "the baptism of grace."
h 13:26 As translated from the Aramaic. The Greek is, "the message of salvation." See Psalm 107:20.

grounds for the death sentence, they pleaded with Pilate to have him executed. [29]And they did to him all that was prophesied they would do.

"Then they took him down from the cross and laid him in a tomb. [30]But God raised him from the dead! [31]And for many days afterward he appeared on numerous occasions to his disciples who knew him well and had followed him from Galilee to Jerusalem. Those disciples are now his witnesses,[a] telling the people the truth about him.

[32]"So here we are to share with you some wonderful news! The promise God made to our forefathers [33]has now been fulfilled for us, their children. For God has raised Jesus from the dead, as it says in Psalm 2:

Today I reveal you as my Son, and I as your Father.[b]

[34]"God had promised to not let him decay in the tomb or face destruction again, so God raised him from the dead. He gave this promise in the Psalms:

I will give to you[c] **what I gave to David:**
Faithful mercies[d] **that you can trust.**[e]

[35]"He explains it further in another Psalm:

You will not allow your holy one
To experience bodily decay.[f]

[36]"This cannot be a reference to David, for after he passionately served God's desires for his generation, he died. He was buried with his ancestors and his body experienced decay. [37]But the one whom God raised from the dead has never experienced corruption in any form.

[38]"So listen, friends! Through this Jesus, the forgiveness[g] of sins is offered to you. [39]Everyone who believes in him is set free from sin and guilt—something

---

a 13:31 The Greek word for "witnesses" can also be translated "martyrs."
b 13:33 See Psalm 2:7.
c 13:34 The Greek is plural, "you all," or "to you and yours."
d 13:34 Or "decrees." See Isaiah 55:3.
e 13:34 The Aramaic is "I will give to you the grace (favor) I gave to faithful David."
f 13:35 See Psalm 16:10.
g 13:38 Or "cancellation."

the law of Moses had no power to do. [40]So be very careful that what the prophets warned about does not happen to you:

> [41]**Be amazed and in agony, you scoffers!**[a]
> **For in your day I will do something so wonderful**
> **That when I perform mighty deeds among you,**
> **You won't even believe that it was I who did it!"**[b]

[42]As Paul and Barnabas started to leave, the people pleaded with them to
share more about these things on the next Sabbath day. [43]When the meeting
had finally broken up, many of those in attendance, both Jews and converts
to Judaism, tagged along with Paul and Barnabas, who continued to persuade
them to go deeper in their understanding of God's grace.

[44]The following week, nearly everyone in the city gathered to hear the
word of God. [45]When the Jewish leaders saw the size of the crowds, vicious
jealousy filled their hearts and they rose up to oppose what Paul was teaching.
They insulted him[c] and argued with him over everything he said.

[46]Yet Paul and Barnabas did not back down. Filled with courage, they boldly
replied, "We were compelled to bring God's Manifestation[d] first to you Jews.
But seeing you've rejected this message and refuse to embrace eternal life,[e] we
will focus instead on the nations and offer it to them. [47]This will fulfill what the
Lord has commanded us:

> **I have destined you to become**
> **A beacon light for the nations**
> **And release salvation to the ends of the earth!"**[f]

[48]When the non-Jewish people in the crowd heard these words, they were
thrilled and they honored[g] the word of the Lord. All who believed that they

---

a 13:41 As translated from the Aramaic. The Greek is "Be amazed and perish, you scoffers."
b 13:41 As translated from the Aramaic. The Greek text seems to quote from the Septuagint version of Habakkuk 1:5, "I am doing a
   work in your days that you won't believe even when it is announced to you."
c 13:45 Or "blasphemed."
d 13:46 Or "word."
e 13:46 Or "You view yourselves as unworthy of eternal life."
f 13:47 See Isaiah 42:6, 49:6, and 60:1–3.
g 13:48 Or "praised."

were destined to experience eternal life received the message.[a] ⁴⁹God's word spread like wildfire throughout the entire region.

⁵⁰The Jewish leaders stirred up a violent mob against Paul and Barnabas, including many prominent and wealthy people of the city. They persecuted them and ran them out of town. ⁵¹As they left, they shook the dust off their feet as a sign of protest against them, and they went on to the city of Iconium.[b] ⁵²They left the new coverts in Antioch overflowing with the joy of the Holy Spirit.

Fourteen

Miracles and Revival in Iconium

¹When Paul and Barnabas arrived at Iconium, the same thing happened there. They went, as they always did, to the Jewish meeting house and preached to the people with such power that a large crowd of both Jews and non-Jews believed.

²Some of the Jews refused to believe, and they began to poison the minds[a] of the non-Jews to discredit the believers. ³Yet Paul and Barnabas stayed there for a long time, preaching boldly and fearlessly about the Lord.[b] Many trusted in the Lord and backed up his message[c] of grace[d] with miracles, signs, and wonders performed by the apostles.

⁴The people of the city were split over the issue. Some sided with the apostles, and others with the Jews who refused to believe.[e] ⁵Eventually, all the opposition factions came together, with their leaders devising a plot[f] to harm Paul and Barnabas and stone them to death. ⁶When the apostles learned about this,[g] they escaped to the region of Lycaonia,[h] to the cities of Lystra[i] and Derby[j] and the nearby villages. ⁷And they continued to preach the hope of the gospel.[k]

---

a   14:2 Or "embittered their souls."
b   14:3 The Aramaic uses the phrase "the Lord Yahweh," referring to Jesus Christ.
c   14:3 The Aramaic is "manifestation of grace."
d   14:3 The Greek word for grace, *charis*, means "that which brings delight, joy, pleasure, and sweetness." See Strong's concordance 5485.
e   14:4 Implied in the text.
f   14:5 The Aramaic is "They issued a decree (death sentence)."
g   14:6 Although not clearly stated, it is possible that it was by supernatural revelation that Paul and Barnabas learned of the plot to kill them.
h   14:6 Lyconia means "land of the wolf."
i   14:6 Lystra means "ransomed" or "set free."
j   14:6 Derbe means "tanner" or "one who covers with skins." The journey from Iconium to these cities would have been about thirty-five kilometers.
k   14:7 As translated from the Aramaic. The Greek is "the good news."

Paul and Barnabas Preach at Lystra

[8]In Lystra, Paul and Barnabas encountered a man who from birth had never walked, for he was crippled in his feet. [9]He listened carefully to Paul as he preached. All of a sudden,[a] Paul discerned that this man had faith in his heart to be healed.[b] [10]So he shouted, "You! In the name of our Lord Jesus,[c] stand up on your feet!" The man instantly jumped to his feet, stood for the first time in his life, and walked!

[11]When the crowds saw the miracle Paul had done, they shouted in their own language,[d] "The gods have come down to us as men!" [12]They addressed Barnabas as "Zeus"[e] and Paul as "Hermes,"[f] because he was the spokesman.

[13]Now, outside of the city stood the temple of Zeus. The priest of the temple, in order to honor Paul and Barnabas, brought bulls with wreaths of flowers draped on them to the gates of the courtyard where they were staying.[g] The crowds clamored to offer them as sacrifices to the apostles. He even brought flower wreaths as crowns to place on their heads.

[14]When the apostles[h] understood what was happening, they were mortified and tore their clothes as a sign of dismay. They rushed into the crowd and shouted, [15]"People, what are you doing? We're only weak human beings like everyone else. This is why we've come to tell you the good news, so that you would turn away from these worthless myths[i] and turn to the living God. He is the Creator of all things: the earth, the heavens, the sea, and everything they contain. [16]In previous generations he allowed the nations to pursue their own

---

a 14:9 There is an implication in the Greek that Paul was watching this man and waited until he saw faith rise in the man's heart for his healing.

b 14:9 The same phrase, "to be healed," is consistently translated elsewhere in the New Testament as "to be saved." To be saved and to be healed are synonymous.

c 14:10 As translated from the Aramaic. This clause is absent in the Greek.

d 14:11 That is, the Lyconian language.

e 14:12 The Aramaic is "the master of deities," and the Latin is "Jupiter." Also found in verse 13.

f 14:12 Hermes was considered to be the messenger god, whom the Romans called Mercury. In Ovid's famous story *Metamorphoses*, there is an account of Philemon and Baucis from Lystra, who took in two strangers (Zeus and Hermes) and welcomed them into their homes. But the rest of the village rejected them, and for that the village was destroyed—only Philemon and Baucis survived. That story was no doubt in the minds of the people when they welcomed Barnabas and Paul. They did not want to make the same mistake as their ancestors. (See Ovid, *Metamorphoses* 8.611–725.) Archeologists have found a stone altar near Lystra with an inscription dedicating it to Zeus and Hermes.

g 14:13 As translated from the Aramaic. The Greek is ambiguous and could be "the gates of the temple" or "the gates of the city."

h 14:14 The book of Acts clearly states that there were more than twelve apostles who were recognized by the church. Barnabas is described multiple times as an apostle. Ephesians 4:11–13 says that apostles and prophets will minister and equip the body of Christ until we are complete and restored into Christ's fullness.

i 14:15 Implied in the text, which is simply "things."

ways, [17]yet he has never left himself without clear evidence of his goodness. For he blesses us with rain from heaven and seasons of fruitful harvests, and he nourishes us with food to meet our needs. He satisfies our lives, and euphoria[a] fills our hearts."

[18]Even after saying these things, they were barely able to restrain the people from offering sacrifices to them.

[19]Some of the Jews who had opposed Paul and Barnabas in Antioch and Iconium arrived and stirred up the crowd against them. They stoned Paul and dragged his body outside the city and left him for dead.

[20]When the believers encircled Paul's body, he was raised from the dead![b] Paul stood and immediately went back into the city. The next day he left with Barnabas for Derbe.

[21]After preaching the wonderful news of the gospel there and winning a large number of followers to Jesus, they retraced their steps and revisited Lystra, Iconium, and Antioch. [22]At each place they went, they strengthened the lives of the believers[c] and encouraged them to go deeper in their faith. And they taught them, "It is necessary for us to enter into the realm of God's kingdom, because that's the only way we will endure our many trials and persecutions."[d]

[23]Paul and Barnabas ordained leaders, known as elders, from among the congregations in every church they visited.[e] After prayer and fasting, they publicly committed them into the care and protection of the Lord of their faith.

[24]After passing through different regions of central Turkey,[f] [25]they went to the city of Perga, preaching the Manifestation of the Lord.[g] Afterward they journeyed down to the coast at Antalya,[h] [26]and from there they sailed back to Antioch.

---

a 14:17 See footnote on Acts 2:28.

b 14:20 The Greek word used here, *anistemi*, is consistently used in the New Testament for people being raised from the dead.

c 14:22 The Aramaic is "They confirmed their spirit of discipleship."

d 14:22 That is, the only way to avoid the oppression of the age is to enter deeper into God's kingdom realm. An alternate translation would be "Through great tribulation we enter into God's kingdom realm." Neither translation of this sentence implies a future kingdom, but a kingdom realm that is presently accessible.

e 14:23 The appointment of elders among the people dates back to the days of Moses in the wilderness. See Exodus 18:21, where the word used to describe these leaders is *khayil*, or "mighty men of valor." The word *khayil* is also used for the radiant church (commonly known as the "virtuous woman" found in Proverbs 31). These elders were the pastors and leaders of the churches, ordained by the apostles. See also Hebrews 13:17, 1 Timothy 3, and Titus 1.

f 14:24 Or "After they had passed through Pisidia, they went into Pamphylia."

g 14:25 Or "the Manifestation of Lord Yahweh," as translated from the Aramaic. The Greek is "the word of the Lord."

h 14:25 Or "Attalia." Antalya is a city on the southwestern coast of Turkey.

With their mission complete, they returned to the church where they had originally been sent out as missionaries, for it was in Antioch where they had been handed over to God's powerful grace. [27]When they arrived in Antioch, they gathered the church together and shared with them all of the wonderful works God had done through them and how God had opened the door of faith for the non-Jews to enter in. [28]Afterward, Paul and Barnabas stayed there for a long time in fellowship with the believers.[a]

---

a 14:28 This would have been AD 47–48, when Paul wrote his letter to the Galatians, the region they had visited during their first missionary journey. Antioch of Syria is here seen as the center of the missionary enterprise as the church hosts the anointed apostles Paul and Barnabas, who taught the church during their time there. For many centuries Antioch of Syria was considered a major Christian center. Into the fourth century, it was noted as having schools of theology and institutions of learning.

The Jerusalem Council of Apostles

¹While Paul and Barnabas were in Antioch, some false teachers[a] came from Judea to trouble the believers. They taught, "Unless you are circumcised, as the law of Moses requires, you cannot be saved." ²This sparked a fierce argument between the false teachers and Paul and Barnabas. So the church appointed a delegation of believers, including Paul and Barnabas, to go to Jerusalem to meet with the apostles and elders of the church and resolve this issue. ³So the church sent them on their way.

As they passed through Lebanon[b] and Samaria, they stopped to share with the believers how God was converting many from among the non-Jewish people.[c] Hearing this report brought great joy to all the churches.

⁴When they finally arrived in Jerusalem, Paul and Barnabas were welcomed by the church, the apostles, and the elders. They explained to them everything God had done among them. ⁵But some of the believers who were of the religious group called "separated ones"[d] were insistent, saying, "We must continue the custom of circumcision and require that the people keep[e] the law of Moses."

⁶So the apostles and elders met privately to discuss the matter further. ⁷After a lengthy debate, Peter rose to his feet and said to them, "Brothers, you know how God has chosen me[f] from the beginning to preach the wonderful

a 15:1 Implied in the context.
b 15:3 Or "Phoenicia."
c 15:3 The Aramaic is "the reconciliation of the Gentiles."
d 15:5 Or "Pharisees." The legalism of the Pharisees continued even among some believers, who were still bound in the expressions of external religion.
e 15:6 The Aramaic is "to put a fence around the Torah"; that is, to guard the Torah and keep it as a sacred duty to man. The apostolic council of Acts 15 makes it clear that Gentile believers had no obligation to keep that "fence" around the Torah (observing the Mosaic laws).
f 15:7 The wording of the Aramaic text is different, stating, "God chose the Gentiles from the beginning to hear the Manifestation of the gospel from my mouth and to believe."

news of the Manifestation to the non-Jewish nations. [8]God, who knows the hearts of every person, confirmed this when he gave them the Holy Spirit, just like he has given the Spirit to us.[a] [9]So now, not one thing separates us as Jews and Gentiles, for when they believe he makes their hearts pure. [10]So why on earth would you now limit God's grace[b] by placing a yoke of religious duties on the shoulders of the believers that neither we nor our ancestors have been able to bear? [11]Don't you believe that we are introduced to eternal life through the grace of our Lord Jesus—the same grace that has brought these people new life?"

[12]Everyone became silent and listened carefully as Paul and Barnabas shared with the council at length about the signs and wonders and miracles God had worked through them while ministering to the non-Jewish people.

[13]When they had finished, James took the floor and said, "Ladies and gentlemen, listen. [14]Peter has explained thoroughly that God has determined to win a people for himself from among the non-Jewish nations. [15]And the prophet's words are fulfilled:

> [16]"After these things I will return to you
> And raise up the tabernacle of David
> That has fallen into ruin.
> I will restore and rebuild what David experienced
> [17]So that all of humanity will be able to encounter the Lord
> Including the Gentiles whom I have called
> To be my very own," says the Lord.
> [18]"For I have made known my works from eternity!"[c]

[19]"So, in my judgment, we should not add any unnecessary burden upon the non-Jewish converts who are turning to God. [20]We will go to them as apostles[d] and teach them to be set free from offering sacrifices to idols, sexual immorality, and eating anything strangled or with any blood.[e] [21]For many gen-

a 15:8 This is in reference to the events of Acts 10–11.
b 15:10 Implied in the context. The text is "testing (provoking) God"; e.g., by limiting his grace among the Gentiles.
c 15:18 As translated from the Aramaic. This prophecy (verses 16–18) is found in Amos 9:11–12 and Isaiah 45:21.
d 15:20 Or "We will be apostles (sent ones) to them." As translated from the Aramaic. The Greek is "to send a message (letter)."
e 15:20 See Leviticus 17:12–16.

erations these words of Moses have been proclaimed every Sabbath day in the Jewish meeting houses."

The Apostles' Letter to the Non-Jewish People

²²The apostles and elders and the church of Jerusalem chose delegates to go to Antioch in Syria. They chose Judas, called Barsabbas, and Silas, both leaders in the church, to accompany Paul and Barnabas. ²³They sent with them this letter:

"Greetings from the apostles and pastors, and from your fellow believers—to our non-Jewish brothers and sisters living in Antioch in Syria and the nearby regions.ᵃ

²⁴"We are aware that some have come to you from the church of Jerusalem. These men were not sent by us, but came with false teachings that have brought confusion and division, telling you to keep the law and be circumcised—things we never commanded them to teach.ᵇ

²⁵⁻²⁷"So after deliberation, we're sending you our beloved brothers Paul and Barnabas, who have risked their livesᶜ for the glory of the name of our Lord Jesus, the Anointed One. They are accompanied by Judas and Silas, whom we have unanimously chosen to send as our representatives to you. They will validate all that we're wanting to share with you.ᵈ

²⁸"For it pleases the Holy Spirit and usᵉ that we not place any unnecessary burden on you, except for the following restrictions: ²⁹Stay away from anything sacrificed to a pagan idol, from eating what is strangled or blood, and from any form of sexual immorality. You will be beautiful believersᶠ if you keep your souls from these things, and you will be true and faithful to our Lord Jesus. May God bless you!"

³⁰They sent the four men off for Antioch, and after gathering the regional church together,ᵍ they delivered the letter. ³¹When the people heard the letter

---

a 15:23 Or "Cilicia," which is the southwestern region of coastal turkey that borders Syria.
b 15:24 As translated from the Aramaic and implied in the Greek. The Greek does not make explicit the false teaching, but says simply, "They have upset and unsettled you."
c 15:25–27 The Aramaic is "They have devoted their souls."
d 15:25–27 Significant changes in the order of the clauses in these three verses have been made for the sake of clarity of the English narrative.
e 15:28 Or "the Holy Spirit and we have determined (decided)."
f 15:29 As translated from the Aramaic.
g 15:30 Implied in the context.

read out loud, they were overjoyed and delighted by its encouraging message. [32]Then Judas and Silas, who were both prophets, spoke to them affirming words[a] that strengthened the believers.[b]

[33]After the four men spent some time there, the church sent them off in peace to return to the apostles in Jerusalem.[c] [34-35]However, only Judas departed;[d] Paul, Barnabas, and Silas stayed in Antioch, where they and many others preached and taught the wonderful message of the word of God.

Paul and Barnabas Disagree

[36]After some days, Paul said to Barnabas, "Let's travel to the regions where we've preached the Manifestation of God[e] and see how the believers are getting along."

[37]Barnabas wished to take Mark (also known as John) along with them, [38]but Paul disagreed. He didn't think it was proper to take the one who had deserted them in south-central Turkey,[f] leaving them to do their missionary work without him. [39]It became a heated argument between them, a disagreement so sharp that they parted from each other. Barnabas took Mark and sailed to Cyprus. [40]And Paul chose Silas[g] as his partner.

After the believers prayed for them, asking for the Lord's favor on their ministry, they left [41]for Syria and southeast Turkey.[h] Every place they went, they left the church stronger and more encouraged than before.

---

a 15:32 The Aramaic is "an abundant word" or "a rich word."

b 15:31 The ministry of the New Testament prophet is to strengthen the church.

c 15:33 Or "sent them with peace back to those who sent them."

d 15:34-35 The most reliable Greek manuscripts do not mention Silas remaining in Antioch. However, many manuscripts include this information, such as the Aramaic, codices D and C, the Harklean Syriac Version of AD 616, the Sahidic Version of the second to third century, and the St. Ephraim of Syria version of the fourth century. Regardless, verse 40 indicates that Silas did remain behind. An argument could be made that copyists inserted the data in verse 34 to explain the presence of Silas from verse 40.

e 15:36 As translated from the Aramaic. The Greek is "word of God."

f 15:38 Or "Pamphylia."

g 15:40 The apostle Silas was acknowledged in church history as one of the seventy apostles whom Jesus sent out. See Luke 10:1-11. After his missionary journey with Paul, he remained in Corinth and ministered there until his death.

h 15:41 Or "Cilicia."

Sixteen

Timothy Joins Paul and Silas

[1]Paul and Silas came to the city of Derbe and then went on to Klistra,[a] the hometown of a believer named Timothy. His mother was a Jewish follower of Jesus, but his father was not a Jew.[b] [2]Timothy was well known and highly respected among all the believers of Klistra and Iconium. [3]Paul recognized God's favor on Timothy's life[c] and wanted him to accompany them in ministry, but Paul had Timothy circumcised first because of the significant Jewish community living in the region, and everyone knew that Timothy's father wasn't a Jew.

[4]They went out together as missionaries, traveling to different cities where they preached and informed the churches of the decrees of the apostolic council of Jerusalem for the non-Jewish converts to observe. [5]All the churches were growing daily and were encouraged and strengthened in their faith.

Paul's Vision of the Man from Macedonia

[6]The Holy Spirit had forbidden Paul and his partners to preach the word in the southwestern provinces of Turkey,[d] so they ministered throughout the region of central and west-central Turkey.[e] [7]When they got as far west as the borders of Mysia, they repeatedly attempted to go north into the province of Bithynia,[f] but

---

a 16:1 Or "Lystra," which is modern-day Klistra, a city in Turkey. Derbe, also in Turkey, was about sixty miles from Klistra (Lystra).
b 16:2 The Aramaic is "His father was a Syrian (an Aramaic speaker)." In the time of Paul's missionary journeys, the Aramaic language was commonly spoken in the region he traveled throughout in the Middle East. The Greek is "His father was a Greek."
c 16:3 Implied in the context.
d 16:6 Or "Asia." This does not refer to the continent of Asia as we know it today, but to the far western and southwestern provinces of Asia Minor (Turkey).
e 16:6 Or "Phrygia" and "Galatia." The modern-day capital of Ankara is situated in the area known as Galatia.
f 16:7 Both Mysia and Bithynia are northwestern regions of Turkey.

again the Spirit of Jesus would not allow them to enter.ª ⁸So instead they went right on through the province of Mysia to the seaport of Troas.

⁹While staying there Paul experienced a supernatural, ecstatic vision during the night. A man from Macedonia appeared before him, pleading with him, "You must come across the sea to Macedonia and help us!"

¹⁰After Paul had this vision, weᵇ immediately prepared to cross over to Macedonia, convinced that God himself was calling us to go and preach the wonderful news of the gospel to them.

Paul Arrives at Philippi

¹¹From Troas we sailed a straight course to the island of Samothrace, and the next day to Neapolis. ¹²Finally we reached Philippi, a major cityᶜ in the Roman colony of Macedonia, and we remained there for a number of days.ᵈ

¹³When the Sabbath day came, we went outside the gates of the city to the nearby river, for there appeared to be a house of prayer and worship there.ᵉ Sitting on the riverbank we struck up a conversation with some of the women who had gathered there. ¹⁴One of them was Lydia, a business woman from the city of Thyatira who was a dealer of exquisite purple clothᶠ and a Jewish convert. While Paul shared the good news with her, God opened her heart to receive Paul's message.ᵍ ¹⁵She devoted herself to the Lord, and we baptized her and her entire family. Afterward she urged us to stay in her home, saying, "Since I am now a believer in the Lord, come and stay in my house." So we were persuaded to stay there.

---

a 16:7 We do not know how the Holy Spirit kept them from going into Bithynia, but it could have been through a warning given by means of a dream or vision. In any case, it is obvious the Holy Spirit was guiding his missionaries. He is the Lord of the Harvest who prepares, imparts gifts, anoints, and sends out his servants to gather the nations to Jesus Christ. The book of Acts is best understood as the book of the Activities of the Holy Spirit. Here he is designated "the Spirit of Jesus." True and lasting fruit in ministry comes through the work and leading of the Spirit of Jesus.

b 16:10 Apparently, Luke now joins the missionary team going to Macedonia (which includes parts of modern-day Bulgaria and former Yugoslavia). This is the first instance in Acts of the gospel going to Europe. Luke likely left the group later, as he is not included in the team starting in verse 40. Portions of Acts appear to be Luke's missionary travel journal.

c 16:12 The Aramaic is "the capital city."

d 16:12 The Aramaic can be translated "In a matter of days we were well known in the city." Other versions of the Aramaic read, "We were there over certain holy days."

e 16:13 Although implied in the Greek text, it is made explicit in the Aramaic, "We saw it was a house (place) of prayer."

f 16:14 Or "purple dye," a rare commodity that would only be purchased by the wealthy.

g 16:14 Or "feared (worshipped) God." The implication is that Lydia was a Gentile convert to Judaism.

The Python Spirit

¹⁶One day, as we were going to the house of prayer, we encountered a young slave girl who had an evil spirit of divination, the spirit of Python.ᵃ She had earned great profits for her owners by being a fortune-teller.

¹⁷She kept following us, shouting, "These men are servants of the Great High God, and they're telling us how to be saved!"

¹⁸Day after day she continued to do this, until Paul, greatly annoyed, turned and said to the spirit indwelling her, "I command you in the name of Jesus, the Anointed One, to come out of her, now!" At that very moment, the spirit came out of her!

¹⁹When her owners realized that their potential of making profit had vanished, they forcefully seized Paul and Silas and dragged them off to the city square to face the authorities.

²⁰When they appeared before the Roman soldiers and magistrates, the slave owners leveled accusations against them, saying, "These Jews are troublemakers. They're throwing our city into confusion. ²¹They're pushing their Jewish religion down our throats. It's wrong and unlawful for them to promote these Jewish ways, for we are Romans living in a Roman colony."

²²A great crowd gathered, and all the people joined in to come against them. The Roman officials ordered that Paul and Silas be stripped of their garments and beaten with rods on their bare backs.

Miracles Can Come Out of Painful Places

²³After they were severely beaten, they were thrown into prison and the jailer was commanded to guard them securely. ²⁴So the jailer placed them in the innermost cell of the prison and had their feet bound and chained.ᵇ

²⁵Paul and Silas, undaunted, prayed in the middle of the night and sang songs of praise to God, while all the other prisoners listened to their worship.

²⁶Suddenly, a great earthquake shook the foundations of the prison. All at once every prison door flung open and the chains of all the prisoners came loose.

---

a 16:16 In the religious context of Greek mythology, she was an "oracle," a medium who had the spirit of the gods speaking through her to foretell the future. The Python spirit was the epithet of Apollo, known as the Greek god of prophecy. An individual (often a young virgin) who became the oracle of Apollo was known as the Python, or Pythia.

b 16:24 Or "placed in stocks."

²⁷Startled, the jailer awoke and saw every cell door standing open. Assuming that all the prisoners had escaped, he drew his sword and was about to kill himself ²⁸when Paul shouted in the darkness, "Stop! Don't hurt yourself. We're all still here."

²⁹The jailer called for a light. When he saw that they were still in their cells, he rushed in and fell trembling at their feet. ³⁰Then he led Paul and Silas outside and asked, "What must I do to be saved?"

³¹They answered, "Believe in the Lord Jesus and you will be saved—you and all your family."ᵃ ³²Then they prophesied the word of the Lord over him and all his family.ᵇ ³³Even though the hour was late, he washed their wounds. Then he and all his family were baptized. He took Paul and Silas into his home and set them at his table and fed them. ³⁴The jailer and all his family were filled with joy in their newfound faith in God.

³⁵At daybreak, the magistrates sent officers to the prison with orders to tell the jailer, "Let those two men go." ³⁶The jailer informed Paul and Silas, "The magistrates have sent orders to release you. So you're free to go now."

³⁷But Paul told the officers, "Look, they had us beaten in public, without a fair trial—and we are Roman citizens.ᶜ Do you think we're just going to quietly walk away after they threw us in prison and violated all of our rights? Absolutely not! You go back and tell the magistrates that they need to come down here themselves and escort us out!"

³⁸When the officers went back and reported what Paul and Silas had told them, the magistrates were appalled, especially upon hearing that they had beaten two Roman citizens without due process. ³⁹So they went to the prison and apologized to Paul and Silas, begging them repeatedly, saying, "Please leave our city."

⁴⁰So Paul and Silas left the prison and went back to Lydia's house, where they met with the believers and comforted and encouraged them before departing.

---

a 16:31 The implication is "you and anyone in your household who believes."
b 16:32 Or "spoke the word of the Lord." This phrase is consistently used in the Old Testament for prophetic utterance of a supernatural origin.
c 16:37 Paul didn't notify them that he and Silas were Romans prior to the their beating, when they could have escaped persecution. Instead, they endured the brutal treatment and ended up leading their jailor to Christ.

Seventeen

A Riot Breaks Out in Thessalonica

[1]After passing through the cities of Amphipolis and Apollonia, Paul and Silas arrived at Thessalonica.[a] [2]As they customarily did, they went to the Jewish meeting house to speak to the Jews from the Torah scrolls. For three weeks [3]Paul challenged them by explaining the truth and proving to them the reality of the gospel—that the Messiah had to suffer and die, then rise again from among the dead. He made it clear to them, saying, "I come to announce to you that Jesus is the Anointed One, the Messiah!"

[4]Some of the Jews were convinced that their message was true, so they joined Paul and Silas, along with quite a few prominent women and a large number of Greeks who worshipped God.[b] [5]But many of the Jews were motivated by bitter jealousy and formed a large mob out of the troublemakers, unsavory characters, and street gangs to incite a riot. They set out to attack Jason's house, for he had welcomed the apostles into his home.[c] The mob was after Paul and Silas and sought to take them by force and bring them out to the people. [6]When they couldn't find them, they took Jason instead, along with some of the brothers in his house church,[d] and dragged them before the city council. Along the way they screamed out, "Those troublemakers who have turned the world upside down have come here to our city. [7]And now Jason and these men have welcomed them as guests. They're traitors to Caesar, teaching that there is another king named Jesus."

---

a 17:1 Known today as Salonica, it was the ancient capital of Macedonia.

b 17:4 It is probable that this is when Timothy arrived in Thessalonica with gifts of money and food from the church of Philippi. See Philippians 4:16, 1 Thessalonians 1:1, and 2 Thessalonians 1:1.

c 17:5 This information is borrowed from verse 7 and inserted here for the sake of English narrative.

d 17:6 Implied in the text. Although not much about Jason is given here, he is known in church history as Jason of Tarsus, who was one of the seventy apostles Jesus sent out and is named as one of Paul's ministry companions. See Luke 10:1–11 and Romans 16:21.

[8]Their angry shouts stirred up the crowds and troubled the city and all its officials. [9]So when Paul and Silas came before the leaders of the city,[a] they refused to let them go until Jason and his men posted bail.

The Gospel Received in Berea

[10]That night the believers sent Paul and Silas off to the city of Berea,[b] where they once again went into the Jewish meeting house. [11]They found that the Jews of Berea were of more noble character and much more open minded than those of Thessalonica. They were hungry to learn and eagerly received the word. Every day they opened the scrolls of Scripture to search and examine them, to verify that what Paul taught them was true. [12]A large number of Jews became believers in Jesus,[c] along with quite a few influential[d] Greek women and men.

[13]When the news reached the Jews in Thessalonica that Paul was now in Berea, preaching the word of God, the troublemakers went there, too, and they agitated and stirred up the crowds against him. [14]The fellow believers helped Paul slip away to the coast of the Aegean Sea,[e] while Silas and Timothy remained in Berea.

[15]Those who accompanied Paul sailed with him as far as Athens. Then Paul sent them back to Berea with instructions[f] for Silas and Timothy to hurry and join him.

The Apostle Paul in Athens

[16]While Paul was waiting for them in Athens, his spirit was deeply troubled[g] when he realized that the entire city was full of idols. [17]He argued the claims of the gospel[h] with the Jews in their meeting house, and with those who were worshippers of God, and every day he preached in the public square with whoever would listen.

---

a 17:9 Implied in the text and added for the sake of English narrative.
b 17:10 Berea (modern-day Veria) was a city in Macedonia about forty-five miles (seventy-five kilometers) from Thessalonica.
c 17:12 Implied in the text.
d 17:12 The Greek word *euschemon* also implies "women of high standing, wealthy, honorable, elegant, and respected." See Strong's concordance 2158.
e 17:14 Implied in the context. The Greek text is simply "the sea."
f 17:15 The Aramaic makes it clear that this message was written as a letter.
g 17:16 Or "deeply pained" or "irritated."
h 17:17 Implied in the text.

[18]Philosophers of the teachings of Epicurus,[a] and others called Stoics,[b] debated[c] with Paul. When they heard him speak about Jesus and his resurrection, they said, "What strange ideas is this babbler trying to present?" Others said, "He's peddling some kind of foreign religion." [19]So they brought him for a public dialogue before the leadership council of Athens,[d] known as the Areopagus.

"Tell us," they said, "about this new teaching that you're bringing to our city. [20]You're presenting strange and astonishing things to our ears, and we want to know what it all means." [21]Now, it was the favorite pastime of the Athenians and visitors to Athens to discuss the newest ideas and philosophies.

Paul Speaks to the Leaders of Athens

[22]So Paul stood in the middle of the leadership council and said, "Respected leaders of Athens,[e] it is clear to me how extravagant you are in your worship of idols.[f] [23]For as I walked through your city, I was captivated by the many shrines and objects of your worship. I even found an inscription on one altar that read, 'To the Unknown God.'[g] I have come to introduce to you this God whom you worship without even knowing anything about him.

[24]"The true God is the Creator of all things. He is the owner and Lord of the heavenly realm and the earthly realm, and he doesn't live in man-made temples. [25]He supplies life and breath and all things to every living being. He doesn't lack a thing that we mortals could supply for him, for he has all things and everything he needs. [26]From one man, Adam, he made every man and woman and every

---

a 17:18 Epicurus was a Greek philosopher (341–270 BC) who espoused a radical materialism that claimed people should live for pleasure and materialistic gain. He denied an afterlife and asserted that the gods had little interest in or concern for humanity.

b 17:18 Stoicism, in contrast to Epicureanism, is a passive determinism of emotional indifference that elevates the virtue of self-control. By mastering human passions and emotions, one could realize peace within himself. The Greek Stoics believed that humans can only reach their full potential when they live by sheer reason and divine principle, or the spark of divinity, which they called *logos*.

c 17:18 The Aramaic is "word wrestling."

d 17:19 The Areopagus was a governing body of intellectuals who were the overseers of Athens. It was equivalent to the board of education, the city council, the ethics committee, the council of foreign relations, and leaders of the religious and philosophical community all rolled into one. The Areopagus, also known as Mars Hill (Mars, or Ares, was the Greek god of war), was not simply a location but a gathering of a council of people overseeing the spiritual atmosphere of Athens. It could best be described as the Greek temple of human thought. The Aramaic here uses the phrase "house of religion."

e 17:22 Or simply, "Athenians."

f 17:22 As translated from the Aramaic, which can also be translated "You excel in the worship of demons (idols)." The Greek is "How very superstitious you are (i.e., extraordinarily religious)."

g 17:23 The Aramaic can be translated "To the Hidden God."

race of humanity, and he spread us over all the earth. He sets the boundaries of people and nations, determining their appointed times in history.[a] 27He has done this so that every person would long for God, feel their way to him,[b] and find him—for he is the God who is easy to discover![c] 28It is through him that we live and function and have our identity; just as your own poets have said,[d] 'Our lineage comes from him.'[e]

29"Since our lineage can be traced back to God, how could we even think that the divine image could be compared to something made of gold, silver, or stone, sculpted by man's artwork and clever imagination?

30"In the past God tolerated[f] our ignorance of these things, but now the time of deception has passed away.[g] He commands us all to repent and turn to God.[h] 31For the appointed day has risen, in which he is going to judge the world in righteousness by the Man he has designated. And the proof given to the world that God has chosen this Man is this: he resurrected him from among the dead!"[i]

32The moment they heard Paul bring up the topic of resurrection, some of them ridiculed him, then got up and left.[j] But others said, "We want to hear you again later about these things." 33So Paul left the meeting. 34But there were some who believed the message and joined him from that day forward. Among them were Dionysius, a judge on the leadership council,[k] and a woman named Damaris.[l]

---

a 17:26 The Aramaic adds an interesting nuance: "He commands the separation of the seasons and sets the lifespan of every person."

b 17:27 The Aramaic is "investigating him in his creation."

c 17:27 Or "the God who is not far from each one of us."

d 17:28 Paul is quoting two classical Greek writers (circa 270 BC): Aratois (Phainomena, 5) and Cleanthes (Hymn to Zeus, 5).

e 17:28 Or "Our nature comes from him," as translated from the Aramaic. The Greek is "We are his offspring." The Greek word is genos, which means "kindred" or "family" (taken from his genes).

f 17:30 Or "deliberately paid no attention to."

g 17:30 As translated from the Aramaic.

h 17:30 That is, to turn away from idolatry and worship the true God.

i 17:31 The Aramaic is "God turns the hearts of men to faith in him (Jesus) and raises them from among the dead."

j 17:32 Implied in the Aramaic.

k 17:34 As translated from the Aramaic. According to the church historian Eusebius, he later became the Bishop of Athens (Eusebius, Historia Ecclesiae III: iv).

l 17:34 The Greek word can also mean "wife," indicating she was possibly the wife of Dionysius. Regardless, she must have been a woman of high social standing to be included in the meeting of the leadership council.

Eighteen

The Apostle Paul in Corinth

¹When Paul left Athens he traveled to Corinth,ᵃ ²where he met a Jewish man named Aquila, who was originally from northeastern Turkey.ᵇ He and his wife, Priscilla, had recently emigrated from Italy to Corinth because Emperor Claudius had expelled all the Jews from Rome. ³Since Paul and Aquila were both tentmakersᶜ by trade, Paul moved in with them and they became business partners.

⁴Every Sabbath day Paul spoke openly in the Jewish meeting house, to both Jews and non-Jews,ᵈ attempting to persuade them to believe the message of Jesus.ᵉ

⁵When Silas and Timothy finally arrived from Macedonia, Paul spent all his time preaching the word of God,ᶠ trying to convince the Jews that Jesus was the Messiah.

⁶When they viciously slandered him and hurled abuse on him, he symbolically shook the dust off his clothes in protest against them. He said to them, "Have it your way then! I am guiltless as to your fate, for the blood-guilt of your actions will be on your own heads, and from now on I will preach to the non-Jews."

⁷Leaving the Jewish meeting house, Paul went to the home of Titus,ᵍ a con-

---

a 18:1 Corinth is about forty-eight miles (seventy-eight kilometers) from Athens. It was a large commercial center with trade links all over the entire ancient world. It was the home of the famous Isthmian Games and the temple of Aphrodite, which held a thousand temple prostitutes. Corinth was known for its debauchery. In the midst of a depraved culture, God birthed a church to become light to the people of their city.

b 18:2 Or "Pontus," a Roman province in northeastern Asia Minor (Turkey).

c 18:3 The Aramaic can also mean "saddle makers."

d 18:4 The Aramaic is "pagans."

e 18:4 Implied in the text.

f 18:5 The Aramaic is "the Manifestation of God."

g 18:7 The Greek text is "Titus Justus," but the Aramaic only has Titus. It is possible that he is the Titus who accompanied Paul in ministry and the one Paul addressed in the book of Titus.

vert to Judaism, for he and his family attended the Jewish meetings [a] and they had all became believers in Jesus.[b] [8]Crispus, the leader of the Jewish congregation, believed in the Lord, together with his entire family, and many of the Corinthians who heard what had happened believed in the Lord[c] and were baptized.

[9]One night, the Lord spoke to Paul in a supernatural vision and said, **"Don't ever be afraid. Speak the words that I give you[d] and don't be intimidated, [10]because I AM with you.**[e] No one will be able to hurt you, for there are many in this city whom I call my own."

[11]For the next year and a half, Paul stayed in Corinth, faithfully teaching the Word, the living expression of God.[f]

Paul Brought before the Roman Official Gallio

[12]Now, at that time, Gallio was the regional governor who ruled over the Roman province of Achaia,[g] and the Jews turned against Paul and came together to seize him and bring him publicly before the governor's court.[h] [13]They accused him before Gallio, saying, "This man is creating a disturbance by persuading people to worship God in ways that are contrary to our laws."

[14]Just as Paul was about to speak in his defense, Gallio interrupted and said, "Wait! If this involved some major crime or fraud, it would be my responsibility to hear the case. [15]But this is nothing more than a disagreement among yourselves over semantics[i] and personalities[j] and traditions of your own Jewish laws.[k] Go and settle it yourselves! I refuse to be the judge of these issues." [16]So Gallio dismissed them from the court.

---

a 18:7 As translated from the Aramaic. The Greek says that Titus Justus lived next door to the Jewish meeting house.
b 18:7 Implied in the text.
c 18:8 Crispus was one of the few people Paul baptized. See 1 Corinthians 1:14. According to church tradition he became the bishop of Aegina.
d 18:9 Implied in the text.
e 18:10 Somewhat more explicit in the Aramaic, this is the great "I Am" who is speaking with Paul, assuring him of God's presence.
f 18:11 As translated from the Aramaic. The Greek is *Logos* (Word).
g 18:12 The province of Achaia included the three most important parts of southern Greece: Attica, Boeotia, and the Peloponnesus. Gallio was the brother of Seneca, the tutor of Nero.
h 18:12 Or "judgment seat." This was a raised platform with a marble bench where judicial and governmental decrees were issued. This bench has been discovered after excavations in the agora.
i 18:15 Or "doctrines."
j 18:15 Or "names."
k 18:15 The Aramaic is "Torah (the first five books of Moses.")

[17]Immediately the crowd turned on Sosthenes,[a] one of the leaders[b] of the Jewish congregation who sided with Paul.[c] They seized him and beat him up right there in the courtroom! But Gallio showed no concern at all over what was happening.

Priscilla and Aquila

[18]After remaining in Corinth several more days, Paul finally bid "Shalom"[d] to the believers and sailed away for the coast of Syria, accompanied by Priscilla and Aquila.[e] Before they left, Paul had his head shaved at Cenchrea,[f] because he had taken a vow of dedication.

[19]When they reached Ephesus,[g] Paul left Priscilla and Aquila behind, then he went into the meeting house and spoke to the Jews. [20]They asked him to stay longer, but he refused [21]and said farewell to them, adding, "I will come back to you, if it is God's will, after I go to Jerusalem to observe the feast."[h] Then he set sail from Ephesus for Caesarea.

[22]When he arrived there he traveled on to Jerusalem to visit the church and pray for them,[i] then he left for Antioch. [23]After spending some time there, Paul continued on through central and west central Turkey, the region of Galatia and Phrygia. And wherever he went he encouraged and strengthened the believers.[j]

---

a 18:17 Sosthenes means "savior of our nation." See 1 Corinthians 1:1.

b 18:17 The Aramaic word used here can mean "priest" or "elder." Crispus is mentioned as the president or leader (verse 8). Some speculate that Crispus's term of service had been completed and Sosthenes took his place.

c 18:17 Implied in the text.

d 18:18 Shalom is the Hebrew and Aramaic word for "peace and well-being." The Greek is "Farewell." The Aramaic can also be translated "Paul brought peace to the brothers."

e 18:18 Priscilla means "Ancient"; Aquila means "Eagle."

f 18:18 Cenchrea was one of two major ports of Corinth, possibly where agricultural goods were exported, for Cenchrea means "millet," a grain similar to quinoa.

g 18:19 Ephesus was in the ancient world, a white marble city, one of the most beautiful in the world. It had the temple of Artemis, one of the seven great wonders of that era. It also had two agoras, a beautiful fountain in the city supplied by an aqueduct, the monument of Phillio, the Koressian Gates, the Bouleuterion, a large stadium, and many terraced houses. It was the capital city of the Roman province of Asia and had a population of well over one hundred thousand at the time Paul visited the city. Ephesus was known historically as the center of powerful magical practices and the casting of spells, as well as the cult center of the worship of the Ephesian goddess Artemis, known as "the supreme power." It was in this backdrop that the apostle Paul and his companions planted the renowned church of Ephesus.

h 18:21 This last clause is only found in the Aramaic.

i 18:22 Although this clause is missing in the Greek, the Aramaic can be translated "to pray for the peace of the congregation." A true spiritual father prays for believers and brings them a message of hope and peace.

j 18:23 The Aramaic can be translated "Wherever he went he made them all disciples."

The Ministry of Apollos

²⁴A Jewish man by the name of Apollos arrived in Ephesus. He was a native of Alexandria*a* and was recognized as an educated and cultured man. He possessed a thorough knowledge*b* of the Scriptures ²⁵and had accepted Jesus, the Manifestation.*c* He was spiritually passionate*d* for Jesus and a convincing teacher, although he only knew about the baptism of John. ²⁶He fearlessly preached*e* in the Jewish meetings. But when Priscilla and Aquila heard Apollos's teachings, they met with him privately*f* and revealed to him the ways of God more completely.*g*

²⁷Then Apollos, with the encouragement of the believers, went to the province of Achaia.*h* He took a letter of recommendation from the brothers of Ephesus so his ministry would be welcomed in the region. He was a tremendous help to the believers and caused them to increase in grace.*i* ²⁸Apollos boldly and publicly confronted the Jews, vigorously debating them, proving undeniably from the Scriptures that Jesus was the Messiah.

---

a 18:24 This is, Alexandria in Egypt.
b 18:24 Or "powerful in the Scriptures."
c 18:25 As translated from the Aramaic. The Manifestation refers to the Word made flesh, Jesus Christ. The Greek is "He had been taught about the Lord."
d 18:25 Or "His spirit boiled."
e 18:26 That is, boldly and powerfully. The Aramaic can be translated "with crystal clarity."
f 18:26 The Aramaic is "They took him into their home."
g 18:27 Or "more accurately." They filled in the gaps in his understanding of the Lord Jesus.
h 18:27 See footnote on 18:12.
i 18:27 As translated from the Aramaic. The Greek is "He helped those who believed by grace."

Nineteen

The Apostle Paul in Ephesus

¹While Apollos was ministering in Corinth, Paul traveled on through the regions of Turkey[a] until he arrived in Ephesus, where he found a group of twelve followers of Jesus.[b] ²The first thing he asked them was "Did you receive the Holy Spirit when you became believers?"

"No," they replied. "We've not even heard of a holy spirit."

³Paul asked, "Then what was the meaning of your baptism?"[c]

They responded, "It meant that we would follow John's teaching."

⁴Paul said, "John's baptism was for those who were turning from their sins,[d] and he taught you to believe in and follow the one who was coming after him: Jesus the Anointed One."[e]

⁵When they understood this, they were baptized into the authority of Jesus, the Anointed One.[f] ⁶⁻⁷And when Paul laid his hands on each of the Twelve, the Holy Spirit manifested and they immediately spoke in tongues[g] and prophesied.[h]

⁸For three months Paul taught openly and fearlessly in the Jewish meeting house, arguing persuasively for them to enter into God's kingdom realm.[i] ⁹But some of them hardened their hearts and stubbornly refused to believe. When

---

a 19:1 Implied in the text. The Greek is "the upper inland country." This was a trek through certain regions of Turkey for him to arrive in Ephesus.

b 19:1 Or "some disciples." Verse 7 states there were twelve. This information is moved here to verse 1 for the sake of the English narrative.

c 19:3 Or "into what (name or authority) were you baptized?"

d 19:4 The Aramaic can be translated "John's baptism was a baptism of grace to the people."

e 19:4 "The Anointed One (Messiah)" is found only in the Aramaic. The Greek is simply "Jesus."

f 19:5 Or "on the name of Jesus Christ," which means they were baptized into the authority of the name of Jesus, who was greater than John.

g 19:6–7 Or "supernaturally given languages."

h 19:6–7 The Aramaic is "They spoke tongue by tongue and gushed out prophecies." The impartation of the Holy Spirit and his gifts are here being transferred from Paul to these believers. See also 1 Timothy 4:14 and 2 Timothy 1:6–7. Jesus taught that when the Holy Spirit comes upon us, it is to impart power for our lives and ministries. See Acts 1:8.

i 19:8 Or "about the kingdom realm of God." It is a big step for both Jews and Christians to come out of their religious identity and focus on the reality of the kingdom of God.

they spoke evil[a] of the Way in front of the congregation, Paul withdrew from them and took the believers with him.

[10]Every day[b] for over two years,[c] he taught them in the lecture hall of Tyrannus,[d] which resulted in everyone living in the province of Asia,[e] Jews and non-Jews, hearing the prophetic word of the Lord.[f]

Extraordinary Miracles in Ephesus

[11]God kept releasing a flow of extraordinary miracles through the hands of Paul. [12]Because of this, people took Paul's handkerchiefs and articles of clothing, even pieces of cloth that had touched his skin, laying them on the bodies of the sick, and diseases and demons left them and they were healed.

[13-14]Now, there were seven itinerant Jewish exorcists, sons of Sceva the high priest, who took it upon themselves to use the name and authority of Jesus over those who were demonized. They would say, "We cast you out in the name of the Jesus that Paul preaches!"

[15]One day, when they said those words, the demon in the man replied, "I know about Jesus, and I recognize Paul, but who do you think you are?"

[16]Then the demonized man jumped on them and threw them to the ground, beating them mercilessly.[g] He overpowered the seven exorcists until they all ran out of the house naked and badly bruised.

Revival Breaks Out

[17]All of the people in Ephesus were awestruck, both Jews and non-Jews, when they heard about what had happened. Great fear fell over the entire city, and the

---

a 19:9 Or "cursed the Christian way of living."

b 19:10 The Greek manuscript D adds, "from the fifth hour (11:00 a.m.) to the tenth hour (4:00 p.m.)."

c 19:10 Counting the three months of focusing on ministry to the Jews, Paul's entire stay in Ephesus came to three years, which would have included a short visit to Corinth. See Acts 20:31.

d 19:10 This was like a college or lecture hall. Tyrannus (whose name means "sovereign") was most likely a philosopher and lecturer who had disciples whom he taught. Apparently Tyrannus welcomed Paul after he left the Jewish congregation and brought him into his school to teach the students.

e 19:10 This "school of ministry" exploded as many came to hear Paul and then went out to preach, expanding the reach of the gospel into all the "province of Asia" (Asia Minor). The province of Asia would have covered no less than one third of Turkey. Many multitudes heard the gospel in the two-year period when Paul taught in Ephesus. The teaching of the apostles resulted in the expansion of the kingdom of God.

f 19:10 Or simply, "the word of the Lord." However, the phrase "the word of the Lord" is a Hebrew expression consistently used for the prophetic utterances given by the prophets.

g 19:16 True authority comes from relationship with Jesus Christ, not just using formulas and techniques. Evil spirits know about the depth of our relationship with God.

authority of the name of Jesus was exalted. [18]Many believers publicly confessed their sins and disclosed their secrets. [19]Large numbers of those who had been practicing magic took all of their books and scrolls of spells and incantations[a] and publicly burned them. When the value of all the books and scrolls was calculated, it all came to several million dollars.[b] [20]The power of God caused the word to spread, and the people were greatly impacted.[c]

A Riot Breaks Out

[21]Paul had it in his heart to go to Jerusalem and, on his way there, to revisit the places in Greece where he had ministered.[d] "After that," he said, "I have to go to Rome also." [22]So he sent ahead of him into Macedonia two of his ministry assistants, Timothy[e] and Erastus,[f] while he remained in western Turkey.[g]

[23]At that time a major disturbance erupted in Ephesus over the people following God's way.[h] [24]It began with a wealthy man named Demetrius, who had built a large business and enriched many craftsmen by manufacturing silver shrines for the Greek goddess Artemis.[i]

[25-26]Demetrius called a meeting of his employees, along with all the various tradespeople of Ephesus, and said, "You know that our prosperous livelihood is being threatened by this Paul, who is persuading crowds of people to turn away from our gods.[j] We make a good living by doing what we do, but everywhere Paul goes, not only here in Ephesus but throughout western Turkey,[k] he convinces people that there's no such thing as a god made with hands. [27]Our businesses are in danger of being discredited. And not only that, but the temple

---

a 19:19 Implied in the text.
b 19:19 Or "fifty thousand silver drachmas." Some historians have said that one lamb would be sold for one silver drachma. The price of a ewe lamb today is about $150 USD. A drachma was one day's wage, and fifty thousand drachmas would be one hundred years' wages. The value of the books could have been millions of dollars.
c 19:20 Chronologically, this would have been the time when Paul wrote his first letter to the Corinthians.
d 19:21 Or "to go through Macedonia and Achaia." The implication is that Paul wanted to revisit the area of Greece he had ministered in; therefore, that is made explicit in the translation.
e 19:22 Timothy's name means "one who honors God." He was Paul's spiritual son and later became an apostolic church planter. See 1 and 2 Timothy.
f 19:22 Erastus means "beloved." He was possibly the treasurer of the city of Corinth. See Romans 16:23 and 2 Timothy 4:20.
g 19:22 Or "the province of Asia (Minor)."
h 19:23 As translated from the Aramaic. The Greek is simply "the way."
i 19:24 Also known as Diana. She was venerated as the daughter of Zeus and the sister of Apollo.
j 19:25-26 Implied in the context. The true worship of God threatens not only the political realm, but the spiritual and economic realm as well. Jesus compels men to adopt new values.
k 19:25-26 Or "the (Roman) province of Asia (Minor)."

of our great goddess Artemis is being dishonored and seen as worthless.[a] She is the goddess of all of western Turkey and is worshipped in all the world. But if this outrage continues, everyone everywhere will suffer the loss of her magnificent greatness."

[28]When the people heard this, they were filled with boiling rage. They shouted over and over, "Artemis, the great goddess of the Ephesians!" [29]The entire city was thrown into chaos as everyone rushed into the stadium together,[b] dragging with them Gaius[c] and Aristarchus,[d] Paul's traveling companions from Macedonia.

[30]When Paul attempted to go in and speak to the massive crowd, the disciples wouldn't let him. [31]Some of the high-ranking governmental officials of the region, because they loved him,[e] sent Paul an urgent message, saying, "Whatever you do, don't step foot into that stadium!"

[32]The frenzied crowd shouted out one thing, and others shouted something else, until they were all in mass confusion, with many not even knowing why they were there!

[33]Some of the Jews pushed forward a Jewish man named Alexander to be their spokesman, and different factions of the crowd shouted instructions at him. He stood before the people and motioned for everyone to be quiet so he could be heard. [34]But when he began to speak, they realized that he was a Jew, so they shouted him down. For nearly two hours they shouted over and over, "Great is Artemis, the goddess of the Ephesians!"[f]

[35]Eventually the mayor of the city[g] was able to quiet them down. He said, "Fellow citizens! Who in the world doesn't know that we are devoted to[h] the

---

a 19:27 The temple of Artemis (Diana) is one of the seven ancient wonders of the world. We must never put buildings or temples above the true worship of God. The Ephesians valued their goddess and economic standards more than truth.

b 19:29 The stadium of Ephesus has recently been discovered and is estimated to have held twenty-four thousand spectators.

c 19:29 Gaius's name is a variant form of "lord." There is speculation that he could be the man to whom the apostle John wrote his third letter (3 John).

d 19:29 Aristarchus's name means "best ruler." He was a native of Thessalonica (Acts 20:4 and 27:2). He traveled often with Paul and is also mentioned in Colossians 4:10 and Philemon 24, called there Paul's "fellow prisoner." Church tradition states that he was martyred by Emperor Nero for loving and serving Jesus Christ.

e 19:31 As translated from the Aramaic.

f 19:28 Artemis, the great goddess of the Ephesians, has faded from history, while we fill stadiums today to say, "Great is the God Most High!"

g 19:35 The Aramaic is "the city governor." The Greek is "city clerk" or "scribe (keeper of the records)." For all practical purposes he would represent the mayor of the city.

h 19:35 As translated from the Aramaic, the Greek is "custodians of the temple."

great temple of Artemis and to her image that fell from Zeus out of heaven?[a] 36Since no one can deny it, you should all just be quiet. Calm down and don't do anything hasty. 37For you have brought these men before us who aren't guilty of any crime. They are neither temple robbers nor blasphemers of our goddess. 38So if Demetrius and the men of his trade have a case against someone, the courts are open. They can appear before the judge and press charges. 39But if you're looking for anything further to bring up, it must be argued before the court and settled there, not here. 40Don't you realize we're putting our city in danger of being accused of a riot by the Roman authorities? There's no good explanation we can give them for all this commotion!"

41After he had said this, he dispersed the crowds and sent them away.

a 19:35 The Aramaic is "her face that fell from heaven." Much conjecture has been made over this statement. Some of the oldest translations have "fell from Zeus (Jupiter)," while most modern translations have "fell from the sky (heaven)." Some believe it was an aerolite that was fashioned into a stature of Artemis; however, Pliny the Elder, a Roman author and philosopher who died trying to save relatives from the eruption of Mount Vesuvius, says it was made from wood, possibly ebony (Naturalis Historia 16.79.213–14).

Twenty

The Apostle Paul Goes to Macedonia and Greece

[1]When the uproar finally died down, Paul gathered the believers and encouraged their hearts. He kissed them,[a] said good-bye, and left for Macedonia. [2]At every place he passed through, he brought words of great comfort and encouragement to the believers. Then he went on to Greece [3]and stayed there for three months.

Just as Paul was about to sail for Syria, he learned of a plot against him by the Jews, so he decided to return by going through Macedonia. [4]Seven men accompanied him as far as western Turkey. They were Sopater,[b] son of Pyrrhus[c] from Berea, Aristarchus[d] and Secundus[e] from Thessalonica, Gaius[f] from Derby, and Timothy,[g] Tychicus,[h] and Trophimus[i] from western Turkey. [5]These men went ahead and were waiting for us at Troas.[j]

[6]As soon as all of the Passover celebrations were over,[k] we sailed from Philippi. After five days we joined the others in Troas, where we stayed another week.[l] [7]On Sunday we gathered to take communion[m] and to hear Paul preach. Because he was planning to leave the next day, he continued speaking until

a 20:1 As translated from the Aramaic.
b 20:4 Sopater, or Sosipiter, is mentioned in Romans 16:21 as one of Paul's relatives. His name means "his father's savior."
c 20:4 Or "son of fiery red flames." This phrase is not found in the Aramaic.
d 20:4 See footnote on 19:29.
e 20:4 Secundus means "fortunate."
f 20:4 Many believe this is the same Gaius mentioned in 19:29. See footnote.
g 20:4 The Aramaic is "Timothy of Lystra." See introduction to 1 and 2 Timothy.
h 20:4 It is likely that Tychicus was a native of Ephesus since he carried the letter Paul wrote to them as well as the letter to Colossae. See Ephesians 6:21 and Colossians 4:7. He is also mentioned in 2 Timothy 4:12 and Titus 3:12. His name means "child of fortune."
i 20:4 Trophimus was not a Jew. He is mentioned in Acts 21:29. His name means "nutritious."
j 20:5 Notice "us," which implies Luke has now rejoined the missionary team.
k 20:6 Or "the Days of Unleavened Bread." This holiday was observed during the week immediately following Passover and was wrapped into the Passover celebration.
l 20:6 This is when the events took place mentioned by Paul in 2 Corinthians 2:12–13.
m 20:7 The Aramaic is "breaking pieces of the Eucharist."

past midnight. [8]Many flickering lamps burned in the upstairs chamber where we were meeting. [9]Sitting in an open window listening was a young man named Lucky.[a] As Paul's sermon dragged on, Lucky became drowsy and fell into a deep slumber. Sound asleep, he fell three stories to his death below.[b]

[10]Paul went downstairs, bent over the boy, and embraced him. Taking him in his arms, he said to all the people gathered, "Stop your worrying. He's come back to life!"[c]

[11]Paul went back upstairs, served communion, and ate a meal with them. Then he picked back up where he left off and taught until dawn.[d] [12]Filled with enormous joy, they took the boy home alive and everyone was encouraged.[e]

Paul's Voyage to Miletus

[13]Continuing our journey, we made our way to the ship and sailed for Assos.[f] Paul had previously arranged to meet us there as he traveled overland by foot. [14]So he rejoined our team there and we took him aboard and sailed for Mitylene.[g] [15]The next day we crossed over to Chios,[h] and the following day we arrived at the island of Samos.[i] We stayed at Trogyllium,[j] and on the day after that we reached Miletus.[k] [16]Paul was in a hurry to arrive in Jerusalem, hoping to make it in time for the Feast of Pentecost, so he decided to bypass Ephesus and not spend any time in that region.[l] [17]However, from Miletus Paul had sent a message to the elders of the church[m] in Ephesus and asked them to come meet with him.

[18]When they arrived, he said to them, "All of you know how I've lived and

---

a 20:8 Or "a preteen named Eutychus," which means "fortunate" or "lucky."
b 20:10 There is no doubt that Lucky died because of his fall. The Greek word *nekros* can only mean that he was lifeless. This boy becomes a picture of some believers today who, because they view themselves as "well off," sit carelessly where they shouldn't, growing drowsy, falling asleep, and enduring a disastrous fall. But God has grace and power to raise even the foolish ones back to life.
c 20:10 Or "His soul is in him." Paul raised him from the dead.
d 20:11 The Aramaic adds "by land (on foot)."
e 20:12 The Greek is "comforted," while the Aramaic is "overjoyed." The translation merges both concepts.
f 20:13 A coastal city in far western Turkey. Assos means "approaching."
g 20:14 A city on the Greek island of Lesbos.
h 20:15 A Greek island in the Aegean Sea off the coast of Turkey.
i 20:15 A Greek island in the Aegean Sea off the coast of Turkey.
j 20:15 As translated from the Aramaic and some Greek manuscripts. Most Greek manuscripts do not have this clause.
k 20:15 An ancient seaport of far western Turkey.
l 20:16 Or "waste any time in the province of Asia (Minor)."
m 20:17 These elders would be equivalent to pastors, leaders of the church.

conducted myself while I was with you. From the first day I set foot in western Turkey [19]I've operated in God's miracle power[a] with great humility and served you[b] with many tears. I've endured numerous ordeals because of the plots of the Jews. [20]You know how I've taught you in public meetings and in your homes, and that I've not held anything back from you that would help you grow. [21]I urged both Jews and non-Jews to turn from sin to God and to have faith in our Lord Jesus. [22]And now I am being compelled by the Holy Spirit[c] to go to Jerusalem, without really knowing what will happen to me there. [23]Yet I know that the Holy Spirit warns me[d] in town after town, saying, **'Chains and afflictions are prepared for you.'**

[24]"But whether I live or die is not important, for I don't esteem my life as indispensable.[e] It's more important for me to fulfill my destiny and to finish the ministry my Lord Jesus has assigned to me, which is to faithfully preach the wonderful news of God's grace. [25]I've been a part of your lives and shared with you many times the message of the kingdom realm of God. But now I leave you, and you will not see my face again. [26]If any of you should be lost, I will not be blamed, for my conscience is clean, [27]because I've taught you everything I could about God's eternal plan and I've held nothing back. [28]So guard your hearts. Be true shepherds[f] over all the flock and feed them well. Remember, it was the Holy Spirit who appointed you to guard and oversee[g] the churches that belong to Jesus, the Anointed One,[h] which he purchased and established by his own blood.

[29]"I know that after I leave, imposters who have no loyalty to the flock[i] will come among you like savage wolves. [30]Even some from among your very own ranks will rise up, twisting the truth[j] to seduce people into following them

---

a 20:19 As translated in the Aramaic, which is literally "I've performed God's miracles." The Greek is "I've served the Lord."

b 20:19 Some manuscripts add, "for more than three years." See also 1 Thessalonians 2:10–12.

c 20:22 Or "shackled by the Holy Spirit."

d 20:23 This warning from the Holy Spirit could have come through prophecies, dreams, visions, or the voice of the Holy Spirit speaking within him.

e 20:24 Or "I do not consider my life worth a single word." That is, Paul viewed his life as not worth mentioning. We don't need to see our lives as precious in our own eyes, for they are precious in the eyes of our Lord Jesus, and that must be enough.

f 20:28 Or "pastors."

g 20:28 The Greek uses the word "overseers" or "guardians." This is the sacred duty of his leaders in the church.

h 20:28 As translated from the Aramaic. Jesus is implied, for the Aramaic is simply "the Anointed One." Some Greek manuscripts and the Western Peshitta read, "the church of God."

i 20:29 As translated from the Aramaic. The Greek is "They won't spare the flock."

j 20:30 Or "speaking crooked things."

instead of Jesus. ³¹So be alert and discerning. Remember that for three years, night and day, I've never stopped warning each of you, pouring out my heart to you with tears.

³²"And so now, I entrust you into God's hands and the message of his grace,ᵃ which is all that you need to become strong.ᵇ All of God's blessings are imparted through the message of his grace, which he provides as the spiritual inheritance given to all of his holy ones.ᶜ

³³"I haven't been after your money or any of your possessions.ᵈ ³⁴You all know that I've worked with my hands to meet my own needs and the needs of those who've served with me. ³⁵I've left you an example of how you should serve and take care of those who are weak.ᵉ For we must always cherish the words of our Lord Jesus, who taught, **'Giving brings a far greater blessing than receiving.'"**ᶠ

³⁶After Paul finished speaking, he knelt down and prayed with them. ³⁷Then they all cried with great weeping as one after another hugged Paul and kissed him. ³⁸What broke their hearts the most were his words "You will not see my face again."

Then they tearfully accompanied Paul back to the ship.

---

a 20:32 The Aramaic is "the Manifestation of Grace."
b 20:32 Or "to build you up," a Greek word taken from the root word for "architect."
c 20:32 Or "sanctified"; that is, those who are devoted to holiness.
d 20:33 Or "silver, gold, or fine apparel."
e 20:35 Or "minister to the sick."
f 20:35 The Aramaic is an idiom that speaks of extravagant generosity. "Blessed are those who try to give more than they've been given."

Twenty-one

Paul's Journey to Jerusalem

[1]After we tore ourselves away from them, we put out to sea and sailed a direct course for the island of Kos, and on the next day to the island of Rhodes,[a] and from there to Patara.[b] [2]There we found a ship that was crossing over to Syria,[c] so we went aboard and sailed away. [3]After we sighted Cyprus and sailed south of it, we docked at Tyre[d] in Syria, where the ship unloaded its cargo.

[4]When we went ashore we found a number of believers and stayed with them for a week. [5]They prophesied to Paul repeatedly,[e] warning him by the Holy Spirit not to set foot in Jerusalem. When it was time for us to leave and be on our way, everyone—men, women, and children—accompanied us out of the city down to the beach. After we all knelt in the sand[f] and prayed together, [6]we kissed one another,[g] said our good-byes, and boarded the ship, while the believers went back to their homes.

[7]From Tyre we sailed[h] on to the town of Akko and greeted the believers there with peace.[i] We stayed with them for a day. [8]Then we went on to Caesarea and stayed for several days[j] in the home of Phillip the evangelist, who was one of the seven deacons[k] and [9]the father of four unmarried daughters who prophesied.

---

a 21:1 Both Kos and Rhodes are Greek islands in the Aegean Sea.
b 21:1 A city on the Mediterranean coast of Turkey.
c 21:2 Or "Phoenicia," a Greek term for coastal Lebanon and Syria.
d 21:3 Tyre was a city in Phoenicia. They would have sailed four or five days from Patara to reach Tyre.
e 21:5 As translated from the Aramaic.
f 21:5 Implied in the text.
g 21:6 As translated from the Aramaic idiom "one to one (kissed)."
h 21:7 The text can mean either "continued our journey" or "completed our journey." If they completed their journey by boat to Akko, they would have gone by land to Caesarea. Akko, or Ptolemais, was named after the Egyptian ruler Ptolemy II Philadelphus in 261 BC (Epistulae Aristeas 115; 1 Macc. 5:15). See also Judges 1:31.
i 21:7 As translated from the Aramaic.
j 21:8 This information is supplied from verse 10.
k 21:8 See Acts 6:1–7. An evangelist is simply "a preacher of the good news" or in Aramaic, "a preacher of the hope." Phillip is described as both an evangelist and a deacon (servant). Every minister must become a servant.

[10]During our stay of several days, Agabus,[a] a prophet from Judea, came to visit us. [11]As a prophetic gesture,[b] he took Paul's belt and tied his own hands and feet with it as he prophesied, "The Holy Spirit says, **'The one who owns this belt will be tied up in this same way by the Jews and they will hand him over to those who are not Jews.'"**[c]

[12]When we heard this, both we and the believers of Caesarea begged Paul not to go on to Jerusalem. [13]But Paul replied, "Why do you cry and break my heart with your tears? Don't you know that I'm prepared not only to be imprisoned but to die in Jerusalem for the sake of the wonder of the name of our Lord Jesus?"

[14]Because we couldn't persuade him, we gave up and said nothing more except "May the will of the Lord be done."

Paul Arrives in Jerusalem

[15]Afterward we packed our bags and set off for Jerusalem, [16]with some of the believers from Caesarea accompanying us. They brought us to a village[d] where they introduced us to Mnason, a Cypriot, one of the original disciples,[e] and he offered us hospitality.

[17]When we finally arrived in Jerusalem, the believers welcomed us with delight. [18]The next day Paul and our team had a meeting with James[f] and all the elders of the Jerusalem church. [19]After greeting everyone, Paul explained in detail what God had accomplished through his ministry among the non-Jewish people.

[20]When they heard Paul's report, they praised God. And they said to him, "You should know, brother, that there are many tens of thousands of Jews who have also embraced the faith and are passionately keeping the law of Moses. [21]But they've heard a rumor that you've been instructing the Jews everywhere to abandon Moses[g] by telling them they don't need to circumcise their children

---

a   21:10 See Acts 11:28.
b   21:11 Implied in the text.
c   21:11 Or "Gentiles"; i.e., the Romans.
d   21:16 Implied in the text and found in a few Greek manuscripts.
e   21:16 That is, one of the first converts. He may have been one of the original converts at Pentecost or one of the first disciples converted by Paul and Barnabas. Mnason means "remembering."
f   21:18 That is, James the brother of our Lord Jesus, not the apostle James who was martyred.
g   21:21 Or "apostasy from (the law of) Moses."

or keep our Jewish customs. ²²They will certainly hear that you've come to Jerusalem. So what is the proper way to proceed? ²³We urge you to follow our suggestion. We have four men here who have taken a vow and are ready to have their heads shaved. ²⁴Now, go with them to the temple and sponsor them in their purification ceremony,ᵃ and pay all their required expenses. Then everyone will know that the rumors they've heard are false. They'll see that you are one who lives according to the law of Moses. ²⁵But in reference to the non-Jewish believers, we've sent them a letter with our decision, stating that they should avoid eating meat that has been offered to an idol, or eating blood or any animal that has been strangled, and to avoid sexual immorality."ᵇ

Paul Arrested in Jerusalem

²⁶The next day, Paul took the four men to the temple and ceremonially purified himself along with them. He publicly gave notice of the date when their vows would end and when sacrifices would be offered for each of them.

²⁷When the seven-day periodᶜ was almost over, a number of Jews from western Turkeyᵈ who had seen him in the temple courts stirred up the whole crowd against him. Seizing him, ²⁸they shouted, "Men of Israel, help us! This is the man who teaches everywhere that he goes against our nation, our law, and this temple. And not only that, but now he brings these non-Jewish men with him into the inner courts of our temple! They have made this sacred place ritually unclean." ²⁹(For Trophimus, an Ephesian, had been seen previously with him, and they assumed that he entered the inner courts with Paul.)

³⁰This ignited a huge riot in the city as all the people came together to seize Paul and drag him out of the temple courts, closing the gates behind him. ³¹But as they were about to kill Paul, the news reached the commander of the Roman garrisonᵉ that the entire city was in an uproar. ³²He immediately ran out

---

a 21:24 This could have been the completion of a Nazarite vow (Numbers 6:1–12) or a reference to the Jewish custom of when a Jew returned from a trip to a foreign (pagan) land, he would purify himself of the defilement of being with unbelievers (Mishnah Oholoth 2:3).

b 21:24 It seems strange that James makes no mention of the offering that Paul brought for the poor saints in Jerusalem, which was the reason for leaving his missionary work to come to Jerusalem. Instead, James wants to ensure the purity of Paul's message. There is at least a hint that Paul's ministry was not always well received in Judea. See Romans 15:30–31.

c 21:27 This could also mean "the Sabbath."

d 21:27 Or "Asia (Minor)." They were possibly in Jerusalem to celebrate the Feast of Pentecost.

e 21:31 The Roman commander was in charge of about six hundred soldiers.

to the crowd with a large number of his officers and soldiers. When the crowd saw them coming, they stopped beating Paul. ³³The commander arrested him and ordered that he be bound with two chains. He then asked, "Who is he and what has he done wrong?"

³⁴Some in the crowd shouted one thing and others something else, just adding to the confusion. Since the commander was unable to get to the truth because of the disturbance, he ordered that Paul be brought back to their head-quarters. ³⁵When they reached the steps leading up to the fortress,ᵃ they had to protect Paul and carry him up because of the violent mob following them, ³⁶and everyone was screaming out, "Away with this man! Kill him!"

³⁷As Paul was being led to the entrance of the compound, he said to the commander in Greek, "May I have a word with you?"

The commander replied, "So you know Greek, do you?ᵇ ³⁸Aren't you that Egyptian fanatic who started a rebellion some time ago and led four thousand assassinsᶜ out into the wilderness?"

³⁹Paul answered, "I am, in fact, a Jew from Tarsus, in Cilicia, a well-known city of southern Turkey where I was born.ᵈ I beg you, sir, please give me a moment to speak to these people."

⁴⁰When the commander gave his permission, Paul stood on the steps and gestured with his hands for the people to listen. When the crowd quieted down, Paul addressed them in Aramaicᵉ and said:

Twenty-two

Paul's Defense

[1]"Ladies and gentlemen, fellow believers and elders[a]—please listen to me as I offer my defense."[b] [2](Now, when everyone realized he was speaking to them in their Judean Aramaic language,[c] the crowd became all the more attentive.)

[3]Then Paul said, "I am a Jewish man who was born in Tarsus, a city of Turkey.[d] However, I grew up in this city and was properly trained in the Mosaic law and tutored by Rabbi Gamaliel according to our ancestral customs. I've been extremely passionate in my desire to please God, just as all of you are today. [4]I've hunted down and killed the followers of this Way. I have seized them and thrown them into prison, both men and women. [5]All of this can be verified by the high priest and the Supreme Council of Elders. For they even wrote letters to our fellow Jews of Damascus, authorizing me to arrest them and bring them back to Jerusalem as prisoners to be punished.

[6]"As I was on the road approaching Damascus, about noon, a brilliant heavenly light suddenly appeared, flashing all around me. [7]As I fell to the ground I heard a voice say, **'Saul, Saul ... why are you persecuting me?'**

[8]"I answered, 'Who are you, my Lord?'

"He said to me, **'I am Jesus, the Victorious.[e] I am the one you are persecuting.'**

[9]"Those who were with me saw the brilliant light, but they didn't hear the voice of the one who spoke to me.[f]

---

a 22:1 Or "fathers (parents)."

b 22:1 The Aramaic is literally "Listen to my soul's outburst."

c 22:2 Or "Hebrew." Throughout the Middle East, Assyria, and Babylon, Aramaic was the lingua franca, the language of the people of that day. Greek and Latin were also spoken but not as prevalent as Aramaic.

d 21:3 Or "Cilicia," which was known as Asia Minor.

e 22:8 Or "Jesus the Nazarene." The word *Nazarene* means "the branch" or "Scion." The Aramaic word implies the title of an heir of a powerful family, or one who is victorious ("Jesus, the Victorious"). Believers are now grafted-in branches of his family tree, victorious ones in Christ.

f 22:9 Some Greek manuscripts add "and they were afraid."

[10]"So I asked, 'Lord, what am I to do?'

"And the Lord said to me, **'Get up and go into Damascus, and there you will be told about all that you are destined to do.'**

[11]"Because of the dazzling glory of the light, I couldn't see—I was left blind. So they had to lead me by the hand the rest of the way into Damascus.

[12]A Jewish man living there named Ananias came to see me. He was a godly man who lived according to the law of Moses and was highly esteemed by the Jewish community. [13]He stood beside me and said, 'Saul! My brother, Saul—open your eyes and see again!' At that very instant I opened my eyes and I could see! [14]Then he said to me, 'The God of our ancestors has destined you[a] to know his plan and for you to see the Holy One[b] and to hear his voice. [15]For you will be his witness[c] to every race of people and will share with them everything that you've seen and heard. [16]So now, what are you waiting for? Get up, be baptized, and wash away your sins as you call upon his name.'

[17]"Then I returned to Jerusalem. And while I was praying in the temple, [18]I entered another realm[d] and saw him. He said to me, **'Hurry and depart from Jerusalem quickly, for the people here will not receive the truths you share about me.'**

[19]"'But Lord,' I argued, 'they all know that I'm the one who went into our Jewish meetings to find those who believe in you and had them beaten[e] and imprisoned. [20]When the blood of your witness[f] Stephen was shed, I stood nearby in full approval of what was happening. I even guarded the cloaks of those who stoned him to death.'[g]

[21]"Then he said to me, **'Go at once, for I am sending you to preach to the non-Jewish nations.'"[h]**

[22]The crowd listened attentively to Paul up to this point. But when they

---

a   22:14 The Aramaic is "raised you up."

b   22:14 Or "the Righteous One" or "the Just One."

c   22:15 Or "martyr."

d   22:18 Or "fell into a trance." The Greek word for trance (*ekstasis*, from which we get the word *ecstasy*) literally means "to be taken to another place (state or realm)." See Strong's concordance 1611. He was actually taken into another realm as a trance came over him.

e   22:19 Or "beat with a whip (flogged)."

f   22:20 Or "martyr."

g   22:20 Implied in the text.

h   22:21 The Aramaic is "the far-away nations." See also Romans 11:13.

heard this, all at once they erupted with loud shouts, saying, "Get rid of this man! Kill him! He doesn't deserve to live!"

The Roman Commander Interrogates Paul

[23]While the crowd was screaming and yelling, removing their outer garments, and throwing handfuls of dust in the air in protest, [24]the commander had Paul brought back into the compound. He ordered that he be whipped with a lash and interrogated to find out what he said that so infuriated the crowd.

[25]When the soldiers stretched Paul out with ropes, he said to the captain, who was standing nearby, "Is it legal for you to torture a Roman citizen like this, without a proper trial?"

[26]When the officer heard this, he immediately went to his commander and reported it, saying, "This man is a Roman citizen. What should we do now?"

[27]The commander came to Paul and asked him, "Tell me the truth, are you a Roman citizen?"

"Yes I am," he replied.

[28]The commander said, "I had to purchase my citizenship with a great sum of money."

Paul replied, "I was born as a citizen!"

[29]All of the soldiers who were about to whip Paul backed away, because they were afraid of the consequences for tying up and holding a Roman citizen against his will.

[30]The next day the commander ordered that the high priest and the supreme Jewish council[a] be convened, because he wanted to find out exactly why the Jews were accusing Paul. So he had him untied and brought out to stand before them all.

---

a 22:30 Or "Sanhedrin," a council of seventy of the elders of Israel.

Twenty-three

Paul before the Supreme Council

[1]Paul fixed his eyes on the members of the council and said, "My brothers, up to this day I have lived my life before God with a perfectly clear conscience."[a]
[2]At that moment, Ananias[b] the high priest ordered those standing near Paul to strike him in the mouth.

[3]Paul responded, "God is going to strike you, you corrupt pretender![c] For you sit there judging me according to the law, yet you broke the law when you ordered me to be struck."

[4]Those standing near Paul said to him, "Do you dare insult the high priest of God?"

[5]Paul answered, "I had no idea, brothers, that he was the high priest.[d] For the Scriptures say, **'Do not curse the ruler of your people.'**"[e]

[6]Just then Paul realized that part of the council were Sadducees, who deny the resurrection of the dead,[f] and others were of the separated ones. So he shouted, "My fellow Jews, I am a separated one,[g] and the son of a separated one. That's why I'm on trial here. It's because of the hope I have that the dead will rise to live again."[h]

---

a 23:1 The Aramaic is "I have been blessed by God in every way unto this day" or "I have been guided by God unto this day."
b 23:2 It is ironic that one Ananias was God's instrument to bring healing and sight to Paul in Damascus, but here it is a different Ananias.
c 23:3 Or "white-washed wall (hypocrite)." See Ezekiel 13:10–16 and Matthew 23:27–28.
d 23:5 It was common for priests and rabbis to wear common clothes except on holy occasions. This could be why Paul did not recognize him as the high priest. There was also uncertainty as to who the high priest was, as Paul had been away from Jerusalem for years.
e 23:5 See Exodus 22:28.
f 23:6 This clause is borrowed from verse 8 and inserted here for the sake of clarity of the English narrative. Of the three major sects of Judaism of that day (Pharisees, Essenes, and Sadducees), the Sadducees were a small but influential group that philosophically denied the supernatural (including the resurrection of the dead, angels, and spirit) and gravitated instead toward political control of the people.
g 23:6 Or "Pharisee," which means "separated one." They were strict keepers of the law and believed in angels and the resurrection.
h 23:6 Or "the hope and the resurrection from the dead." This is most likely a hendiadys. The Aramaic is "I have faith in the (miracle) of the resurrection from the dead."

[7]When he said this, a heated argument started among them, dividing the council between the Sadducees and the separated ones. [8]Paul knew[a] that the Sadducees teach there is no resurrection and do not believe in angels or spirits, but the separated ones believe in them all. [9]This sparked an even greater uproar among them.

Finally, some of the separated ones who were religious scholars[b] stood up and protested strongly, saying, "We find nothing wrong with this man. It could be that the Spirit[c] has spoken to him or an angel came to him."

[10]When the shouting match became intense, the commander, fearing they would tear Paul to pieces, intervened and ordered his soldiers to go in to their meeting and seize him and take him back to their headquarters.

[11]That night our Lord appeared to Paul and stood before him and said,[d] **"Receive miracle power.[e] For just as you have spoken for me in Jerusalem, you will also speak for me in Rome."[f]**

The Plot to Kill Paul

[12-13]The next day, more than forty Jews formed a conspiracy and bound themselves under an oath[g] to have no food or water until they had killed Paul. [14]They went to the high priest and the elders to divulge their plans and said to them, "We have united in a solemn oath not to eat or drink until Paul is dead. [15]So we urge you to have the commander bring him to you as though you were to determine his case with a more thorough inquiry. And we will kill him before he even gets here!"

[16]When Paul's nephew, his sister's son, overheard their plot to kill him, he came to the headquarters and informed him of their plans. [17]Paul called for one

---

a 23:8 Implied in the text and added for the sake of clarity of the English narrative.
b 23:9 Or "scribes (experts in the law)."
c 23:9 The Spirit referred to was obviously sent from God (the Holy Spirit).
d 23:11 The Lord Jesus works with his apostolic servants and appeared to them throughout church history to encourage and give them direction for the expansion of the kingdom realm of God. See also Mark 16:15, Acts 18:9–10, 22:17–18, 27:23–24, and 2 Corinthians 12:1.
e 23:11 As translated from the Aramaic. The Greek is "Have courage."
f 23:11 The Aramaic is "You are destined to speak for me in Rome also."
g 23:12–13 Or "with a curse." That is, they pronounced a curse upon themselves, calling down heaven's punishment if they did not murder Paul. One wonders what happened to them when their plot failed.

of the captains[a] and said, "Take this boy[b] to the commander, for he has something important to report to him."

[18]The captain took him to the commander and informed him, "Paul the prisoner asked me to bring this boy to you because he has something important for you to know."

[19]The commander took him by the arm and led him aside in private and asked him, "What do you have to tell me?"

[20]He replied, "The Jews have plotted to kill Paul. Tomorrow they will ask you to bring him again to the supreme council under the pretense of wanting to question him further. [21]Don't believe them, because they have forty men lying in wait to ambush Paul. These men have sworn an oath not to eat or drink until they have killed him. They're all waiting for you to agree to their request so they can carry out their plot."[c]

[22]The commander dismissed Paul's nephew after directing him, "Tell no one that you've reported these things to me." [23-24]Then he summoned two of his captains and said to them, "I want you to take Paul by horseback to Caesarea tonight at nine o'clock. Dispatch two hundred infantrymen, seventy horsemen, and another two hundred spearmen to provide security and deliver him safely to Governor Felix." [25]He sent with them a letter that read:

[26]From Claudias Lysias, to His Excellency, Governor Felix:[d]

> Dear Governor,
>
> [27]I rescued this man, who was seized by the Jews as they were about to put him to death. I intervened with my troops because I understand that he is a Roman citizen. [28]I was determined to learn exactly what charge they were accusing him of, so I brought him to stand before the Jewish supreme council. [29]I discovered that he was being accused with reference to violating controversial issues about their law, but I found no charge

---

a 23:17 Or "centurions." See also verse 18.
b 23:17 The Aramaic is "preteen boy." The Greek is "young man."
c 23:21 Implied and added to complete the ellipsis.
d 23:26 This was Antonius Felix, the governor of Caesarea who had jurisdiction over Israel and parts of Syria. He was known as a corrupt and cruel tyrant. However, he was married to a Jewish woman and was well acquainted with Jewish laws and traditions. It was important that Paul, a Roman citizen, be tried by Roman authorities.

against him that deserved death or imprisonment. ³⁰When I was informed of an imminent plot to kill him, I sent him to you at once, and I have ordered his accusers to also come before you and state their charges against him.

Sincerely,
Claudius Lysias

³¹The soldiers carried out their orders and escorted Paul during the night until they reached the city of Antipatris.ᵃ ³²The next day the horsemen continued on with Paul and the rest of the soldiers were dismissed to return to their headquarters.

³³Upon their arrival in Caesarea, they presented the letter to the governor and brought Paul before him. ³⁴After reading the letter, he asked Paul what province he was from.

Paul answered, "Southeast Turkey."ᵇ

³⁵The governor said, "I will give you a full hearing when your accusers arrive here also." Then he ordered that Paul be kept under guard in Herod's palace.

a 23:31 This was over halfway from Jerusalem to Caesarea.
b 23:34 Or "Cilicia."

Twenty-four

Paul's Trial before Felix

¹Five days later, Ananias the high priest arrived in Caesarea, accompanied by some Jewish elders and Tertullus, their prosecuting attorney.ᵃ They were brought before the governor to present formal charges against Paul. ²After Paul was summoned, Tertullus accused him, saying, ³"Your Excellency Felix, under the shadow of your wise leadershipᵇ we Jews have experienced a long period of peace. Because of your wise foresight, many reforms are coming to pass in our nation because of you, Most Honorable Felix. We deeply appreciate this and thank you very much.

⁴"So that I won't weary you with a lengthy presentation, I beg you to hear our brief summary, with your customary graciousness. ⁵For we have found this man to be a contagious plague,ᶜ a seditious man who continually stirs up riots among the Jews all over the world. He has become a ringleader of the sect known as the Nazarenes.ᵈ ⁶He has even attempted to desecrate our temple, which is why we had him arrested. We sought to judge him according to our law, ⁷but Commander Lysias came with great force, snatched him away from our hands, and sent him here to you. ⁸He has ordered his accusers to come to you so that you could interrogate him and ascertain for yourself that all these charges we are bringing against him are true."ᵉ

⁹All the Jews present joined in the verbal attack, saying, "Yes, it's true!"

Paul's Defense before Felix

[10]The governor motioned that it was Paul's turn to speak, so he began to answer the accusations.

"Because I know that you have been a judge over this nation for many years, I gladly respond in my defense. [11]You can easily verify that about twelve days ago, I went to Jerusalem to worship. [12]No one found me arguing with anyone or causing trouble among the people in the Jewish meeting houses or in the temple or anywhere in the city. [13]They are completely unable to prove these accusations they make against me.

[14]"But I do confess this to you: I worship the God of our Jewish ancestors as a follower of the Way, which they call a sect. For I believe everything that is written in the Law and the Prophets. [15]And my hope is in God, the same hope that even my accusers have embraced, the hope of a resurrection from the dead of both the righteous and the unrighteous. [16]That's why I seek with all my heart to have a clean conscience toward God and toward others.

[17]"After being away from Jerusalem for several years, I returned to bring to my people gifts for the poor.[a] [18]I was in the temple, ritually purified and presenting my offering to God, when they seized me. I had no noisy crowd around me, and I wasn't causing trouble or making any kind of disturbance whatsoever. [19]It was a group of Jews from western Turkey[b] who were being unruly; they are the ones who should be here now to bring their charges if they have anything against me. [20]Or at least these men standing before you should clearly state what crime they found me guilty of when I stood before the Jewish supreme council, [21]unless it's the one thing I passionately spoke out when I stood among them. I am on trial today only because of my belief in the resurrection of the dead."

[22]Felix, who was well acquainted with the facts about the Way, concluded the hearing with these words: "I will decide your case after Commander Lysias arrives." [23]He then ordered the captain to keep Paul in protective custody, but to give him a measure of freedom, he allowed any of his friends to visit him and help take care of his needs.

---

a 24:17–18 The Aramaic is "For many years I brought to my people gifts for the poor."
b 24:19 Or "Asia (Minor)."

Paul Speaks to Felix and Drusilla

²⁴Several days later, Felix came back with his wife, Drusilla,ᵃ who was Jewish. They sent for Paul and listened as he shared with them about faith in Jesus, the Anointed One. ²⁵As Paul spoke about true righteousness, self-control, and the coming judgment, Felix became terrified and said, "Leave me for now. I'll send for you later when it's more convenient."ᵇ

²⁶He expected to receive a bribe from Paul for his release, so for that reason he would send for Paul from time to time to converse with him.

²⁷Two years later, Felix was succeeded by Porcius Festus. Before he left office he decided to leave Paul in prison as a political favor to the Jews.

---

a 24:24 Drusilla was the youngest daughter of Herod Agrippa I and sister of Agrippa II. As a Jewess, she was likely the source of Felix's understanding of the Way.

b 24:25 The Aramaic can be translated "When my conscience is clear I will call for you."

Twenty-five

Paul Appeals to Caesar

¹Three days after Festus assumed his duties in Caesarea, he made the journey to Jerusalem.ᵃ ²Religious authorities and prominent leaders among the Jews brought formal charges against Paul before Festus. ³They came asking him for a favor—that he would transfer Paul from Caesarea to Jerusalem—all the while plotting to ambush and kill Paul along the way.

⁴Festus responded to their request by informing them that he planned to return to Caesarea shortly. ⁵He told them, "Your leaders can come with me to Caesarea. If this man has broken any laws, you can bring charges against him there."

⁶After Festus had stayed in Jerusalem no more than eight to ten days, he left for Caesarea. The day after he arrived, he convened the court and took his seat on the bench as judge over the proceedings. After he ordered Paul brought into the courtroom, ⁷the Jewish leaders who came from Jerusalem encircled him and leveled against him many serious charges, which they were unable to substantiate.

⁸In his defense, Paul said by the Holy Spirit,ᵇ "I have done nothing wrong.ᶜ I've committed no offense against Jewish law, or against the temple, or against Caesar."

⁹Festus, because he wanted to curry favor with the Jews, asked Paul, "Are you willing to go with me to Jerusalem and be tried for these charges?"

¹⁰Paul replied, "I am standing here before Caesar's tribunal. This is where I should be tried. As you well know, I have done no harm to the Jews. ¹¹If I have

---

a 25:1 This was a journey of about sixty-five miles (over one hundred kilometers).
b 25:8 As translated from the Aramaic.
c 25:8 Or "I have not sinned in anything."

committed a crime worthy of death, I won't seek to escape the death penalty. But if none of their charges is true, no one has the right to hand me over to them. I appeal to Caesar!"

[12]After conferring with the members of his council, Festus replied, "Since you have appealed to Caesar, to Caesar you will go!"

Festus and King Agrippa

[13]Several days later, King Agrippa and Bernice[a] arrived at Caesarea for a visit with Festus. [14]During their stay of many days, Festus explained Paul's situation to the king to get his opinion on the matter, saying, "There is a man here whom Felix left as a prisoner. [15]When I was in Jerusalem, the leading priests and Jewish elders pressed charges against him and demanded that I issue a guilty verdict against him. [16]I explained to them that it is not our Roman custom to condemn any man before he has an opportunity to face his accusers and present his defense. [17]So they returned here with me. I didn't postpone the trial, but convened the court the very next day and ordered the man to be brought before me. [18]I listened to their accusations against him, but they were not what I expected to hear, for he had committed no crime. [19]Rather, their issues centered around disagreements with him over their religion, and about a dead man named Jesus, who Paul claimed was alive. [20]Because I was perplexed about how to proceed, I asked him if he would be willing to go to Jerusalem to stand trial on these charges. [21]When Paul appealed his case to the emperor for a decision, I ordered him to be held in custody until I could send him to Caesar."

[22]King Agrippa said to Festus, "I would like to listen to this man myself."

"Tomorrow," he replied, "you will have that opportunity."

Paul before King Agrippa

[23]The next day King Agrippa and Bernice entered the audience hall with much pomp and pageantry. Accompanying them were the senior military officers and prominent citizens. Festus ordered that Paul be brought before them all.

[24]Then Festus said, "King Agrippa, and esteemed guests, here is the man whom the entire Jewish community, both here and in Jerusalem, has asked

a 25:13 Bernice, a Jewess, was the sister of King Agrippa and the older sister of Drusilla, wife of Felix (Acts 24:24).

me to condemn to death. They have screamed and shouted at me, demanding that I end his life. [25]Yet upon investigation I couldn't find one thing that he has done to deserve the death penalty. When he appealed to His Majesty the emperor, I determined to send him. [26]But I have nothing concrete to write to His Majesty, so I have now brought him before you all, and especially before you, King Agrippa. After this preliminary hearing I should have something to write, [27]for it seems absurd to me to send a prisoner without specifying the charges against him."

Twenty-six

Paul's Defense before King Agrippa

¹King Agrippa said to Paul, "You may now state your case." Paul motioned with his hand for silence, then began his defense.ª

²"King Agrippa, I consider myself highly favored to stand before you today and answer the charges made against me by the Jews. ³Because you, more than anyone else, are very familiar with the customs and controversies among the Jewish people, I now ask for your patience as I state my case.ᵇ

⁴"All the Jews know how I have been raised as a young man, living among my own people from the beginning and in Jerusalem. ⁵If my accusers are willing to testify, they must admit that they've known me all along as a Pharisee, a member of the most strict and orthodox sect within Judaism.ᶜ ⁶And now, here I am on trial because I believe in the hopeᵈ of God's promises made to our ancestors. ⁷This is the promise the twelve tribes of our people hope to see fulfilled as they sincerely strive to serve God with prayers night and day.ᵉ

"So, Your Highness, it is because of this hope that the Jews are accusing me. ⁸And how should you judge this matter?ᶠ Why is it that any of you think it unbelievable that God raises the dead? ⁹I used to think that I should do all that was in my power to oppose the name of Jesus of Nazareth. ¹⁰And that's exactly what I did in Jerusalem, for I not only imprisoned many of the holy believers by the authority of the chief priests, I also cast my vote against them, sentencing them to death. ¹¹I punished them often in every Jewish meeting hall and

---

a 26:1 An alternate reading of the Aramaic is "The (Holy) Spirit issued from his mouth."
b 26:3 An alternate reading of the Aramaic is "I beg you to allow the Spirit to flow so that you can hear me."
c 26:5 The Aramaic is "I have lived by the elite knowledge of the Pharisees."
d 26:6 The Aramaic can also be translated "good news."
e 26:7 As translated from the Aramaic.
f 26:8 As translated from the Aramaic.

attempted to force them to blaspheme. I boiled with rage against them, hunting them down in distant foreign cities to persecute them.

¹²"For that purpose I went to Damascus, with the authority granted to me by the chief priests. ¹³While traveling on the road at noon, Your Highness, I saw a light brighter than the sun flashing from heaven all around me and those who were with me. ¹⁴We all fell to the ground, and I heard a voice speaking to me in Aramaic, saying, **'Saul, Saul, why are you persecuting me? You are only hurting yourself when you resist your calling.'**ᵃ

¹⁵"I asked, 'Who are you, Lord?'

"And the Lord replied, **'I am Jesus,**ᵇ **the one you are persecuting. ¹⁶Get up and stand to your feet, for I have appeared to you to reveal your destiny and to commission you**ᶜ **as my assistant.**ᵈ **You will be a witness to what you have seen and to the things I will reveal whenever I appear to you.**ᵉ **¹⁷I will rescue you from the persecution of your own people and from the hostility of the other nations that I will send you to. ¹⁸And you will open their eyes to their true condition, so that they may turn from darkness to the Light**ᶠ **and from the power**ᵍ **of Satan to the power of God. By placing their faith in me they will receive the total forgiveness**ʰ **of sins and be made holy, taking hold of the inheritance that I give to my children!'**ⁱ

¹⁹"So you see, King Agrippa, I have not been disobedient to what was revealed to me from heaven. ²⁰For it was in Damascus that I first declared the truth. And then I went to Jerusalem and throughout our nation,ʲ and even to other nations, telling people everywhere that they must repent and turn to God and demonstrate it with a changed life.ᵏ ²¹That's why the Jews seized me when I was in the temple and tried to murder me.

---

a 26:14 Or "Why are you hurting yourself by kicking against the ox-goads?"
b 26:15 The Aramaic is "Jesus, the Victorious." See Acts 22:8 with footnote.
c 26:16 Implied in the context.
d 26:16 The Greek word *hypēretēs* is also used for John Mark as the "assistant" to Barnabas in Acts 13:5.
e 26:16 As translated from the Aramaic, which is literally "a witness that you have seen me and are going to see me again." The Greek is "to what shall yet appear before your eyes" or "to the things in which I will appear to you." Both Greek and Aramaic are somewhat combined in the translation of this verse. Jesus promised future appearances to Paul.
f 26:18 See Isaiah 35:5, 42:6–7, and 16.
g 26:18 Or "authority" or "dominion."
h 26:18 Or "cancellation of sins."
i 26:18 Implied in the text.
j 26:20 Or "Judea."
k 26:20 Or "with fruits in keeping with repentance."

²²"But in spite of all this, I have experienced the supernatural help of God up to this very moment. So I'm standing here saying the same thing that I've shared with everyone, from the least to the greatest. For I teach nothing but what ²³Moses and the prophets have said was destined to happen: that our Messiah had to suffer and die and be the first to rise from the dead,[a] to release the bright light of truth both to our people and to the non-Jewish nations."[b]

²⁴Festus interrupted Paul's defense,[c] blurting out, "You're out of your mind! All this great learning of yours is driving you crazy."[d]

²⁵Paul replied, "No, Your Excellency Festus, I am not crazy. I speak the words of truth and reason.[e] ²⁶King Agrippa, I know I can speak frankly and freely with you, for you understand these matters well, and none of these things has escaped your notice. After all, it's not like it was a secret! ²⁷Don't you believe the prophets, King Agrippa? I know that you do."

²⁸Agrippa responded, "In such a short time you are nearly persuading me to become a Christian."

²⁹Paul replied, "I pray to God that both you and those here listening to me would one day become the same as I am, except, of course, without these chains."

³⁰The king, the governor, Bernice, and all the others got up. ³¹As they were leaving the chamber, they commented to one another, "This man has done nothing that deserves death or even imprisonment."

³²King Agrippa said to Festus, "If he hadn't appealed to Caesar, he could have been released."

---

a 26:23 The Aramaic is "to inaugurate (or be the origin of) the resurrection from the dead."
b 26:23 See Luke 2:32.
c 26:24 The Aramaic can be translated "As the Holy Spirit spoke through Paul, Festus interrupted."
d 26:24 Or "So much Scripture has made you senseless!"
e 26:25 Or "words of sober truth."

Twenty-seven

Paul Sails to Italy

¹When it was decided that we[a] were to sail for Italy, Festus handed over Paul and a number of other prisoners to the custody of a Roman officer named Julius, a member of the imperial guard. ²We went on board a ship from the port of Adramyttium[b] that was planning to stop at various ports along the coast of southwestern Turkey.[c] We put out to sea and were accompanied by Aristarchus[d] from Thessalonica in Macedonia.

³The next day we docked at Sidon,[e] and Julius, being considerate of Paul, allowed him to disembark and be refreshed by his friends living there. ⁴From there we put out to sea, but because the winds[f] were against us, we sailed under the lee of Cyprus.[g] ⁵After sailing across the open sea off Cilicia and Pamphylia, we docked at the port of Myra in Lycia. ⁶While we were there, the commanding officer found an Egyptian ship from Alexandria that was bound for Italy, and he put us on board.

⁷We made little headway for several days, and with difficulty we made it to Knidus.[h] The strong winds kept us from holding our course, so from there we sailed along the lee of Crete,[i] opposite Cape Salome. ⁸Hugging the coast, we struggled on to a place called Fair Haven, near the town of Lasea. ⁹We remained there a long time, until we passed the day of the Jewish fast.[j]

---

a 27:1 It is likely that Luke rejoined Paul here and sailed with him to Rome.
b 27:2 Adramyttium (modern-day Edrimit, Turkey) was a seaport in the Roman colony of Mysia. Adramyttium means "I will abide in death."
c 27:2 Or "the coast of the province of Asia (Minor)."
d 27:2 Aristarchus means "the best leader."
e 27:3 A Phoenician city now in modern-day Lebanon.
f 27:4 The Aramaic can be translated "The spirits were against us."
g 27:4 That is, east and north of the island.
h 27:7 Or "Cnidus," an ancient port city on the Gulf of Gökova on the coast of Turkey.
i 27:7 The Aramaic is "We circled Crete."
j 27:9 This was possibly the Day of Atonement, when every Jew fasts.

Paul advised the frightened sailors that they should not put out to sea in such dangerous weather,[a] saying, [10]"Men, I can see that our voyage would be disastrous for us and bring great loss, not only to our ship and cargo but also to our own lives. We should remain here."[b]

[11]But the officer in charge was persuaded more by the ship's helmsman and captain[c] than he was by Paul. [12]So the majority decided to put out to sea, since Fair Haven was an exposed harbor and not suitable to winter in. They had hoped to somehow reach the Cretan port of Phineka,[d] which was a more suitable port because it was facing south.[e]

[13]When a gentle south breeze began to blow, they assumed they could make it, so they pulled up anchor and sailed close to Crete. [14]But it wasn't long before the weather abruptly worsened and a storm of hurricane force called the Nor'easter[f] tore across the island and blew us out to sea. [15]The sailors weren't able to turn the ship into the wind, so they gave up and let it be driven by the gale winds.[g]

[16]As we passed to the lee of a small island called Cauda,[h] we were barely able to get the ship's lifeboat under control, [17]so the crew hoisted the dinghy aboard. The sailors used ropes and cables to undergird the ship,[i] fearing they would run aground on the shoals of Syrtis.[j] They lowered the drag anchor to slow its speed and let the ship be driven along.

[18]The next day, because of being battered severely by the storm, the sailors jettisoned the cargo,[19] and by the third day they even threw the ship's tackle and rigging overboard. [20]After many days of seeing neither the sun nor the stars, and with the violent storm continuing to rage against us, all hope of ever getting through it alive was abandoned.

---

a   27:9 As translated from the Aramaic. This was the season the Romans called *mare clausum*, the closed sea, when the Mediterranean was not navigable.

b   27:10 This was clearly prophetic revelation given to the apostle Paul. The last sentence is implied in the context (see verse 21) and important for the sake of English narrative.

c   27:11 Or "ship's owner."

d   27:12 Or "Phoenix."

e   27:12 As translated from the Aramaic. The Greek is "looking toward Lips and Choros." Lips was the Greek term for the winds from the southwest, and *Choros* the word for winds from the northwest.

f   27:14 The Aramaic is "Euroclydon's typhoon."

g   27:15 The Aramaic is "We surrendered to its power."

h   27:16 Or "Gaudos."

i   27:17 The Aramaic is "They tied down the lifeboat on the ship, lest it fall into the sea."

j   27:17 This was a shallow region full of reefs and sandbars off the coast of Libya between Benghazi and Tripoli.

21After being without food for a long time, Paul stepped before them all and said, "Men, you should have obeyed[a] me and avoided all of this pain and suffering by not leaving Crete. 22Now listen to me. Don't be depressed, for no one will perish—only the ship will be lost. 23For God's angel visited me last night, the angel of my God, the God I passionately serve. He came and stood in front of me 24and said, 'Don't be afraid, Paul. You are destined to stand trial before Caesar. And because of God's favor on you, he has given you the lives of everyone who is sailing with you.' 25So men, keep up your courage! I know that God will protect you, just as he told me he would. 26But we must run aground on some island to be saved."[b]

27On the fourteenth night of being tossed about the Adriatic Sea, about midnight, the sailors sensed we were approaching land. 28So they took soundings and discovered that the water was about 120 feet deep.[c] After sailing a short distance, they again took soundings and found it was only ninety feet deep.[d] 29Fearing we would be dashed against a rocky coast, they dropped four anchors from the stern and waited for morning to come.

30Some sailors pretended to go down to drop anchors from the bow when in fact they wanted to lower the lifeboat into the sea and escape, abandoning ship. 31Paul said to the Roman officer and his soldiers, "Unless you all stay together onboard the ship, you have no chance of surviving." 32At the moment they heard this, the soldiers cut the ropes of the dinghy and let it fall away.

33Just before daybreak, Paul urged everyone to eat. He said, "Today makes two full weeks that you've been in fearful peril and hunger, unable to eat a thing. 34Now eat and be nourished. For you'll all come through this ordeal without a scratch."[e]

35Then Paul took bread and gave thanks to God[f] in front of them, broke it and passed it around for everyone to eat. 36-38Paul fed 276 people with the

---

a 27:21 The Greek word *peitharkheo* means "to obey one who is in authority." Paul was the true captain of the ship and carried the weight of authority.
b 27:26 Implied in the text.
c 27:28 Or "twenty fathoms."
d 27:28 Or "fifteen fathoms."
e 27:34 Or "Not one hair of your heads will perish."
f 27:35 The Aramaic is "glorified God."

bread, and they all ate until they were filled, and were strengthened and encouraged.[a] Afterward, they threw the grain into the sea to lighten the ship.

Paul Is Shipwrecked

[39]When daylight came, the sailors didn't recognize the land, but they noticed a cove with a sandy beach, so they decided to run the ship ashore. [40]They cut away the anchors, leaving them in the sea, untied the ropes holding the rudders, and hoisted the foresail to the breeze to head for the beach. [41]But they drifted into the rocky shoals between two depths of the sea, causing the ship to flounder still a distance from shore. The bow was stuck fast, jammed on the rocks, while the stern was being smashed by the pounding of the surf.

[42]The soldiers wanted to kill all the prisoners to prevent them from escaping. [43]But the Roman officer was determined to bring Paul safely through, so he foiled their attempts. He commanded the prisoners and crew who could swim to jump overboard and swim ashore.[b] [44]The rest all managed to survive by clinging to planks and broken pieces of the ship, so that everyone scrambled to the shore uninjured.

---

a 27:36–37 Paul served communion on board the ship and fed every passenger and crew member. (Did God multiply the bread?) The language used is vividly Eucharistic. There is a variation among many Greek manuscripts as to the total of those who were fed. Some have as few as sixty-nine or seventy. The majority of reliable manuscripts in Greek and Aramaic have 276.

b 27:43 As translated from the Aramaic.

Paul on the Island of Malta

¹After we had safely reached land, we discovered that the island we were on was Malta. ²The people who lived there showed us extraordinary kindness, for they welcomed us around the fire they had built because it was cold and rainy.

³When Paul had gathered an armful of brushwood and was setting it on the fire, a venomous snake was driven out by the heat and latched onto Paul's hand with its fangs. ⁴When the islanders saw the snake dangling from Paul's hand, they said to one another, "No doubt about it, this guy is a murderer. Even though he escaped death at sea, Justice[a] has now caught up with him!"

⁵But Paul shook the snake off, flung it into the fire, and suffered no harm at all. ⁶Everyone watched him, expecting him to swell up or suddenly drop dead. After observing him for a long time and seeing that nothing unusual happened, they changed their minds and said, "He must be a god!"

⁷The Roman governor of the island, named Publius, had his estate nearby. He graciously welcomed us as his houseguests and showed us hospitality for the three days that we stayed with him. ⁸His father lay sick in bed, suffering from fits of high fever and dysentery. So Paul went into his room, and after praying, placed his hands on him. He was instantly healed. ⁹When the people of the island heard about this miracle, they brought all the sick to Paul, and they were also healed.[b] ¹⁰The islanders honored us greatly,[c] and when we were preparing to set sail again, they gave us all the supplies we needed for our journey.

---

a 28:4 The implication in the Greek text is that they were referring to a "goddess of justice," perhaps a local deity.

b 28:9 Although Paul was technically a prisoner, he was the one setting everyone free. No doubt he preached the gospel with signs and wonders, leaving the island healed in more ways than one.

c 28:10 Or "They honored us with many honors."

Paul Reaches Rome

[11]After three months we put out to sea on an Egyptian ship from Alexandria that had wintered at the island. The ship had carved on its prow as its emblem the "Heavenly Twins."[a]

[12]When we landed at Syracuse,[b] we stayed there for three days. [13]From there we set sail for the Italian city of Rhegium. The day after we landed, a south wind sprang up that enabled us to reach Puteoli[c] in two days. [14]There we found some believers, who begged us to stay with them for a week. Afterward, we made our way to Rome.

[15]When the believers were alerted we were coming, they came out to meet us at the Forum of Appius, while we were still a great distance from Rome.[d] Another group met us[e] at the Three Taverns. When Paul saw the believers, his heart was greatly encouraged and he thanked God.

[16]When we finally entered Rome, Paul was turned over to the authorities and was allowed to live where he pleased, with one soldier assigned to guard him.

Paul Speaks to Prominent Jews of Rome

[17]After three days Paul called together all the prominent members of the Jewish community of Rome.[f] When they had all assembled, Paul said to them, "My fellow Jews, while I was in Jerusalem, I was handed over as a prisoner of the Romans for prosecution, even though I had done nothing against any of our people or our Jewish customs. [18]After hearing my case, the Roman authorities wanted to release me since they found nothing that deserved a death sentence. [19]When the Jews objected to this, I felt it necessary, with no malice against them,[g] to appeal to Caesar. [20]This, then, is the reason I've asked to speak with

---

a 28:11 These were the twin sons of Zeus, Castor and Pollux. The Aramaic is "flying the flag of Gemini." This was a widespread cult in Egypt in that era.

b 28:12 This was the city on the eastern coast of Sicily.

c 28:13 This was on the western coast of Italy, with a road leading to Rome, about 145 miles to the north.

d 28:15 Implied in the text. The Forum of Appius was about forty-three miles away from Rome.

e 28:15 Implied in the text. Three Taverns was about thirty-three miles from Rome.

f 28:17 Some believe there could have been as many as fifty thousand Jews living in Rome at the time of Paul's visit.

g 28:19 Or "not that I had any feud against my own nation."

238 • THE PASSION TRANSLATION

you, so that I could explain these things. It is only because I believe in the Hope of Israel that I am in chains before you."

²¹They replied, "We haven't received any letters from the Jews of Judea, nor has anyone come to us with a bad report about you. ²²But we are anxious to hear you present your views regarding this Christian sect we've been hearing about, for people everywhere are speaking against it."

²³So they set a time to meet with Paul. On that day an even greater crowd gathered where he was staying. From morning until evening Paul taught them, opening up the truths of the kingdom realm of God. With convincing arguments from both the Law and the Prophets, he tried to convince them about Jesus.ª ²⁴Some were converted, but others refused to believe. They argued back and forth, still unable to agree among themselves.

²⁵They were about to leave when Paul made one last statement to them: "The Holy Spirit stated it wellᵇ when he spoke to your ancestors through the prophet Isaiah:ᶜ

²⁶**I send you to this people to say to them, "You keep learning,ᵈ but not understanding. You keep staring at truth but not perceiving it. ²⁷For your hearts are hard and insensitive to me—you must be hard of hearing! For you've closed your eyes so that you won't be troubled by the truth, and you've covered your ears so that you won't have to listen and be pierced by what I say. For then you would have to respond and repent, so that I could heal your hearts."**

²⁸"So listen well. This wonderful salvation given by God is now being presented to the non-Jewish nations, and they will believe and receive it!"ᵉ

---

a 28:23 That is, about the purpose of Jesus' coming, which would include his life, ministry, death for our sins, and glorious resurrection.

b 28:25 The Aramaic can be translated "The Holy Spirit spoke beautifully through the mouth of Isaiah the prophet."

c 28:25 See Isaiah 6:9–10.

d 28:26 Or "listening."

e 28:28 Verse 29 is not included in the oldest and most reliable Greek manuscript, and it is omitted from almost every modern translation, including the Aramaic. Verse 29, if included, would read, "After hearing this, the Jews left with a heated argument among themselves."

³⁰Paul lived two more years in Rome, in his own rented quarters, welcoming all who came to visit. ³¹He continued to proclaim to all the truths of the kingdom realm of God, teaching them about the Lord Jesus, the Anointed One, speaking triumphantly and without any restriction.ᵃ

---

a 28:31 Tradition says that Paul was eventually released from house arrest and traveled to Spain. But the inspired account ends here, with Paul ministering to all who came to him. This completes the Acts of the Holy Spirit as recorded by Luke. Although the book of Acts is finished, the acts of God continue to be accomplished through his apostolic company of surrendered lovers. Every believer has the same Holy Spirit and can do the works of Jesus on the earth today.

About the Translator

Dr. Brian Simmons is known as a passionate lover of God. After a dramatic conversion to Christ, Brian knew that God was calling him to go to the unreached people of the world and present the gospel of God's grace to all who would listen. With his wife Candice and their three children, he spent nearly eight years in the tropical rain forest of the Darien Province of Panama as a church planter, translator, and consultant. Brian was involved in the Paya-Kuna New Testament translation project. He studied linguistics and Bible translation principles with New Tribes Mission. After their ministry in the jungle, Brian was instrumental in planting a thriving church in New England (U.S.), and now travels full time as a speaker and Bible teacher. He has been happily married to Candice for over forty-two years and is known to boast regularly of his children and grandchildren. Brian and Candice may be contacted at:

brian@passiontranslation.com

Facebook.com/passiontranslation

Twitter.com/tPtBible

For more information about the translation project or any of Brian's books, please visit:

www.thepassiontranslation.com

www.stairwayministries.org